Cram101 Textbook Outlines to accompany:

Contemporary Business

Boone and Kurtz, 1st Edition

An Academic Internet Publishers (AIPI) publication (c) 2007.

You have a discounted membership at www.Cram101.com with this book.

Get all of the practice tests for the chapters of this textbook, and access in-depth reference material for writing essays and papers. Here is an example from a Cram101 Biology text:

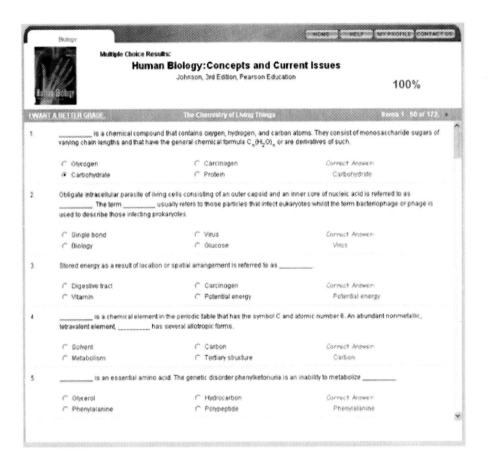

When you need problem solving help with math, stats, and other disciplines, www.Cram101.com will walk through the formulas and solutions step by step.

With Cram101.com online, you also have access to extensive reference material.

You will nail those essays and papers. Here is an example from a Cram101 Biology text:

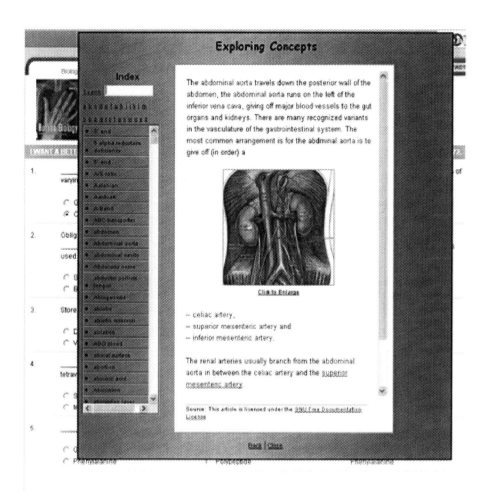

Learning System

Cram101 Textbook Outlines is a learning system. The notes in this book are the highlights of your textbook, you will never have to highlight a book again.

How to use this book. Take this book to class, it is your notebook for the lecture. The notes and highlights on the left hand side of the pages follow the outline and order of the textbook. All you have to do is follow along while your intructor presents the lecture. Circle the items emphasized in class and add other important information on the right side. With Cram101 Textbook Outlines you'll spend less time writing and more time listening. Learning becomes more efficient.

Cram101.com Online

Increase your studying efficiency by using Cram101.com's practice tests and online reference material. It is the perfect complement to Cram101 Textbook Outlines. Use self-teaching matching tests or simulate in-class testing with comprehensive multiple choice tests, or simply use Cram's true and false tests for quick review. Cram101.com even allows you to enter your in-class notes for an integrated studying format combining the textbook notes with your class notes.

Visit **www.Cram101.com**, click Sign Up at the top of the screen, and enter **DK73DW485** in the promo code box on the registration screen. Access to www.Cram101.com is normally $9.95, but because you have purchased this book, your access fee is only $4.95. Sign up and stop highlighting textbooks forever.

Contemporary Business
Boone and Kurtz, 1st

CONTENTS

Technology	The body of knowledge and techniques that can be used to combine economic resources to produce goods and services is called technology.
Partnership	In the common law, a partnership is a type of business entity in which partners share with each other the profits or losses of the business undertaking in which they have all invested.
Chief operating officer	A chief operating officer is a corporate officer responsible for managing the day-to-day activities of the corporation. The chief operating officer is one of the highest ranking members of an organization, monitoring the daily operations of the company and reporting to the chief executive officer directly.
Trial	An examination before a competent tribunal, according to the law of the land, of the facts or law put in issue in a cause, for the purpose of determining such issue is a trial. When the court hears and determines any issue of fact or law for the purpose of determining the rights of the parties, it may be considered a trial.
Competitor	Other organizations in the same industry or type of business that provide a good or service to the same set of customers is referred to as a competitor.
Market	A market is, as defined in economics, a social arrangement that allows buyers and sellers to discover information and carry out a voluntary exchange of goods or services.
Firm	An organization that employs resources to produce a good or service for profit and owns and operates one or more plants is referred to as a firm.
Entrepreneur	The owner/operator. The person who organizes, manages, and assumes the risks of a firm, taking a new idea or a new product and turning it into a successful business is an entrepreneur.
Corporation	A legal entity chartered by a state or the Federal government that is distinct and separate from the individuals who own it is a corporation. This separation gives the corporation unique powers which other legal entities lack.
Stock	In financial terminology, stock is the capital raized by a corporation, through the issuance and sale of shares.
Stock market	An organized marketplace in which common stocks are traded. In the United States, the largest stock market is the New York Stock Exchange, on which are traded the stocks of the largest U.S. companies.
Slowdown	A slowdown is an industrial action in which employees perform their duties but seek to reduce productivity or efficiency in their performance of these duties. A slowdown may be used as either a prelude or an alternative to a strike, as it is seen as less disruptive as well as less risky and costly for workers and their union.
Service	Service refers to a "non tangible product" that is not embodied in a physical good and that typically effects some change in another product, person, or institution. Contrasts with good.
Domestic	From or in one's own country. A domestic producer is one that produces inside the home country. A domestic price is the price inside the home country. Opposite of 'foreign' or 'world.'.
Economic growth	Economic growth refers to the increase over time in the capacity of an economy to produce goods and services and to improve the well-being of its citizens.
Shares	Shares refer to an equity security, representing a shareholder's ownership of a corporation. Shares are one of a finite number of equal portions in the capital of a company, entitling the owner to a proportion of distributed, non-reinvested profits known as dividends and to a portion of the value of the company in case of liquidation.
Revenue	Revenue is a U.S. business term for the amount of money that a company receives from its activities, mostly from sales of products and/or services to customers.
Deficit	The deficit is the amount by which expenditure exceed revenue.
Federal deficit	The excess of federal government expenditures over federal government revenues are referred to as

	federal deficit.
Budget	Budget refers to an account, usually for a year, of the planned expenditures and the expected receipts of an entity. For a government, the receipts are tax revenues.
Federal budget	The annual statement of the expenditures and tax revenues of the government of the United States together with the laws and regulations that approve and support those expenditures and taxes is the federal budget.
National debt	National debt refers to total of outstanding federal government bonds on which the federal government must pay interest.
Household	An economic unit that provides the economy with resources and uses the income received to purchase goods and services that satisfy economic wants is called household.
Economy	The income, expenditures, and resources that affect the cost of running a business and household are called an economy.
Inflation	An increase in the overall price level of an economy, usually as measured by the CPI or by the implicit price deflator is called inflation.
Instrument	Instrument refers to an economic variable that is controlled by policy makers and can be used to influence other variables, called targets. Examples are monetary and fiscal policies used to achieve external and internal balance.
Microsoft	Microsoft is a multinational computer technology corporation with 2004 global annual sales of US$39.79 billion and 71,553 employees in 102 countries and regions as of July 2006. It develops, manufactures, licenses, and supports a wide range of software products for computing devices.
Gap	In December of 1995, Gap became the first major North American retailer to accept independent monitoring of the working conditions in a contract factory producing its garments. Gap is the largest specialty retailer in the United States.
Manufacturing	Production of goods primarily by the application of labor and capital to raw materials and other intermediate inputs, in contrast to agriculture, mining, forestry, fishing, and services a manufacturing.
Nextel	Nextel is the former wireless brand of NEXTEL Communications, and it operates on Motorola's iDEN protocol which uses time division multiple access (TDMA) based technology. Unlike other cellular operators, Nextel utilizes the specialized mobile radio band (SMR) and was one of the first operators in the United States to offer nationwide digital-cellular radio coverage.
Utility	Utility refers to the want-satisfying power of a good or service; the satisfaction or pleasure a consumer obtains from the consumption of a good or service.
General Motors	General Motors is the world's largest automaker. Founded in 1908, today it employs about 327,000 people around the world. With global headquarters in Detroit, it manufactures its cars and trucks in 33 countries.
Merchant	Under the Uniform Commercial Code, one who regularly deals in goods of the kind sold in the contract at issue, or holds himself out as having special knowledge or skill relevant to such goods, or who makes the sale through an agent who regularly deals in such goods or claims such knowledge or skill is referred to as merchant.
Profit	Profit refers to the return to the resource entrepreneurial ability; total revenue minus total cost.
Economic system	Economic system refers to a particular set of institutional arrangements and a coordinating mechanism for solving the economizing problem; a method of organizing an economy, of which the market system and the command system are the two general types.
Enterprise	Enterprise refers to another name for a business organization. Other similar terms are business firm,

Go to **Cram101.com** for the Practice Tests for this Chapter.

	sometimes simply business, sometimes simply firm, as well as company, and entity.
Insurance	Insurance refers to a system by which individuals can reduce their exposure to risk of large losses by spreading the risks among a large number of persons.
Tangible	Having a physical existence is referred to as the tangible. Personal property other than real estate, such as cars, boats, stocks, or other assets.
Per capita	Per capita refers to per person. Usually used to indicate the average per person of any given statistic, commonly income.
Buyer	A buyer refers to a role in the buying center with formal authority and responsibility to select the supplier and negotiate the terms of the contract.
Expense	In accounting, an expense represents an event in which an asset is used up or a liability is incurred. In terms of the accounting equation, expenses reduce owners' equity.
Incentive	An incentive is any factor (financial or non-financial) that provides a motive for a particular course of action, or counts as a reason for preferring one choice to the alternatives.
Yahoo	Yahoo is an American computer services company. It operates an Internet portal, the Yahoo Directory and a host of other services including the popular Yahoo Mail. Yahoo is the most visited website on the Internet today with more than 400 million unique users. The global network of Yahoo! websites received 3.4 billion page views per day on average as of October 2005.
America Online	In 2000 America Online and Time Warner announced plans to merge, and the deal was approved by the Federal Trade Commission on January 11, 2001. This merger was primarily a product of the Internet mania of the late-1990s, known as the Internet bubble. The deal is known as one of the worst corporate mergers in history, destroying over $200 billion in shareholder value.
Users	Users refer to people in the organization who actually use the product or service purchased by the buying center.
Sweepstakes	Sales promotions consisting of a game of chance requiring no analytical or creative effort by the consumer is a sweepstakes.
Sweepstake	A sweepstake is technically a lottery in which the prize is financed through the tickets sold. In the United States the word has become associated with promotions where prizes are given away for free.
Long run	In economic models, the long run time frame assumes no fixed factors of production. Firms can enter or leave the marketplace, and the cost (and availability) of land, labor, raw materials, and capital goods can be assumed to vary.
Public sector	Public sector refers to the part of the economy that contains all government entities; government.
Labor	People's physical and mental talents and efforts that are used to help produce goods and services are called labor.
Union	A worker association that bargains with employers over wages and working conditions is called a union.
Labor union	A group of workers organized to advance the interests of the group is called a labor union.
Fund	Independent accounting entity with a self-balancing set of accounts segregated for the purposes of carrying on specific activities is referred to as a fund.
Grant	Grant refers to an intergovernmental transfer of funds . Since the New Deal, state and local governments have become increasingly dependent upon federal grants for an almost infinite variety of programs.
Advertising	Advertising refers to paid, nonpersonal communication through various media by organizations and individuals who are in some way identified in the advertising message.
Management	Management characterizes the process of leading and directing all or part of an organization, often a

business, through the deployment and manipulation of resources. Early twentieth-century management writer Mary Parker Follett defined management as "the art of getting things done through people."

Federal government	Federal government refers to the government of the United States, as distinct from the state and local governments.
Pledge	In law a pledge (also pawn) is a bailment of personal property as a security for some debt or engagement.
General manager	A manager who is responsible for several departments that perform different functions is called general manager.
Interest	In finance and economics, interest is the price paid by a borrower for the use of a lender's money. In other words, interest is the amount of paid to "rent" money for a period of time.
Marketing	Promoting and selling products or services to customers, or prospective customers, is referred to as marketing.
Conflict of interest	A conflict that occurs when a corporate officer or director enters into a transaction with the corporation in which he or she has a personal interest is a conflict of interest.
Option	A contract that gives the purchaser the option to buy or sell the underlying financial instrument at a specified price, called the exercise price or strike price, within a specific period of time.
Capital	Capital generally refers to financial wealth, especially that used to start or maintain a business. In classical economics, capital is one of four factors of production, the others being land and labor and entrepreneurship.
Stock option	A stock option is a specific type of option that uses the stock itself as an underlying instrument to determine the option's pay-off and therefore its value.
Health maintenance organizations	Health care providers that contract with employers, insurance companies, labor unions, or government units to provide health care for their workers or others who are insured are referred to as health maintenance organizations.
Health maintenance organization	A Health Maintenance Organization is a fixed, prepaid health care plan that provides comprehensive benefits for employees who are required to use a network of participating providers for all health services.
American Medical Association	The American Medical Association is the largest association of medical doctors in the United States. Its purpose is to advance the interests of physicians, to promote public health, to lobby for medical legislation, and to raise money for medical education.
Investment	Investment refers to spending for the production and accumulation of capital and additions to inventories. In a financial sense, buying an asset with the expectation of making a return.
Chief executive officer	A chief executive officer is the highest-ranking corporate officer or executive officer of a corporation, or agency. In closely held corporations, it is general business culture that the office chief executive officer is also the chairman of the board.
Endowment	Endowment refers to the amount of something that a person or country simply has, rather than their having somehow to acquire it.
Gain	In finance, gain is a profit or an increase in value of an investment such as a stock or bond. Gain is calculated by fair market value or the proceeds from the sale of the investment minus the sum of the purchase price and all costs associated with it.
Trend	Trend refers to the long-term movement of an economic variable, such as its average rate of increase or decrease over enough years to encompass several business cycles.
Preparation	Preparation refers to usually the first stage in the creative process. It includes education and formal training.

8

Go to **Cram101.com** for the Practice Tests for this Chapter.

Production	The creation of finished goods and services using the factors of production: land, labor, capital, entrepreneurship, and knowledge.
Operation	A standardized method or technique that is performed repetitively, often on different materials resulting in different finished goods is called an operation.
Inputs	The inputs used by a firm or an economy are the labor, raw materials, electricity and other resources it uses to produce its outputs.
Factors of production	Economic resources: land, capital, labor, and entrepreneurial ability are called factors of production.
Capitalism	Capitalism refers to an economic system in which capital is mostly owned by private individuals and corporations. Contrasts with communism.
Entrepreneurship	The assembling of resources to produce new or improved products and technologies is referred to as entrepreneurship.
Human resources	Human resources refers to the individuals within the firm, and to the portion of the firm's organization that deals with hiring, firing, training, and other personnel issues.
Production line	A production line is a set of sequential operations established in a factory whereby materials are put through a refining process to produce an end-product that is suitable for onward consumption; or components are assembled to make a finished article.
Critical success factor	Critical Success Factor is a business term for an element which is necessary for an organization or project to achieve its mission.
Success factor	The term success factor refers to the characteristics necessary for high performance; knowledge, skills, abilities, behaviors.
Innovation	Innovation refers to the first commercially successful introduction of a new product, the use of a new method of production, or the creation of a new form of business organization.
Yield	The interest rate that equates a future value or an annuity to a given present value is a yield.
Raw material	Raw material refers to a good that has not been transformed by production; a primary product.
Purchasing	Purchasing refers to the function in a firm that searches for quality material resources, finds the best suppliers, and negotiates the best price for goods and services.
Supply	Supply is the aggregate amount of any material good that can be called into being at a certain price point; it comprises one half of the equation of supply and demand. In classical economic theory, a curve representing supply is one of the factors that produce price.
Ford	Ford is an American company that manufactures and sells automobiles worldwide. Ford introduced methods for large-scale manufacturing of cars, and large-scale management of an industrial workforce, especially elaborately engineered manufacturing sequences typified by the moving assembly lines.
Assembly line	An assembly line is a manufacturing process in which interchangeable parts are added to a product in a sequential manner to create a finished product.
Industry	A group of firms that produce identical or similar products is an industry. It is also used specifically to refer to an area of economic production focused on manufacturing which involves large amounts of capital investment before any profit can be realized, also called "heavy industry".
Devise	In a will, a gift of real property is called a devise.
Bill Gates	Bill Gates is the co-founder, chairman, former chief software architect, and former CEO of Microsoft Corporation. He is one of the best-known entrepreneurs of the personal computer revolution and he is widely respected for his foresight and ambition.
Factor of	Factor of production refers to economic resources used in production such as land, labor, and capital.

production	
Information system	An information system is a system whether automated or manual, that comprises people, machines, and/or methods organized to collect, process, transmit, and disseminate data that represent user information.
Sales forecast	Sales forecast refers to the maximum total sales of a product that a firm expects to sell during a specified time period under specified environmental conditions and its own marketing efforts.
Channel	Channel, in communications (sometimes called communications channel), refers to the medium used to convey information from a sender (or transmitter) to a receiver.
Communism	Communism refers to an economic system in which capital is owned by private government. Contrasts with capitalism.
Invisible hand	Invisible hand refers to a phrase coined by Adam Smith to describe the process that turns self-directed gain into social and economic benefits for all.
Adam Smith	Adam Smith (baptized June 5, 1723 O.S. (June 16 N.S.) – July 17, 1790) was a Scottish political economist and moral philosopher. His Inquiry into the Nature and Causes of the Wealth of Nations was one of the earliest attempts to study the historical development of industry and commerce in Europe. That work helped to create the modern academic discipline of economics
Preference	The act of a debtor in paying or securing one or more of his creditors in a manner more favorable to them than to other creditors or to the exclusion of such other creditors is a preference. In the absence of statute, a preference is perfectly good, but to be legal it must be bona fide, and not a mere subterfuge of the debtor to secure a future benefit to himself or to prevent the application of his property to his debts.
Brand	A name, symbol, or design that identifies the goods or services of one seller or group of sellers and distinguishes them from the goods and services of competitors is a brand.
Private property	The right of private persons and firms to obtain, own, control, employ, dispose of, and bequeath land, capital, and other property is referred to as private property.
Property	Assets defined in the broadest legal sense. Property includes the unrealized receivables of a cash basis taxpayer, but not services rendered.
Welfare	Welfare refers to the economic well being of an individual, group, or economy. For individuals, it is conceptualized by a utility function. For groups, including countries and the world, it is a tricky philosophical concept, since individuals fare differently.
Fraud	Tax fraud falls into two categories: civil and criminal. Under civil fraud, the IRS may impose as a penalty of an amount equal to as much as 75 percent of the underpayment.
Price discrimination	Price discrimination refers to the sale by a firm to buyers at two different prices. When this occurs internationally and the lower price is charged for export, it is regarded as dumping.
Financial market	In economics, a financial market is a mechanism which allows people to trade money for securities or commodities such as gold or other precious metals. In general, any commodity market might be considered to be a financial market, if the usual purpose of traders is not the immediate consumption of the commodity, but rather as a means of delaying or accelerating consumption over time.
Economic risk	The likelihood that events, including economic mismanagement, will cause drastic changes in a country's business environment that adversely affects the profit and other goals of a particular business enterprise is referred to as economic risk.
Publicity	Publicity refers to any information about an individual, product, or organization that's distributed to the public through the media and that's not paid for or controlled by the seller.
Market opportunities	Market opportunities refer to areas where a company believes there are favorable demand trends, needs, and/or wants that are not being satisfied, and where it can compete effectively.

13

Bureaucracy	Bureaucracy refers to an organization with many layers of managers who set rules and regulations and oversee all decisions.
Leadership	Management merely consists of leadership applied to business situations; or in other words: management forms a sub-set of the broader process of leadership.
Infant industry	Infant industry refers to a young industry that may need temporary protection from competition from the established industries of other countries to develop an acquired comparative advantage.
Business operations	Business operations are those activities involved in the running of a business for the purpose of producing value for the stakeholders. The outcome of business operations is the harvesting of value from assets owned by a business.
Industrial revolution	The Industrial Revolution is the stream of new technology and the resulting growth of output that began in England toward the end of the 18th century.
Factory system	The factory system was a method of manufacturing adopted in England during the Industrial Revolution. Workers would come to work in a city factory, often making low-quality goods in mass amounts.
Production efficiency	A situation in which the economy cannot produce more of one good without producing less of some other good is referred to as production efficiency.
Manufactured good	A manufactured good refers to goods that have been processed in any way.
Mass production	The process of making a large number of a limited variety of products at very low cost is referred to as mass production.
Andrew Carnegie	Andrew Carnegie (November 25, 1835 – August 11, 1919) was a Scottish-born American businessman, a major philanthropist, and the founder of U.S. Steel.
Standard of living	Standard of living refers to the level of consumption that people enjoy, on the average, and is measured by average income per person.
Henry Ford	Henry Ford was the founder of the Ford Motor Company. His introduction of the Model T automobile revolutionized transportation and American industry.
Great Depression	The period of severe economic contraction and high unemployment that began in 1929 and continued throughout the 1930s is referred to as the Great Depression.
Depression	Depression refers to a prolonged period characterized by high unemployment, low output and investment, depressed business confidence, falling prices, and widespread business failures. A milder form of business downturn is a recession.
Consumer good	Products and services that are ultimately consumed rather than used in the production of another good are a consumer good.
Marketing research	Marketing research refers to the analysis of markets to determine opportunities and challenges, and to find the information needed to make good decisions.
Franchise	A contractual right to sell certain products or services, use certain trademarks, or perform activities in a geographical region is called a franchise.
Smart card	A stored-value card that contains a computer chip that allows it to be loaded with digital cash from the owner's bank account whenever needed is called a smart card.
Information technology	Information technology refers to technology that helps companies change business by allowing them to use new methods.
Advertisement	Advertisement is the promotion of goods, services, companies and ideas, usually by an identified sponsor. Marketers see advertising as part of an overall promotional strategy.
Exchange	The trade of things of value between buyer and seller so that each is better off after the trade is

called the exchange.

Coupon	In finance, a coupon is "attached" to a bond, either physically (as with old bonds) or electronically. Each coupon represents a predetermined payment promized to the bond-holder in return for his or her loan of money to the bond-issuer. .
Discount	The difference between the face value of a bond and its selling price, when a bond is sold for less than its face value it's referred to as a discount.
Commodity	Could refer to any good, but in trade a commodity is usually a raw material or primary product that enters into international trade, such as metals or basic agricultural products.
Brokerage firm	A company that conducts various aspects of securities trading, analysis and advisory services is a brokerage firm.
Inventory	Tangible property held for sale in the normal course of business or used in producing goods or services for sale is an inventory.
Aid	Assistance provided by countries and by international institutions such as the World Bank to developing countries in the form of monetary grants, loans at low interest rates, in kind, or a combination of these is called aid. Aid can also refer to assistance of any type rendered to benefit some group or individual.
Ordering costs	Costs of preparing, issuing, and paying purchase orders, plus receiving and inspecting the items included in the orders are ordering costs.
Customer service	The ability of logistics management to satisfy users in terms of time, dependability, communication, and convenience is called the customer service.
Comprehensive	A comprehensive refers to a layout accurate in size, color, scheme, and other necessary details to show how a final ad will look. For presentation only, never for reproduction.
Foundation	A Foundation is a type of philanthropic organization set up by either individuals or institutions as a legal entity (either as a corporation or trust) with the purpose of distributing grants to support causes in line with the goals of the foundation.
Electronic mail	Electronic mail refers to electronic written communication between individuals using computers connected to the Internet.
Attachment	Attachment in general, the process of taking a person's property under an appropriate judicial order by an appropriate officer of the court. Used for a variety of purposes, including the acquisition of jurisdiction over the property seized and the securing of property that may be used to satisfy a debt.
Intranet	Intranet refers to a companywide network, closed to public access, that uses Internet-type technology. A set of communications links within one company that travel over the Internet but are closed to public access.
Mentoring	Mentoring refers to a developmental relationship between a more experienced mentor and a less experienced partner referred to as a mentee or protégé. Usually - but not necessarily - the mentor/protégé pair will be of the same sex.
Leverage	Leverage is using given resources in such a way that the potential positive or negative outcome is magnified. In finance, this generally refers to borrowing.
Competitive advantage	A business is said to have a competitive advantage when its unique strengths, often based on cost, quality, time, and innovation, offer consumers a greater percieved value and there by differtiating it from its competitors.
Relationship management	A method for developing long-term associations with customers is referred to as relationship management.
Core	A core is the set of feasible allocations in an economy that cannot be improved upon by subset of the

Go to **Cram101.com** for the Practice Tests for this Chapter.

set of the economy's consumers (a coalition). In construction, when the force in an element is within a certain center section, the core, the element will only be under compression.

General Electric	In 1876, Thomas Alva Edison opened a new laboratory in Menlo Park, New Jersey. Out of the laboratory was to come perhaps the most famous invention of all—a successful development of the incandescent electric lamp. By 1890, Edison had organized his various businesses into the Edison General Electric Company.
Distribution	Distribution in economics, the manner in which total output and income is distributed among individuals or factors.
Product design	Product Design is defined as the idea generation, concept development, testing and manufacturing or implementation of a physical object or service. It is possibly the evolution of former discipline name - Industrial Design.
Contract	A contract is a "promise" or an "agreement" that is enforced or recognized by the law. In the civil law, a contract is considered to be part of the general law of obligations.
Strategic alliance	Strategic alliance refers to a long-term partnership between two or more companies established to help each company build competitive market advantages.
Affiliation	A relationship with other websites in which a company can cross-promote and is credited for sales that accrue through their site is an affiliation.
Retailing	All activities involved in selling, renting, and providing goods and services to ultimate consumers for personal, family, or household use is referred to as retailing.
Bond	Bond refers to a debt instrument, issued by a borrower and promising a specified stream of payments to the purchaser, usually regular interest payments plus a final repayment of principal.
Balance	In banking and accountancy, the outstanding balance is the amount of money owned, (or due), that remains in a deposit account (or a loan account) at a given date, after all past remittances, payments and withdrawal have been accounted for. It can be positive (then, in the balance sheet of a firm, it is an asset) or negative (a liability).
Real value	Real value is the value of anything expressed in money of the day with the effects of inflation removed.
Mistake	In contract law a mistake is incorrect understanding by one or more parties to a contract and may be used as grounds to invalidate the agreement. Common law has identified three different types of mistake in contract: unilateral mistake, mutual mistake, and common mistake.
Enabling	Enabling refers to giving workers the education and tools they need to assume their new decision-making powers.
Customer satisfaction	Customer satisfaction is a business term which is used to capture the idea of measuring how satisfied an enterprise's customers are with the organization's efforts in a marketplace.
Misuse	A defense that relieves a seller of product liability if the user abnormally misused the product is called misuse. Products must be designed to protect against foreseeable misuse.
Credit	Credit refers to a recording as positive in the balance of payments, any transaction that gives rise to a payment into the country, such as an export, the sale of an asset, or borrowing from abroad.
Warehouse	Warehouse refers to a location, often decentralized, that a firm uses to store, consolidate, age, or mix stock; house product-recall programs; or ease tax burdens.
Complaint	The pleading in a civil case in which the plaintiff states his claim and requests relief is called complaint. In the common law, it is a formal legal document that sets out the basic facts and legal reasons that the filing party (the plaintiffs) believes are sufficient to support a claim against another person, persons, entity or entities (the defendants) that entitles the plaintiff(s) to a remedy

	(either money damages or injunctive relief).
Interdependence	The extent to which departments depend on each other for resources or materials to accomplish their tasks is referred to as interdependence.
Appeal	Appeal refers to the act of asking an appellate court to overturn a decision after the trial court's final judgment has been entered.
Foreign ownership	Foreign ownership refers to the complete or majority ownership/control of businesses or resources in a country, by individuals who are not citizens of that country, or by companies whose headquarters are not in that country.
Competitiveness	Competitiveness usually refers to characteristics that permit a firm to compete effectively with other firms due to low cost or superior technology, perhaps internationally.
Productivity	Productivity refers to the total output of goods and services in a given period of time divided by work hours.
Productivity ratios	Productivity ratios refer to ratios that are used in measuring the extent to which a firm effectively uses its resources.
Labor productivity	In labor economics labor productivity is a measure of the efficiency of the labor force. It is usually measured as output per hour of all people. When comparing labor productivity one mostly looks at the change over time.
Gross domestic product	Gross domestic product refers to the total value of new goods and services produced in a given year within the borders of a country, regardless of by whom.
Layoff	A layoff is the termination of an employee or (more commonly) a group of employees for business reasons, such as the decision that certain positions are no longer necessary.
Closing	The finalization of a real estate sales transaction that passes title to the property from the seller to the buyer is referred to as a closing. Closing is a sales term which refers to the process of making a sale. It refers to reaching the final step, which may be an exchange of money or acquiring a signature.
Peak	Peak refers to the point in the business cycle when an economic expansion reaches its highest point before turning down. Contrasts with trough.
Contribution	In business organization law, the cash or property contributed to a business by its owners is referred to as contribution.
Unemployment rate	The unemployment rate is the number of unemployed workers divided by the total civilian labor force, which includes both the unemployed and those with jobs (all those willing and able to work for pay).
Applicant	In many tribunal and administrative law suits, the person who initiates the claim is called the applicant.
Policy	Similar to a script in that a policy can be a less than completely rational decision-making method. Involves the use of a pre-existing set of decision steps for any problem that presents itself.
Immigration	Immigration refers to the migration of people into a country.
Points	Loan origination fees that may be deductible as interest by a buyer of property. A seller of property who pays points reduces the selling price by the amount of the points paid for the buyer.
Department of Labor	The United States Department of Labor is a Cabinet department of the United States government responsible for occupational safety, wage and hour standards, unemployment insurance benefits, re-employment services, and some economic statistics.
Human capital	Human capital refers to the stock of knowledge and skill, embodied in an individual as a result of education, training, and experience that makes them more productive. The stock of knowledge and skill

embodied in the population of an economy.

Corporate culture	The whole collection of beliefs, values, and behaviors of a firm that send messages to those within and outside the company about how business is done is the corporate culture.
Federal Express	The company officially began operations on April 17, 1973, utilizing a network of 14 Dassault Falcon 20s which connected 25 U.S. cities. FedEx, the first cargo airline to use jet aircraft for its services, expanded greatly after the deregulation of the cargo airlines sector. Federal Express use of the hub-spoke distribution paradigm in air freight enabled it to become a world leader in its field.
Vendor	A person who sells property to a vendee is a vendor. The words vendor and vendee are more commonly applied to the seller and purchaser of real estate, and the words seller and buyer are more commonly applied to the seller and purchaser of personal property.
Telecommuting	Telecommuting is a work arrangement in which employees enjoy limited flexibility in working location and hours.
Telecommute	To work at home and keep in touch with the company through telecommunications is referred to as telecommute.
Outsourcing	Outsourcing refers to a production activity that was previously done inside a firm or plant that is now conducted outside that firm or plant.
Staffing	Staffing refers to a management function that includes hiring, motivating, and retaining the best people available to accomplish the company's objectives.
Customer value	Customer value refers to the unique combination of benefits received by targeted buyers that includes quality, price, convenience, on-time delivery, and both before-sale and after-sale service.
Affirmative action	Policies and programs that establish procedures for increasing employment and promotion for women and minorities are called affirmative action.
Financial statement	Financial statement refers to a summary of all the transactions that have occurred over a particular period.
Strike	The withholding of labor services by an organized group of workers is referred to as a strike.
Nike	Because Nike creates goods for a wide range of sports, they have competition from every sports and sports fashion brand there is. Nike has no direct competitors because there is no single brand which can compete directly with their range of sports and non-sports oriented gear, except for Reebok.
Logistics	Those activities that focus on getting the right amount of the right products to the right place at the right time at the lowest possible cost is referred to as logistics.
Auction	A preexisting business model that operates successfully on the Internet by announcing an item for sale and permitting multiple purchasers to bid on them under specified rules and condition is an auction.
Oracle	In 2004, sales at Oracle grew at a rate of 14.5% to $6.2 billion, giving it 41.3% and the top share of the relational-database market. Their main competitors in the database arena are IBM DB2 and Microsoft SQL Server, and to a lesser extent Sybase, Teradata, Informix, and MySQL. In the applications arena, their main competitor is SAP.

Technology	The body of knowledge and techniques that can be used to combine economic resources to produce goods and services is called technology.
Service	Service refers to a "non tangible product" that is not embodied in a physical good and that typically effects some change in another product, person, or institution. Contrasts with good.
Agent	A person who makes economic decisions for another economic actor. A hired manager operates as an agent for a firm's owner.
Business ethics	The study of what makes up good and bad conduct as related to business activities and values is business ethics.
Ethical dilemma	An ethical dilemma is a situation that often involves an apparent conflict between moral imperatives, in which to obey one would result in transgressing another.
Social responsibility	Social responsibility is a doctrine that claims that an entity whether it is state, government, corporation, organization or individual has a responsibility to society.
Regulation	Regulation refers to restrictions state and federal laws place on business with regard to the conduct of its activities.
Firm	An organization that employs resources to produce a good or service for profit and owns and operates one or more plants is referred to as a firm.
Profit	Profit refers to the return to the resource entrepreneurial ability; total revenue minus total cost.
Public relations	Public relations refers to the management function that evaluates public attitudes, changes policies and procedures in response to the public's requests, and executes a program of action and information to earn public understanding and acceptance.
Standards of conduct	Standards of conduct refers to a compendium of ethical norms promulgated by an organization to guide the behavior of its members. Many government agencies have formal codes of conduct for their employees.
Brand	A name, symbol, or design that identifies the goods or services of one seller or group of sellers and distinguishes them from the goods and services of competitors is a brand.
Management	Management characterizes the process of leading and directing all or part of an organization, often a business, through the deployment and manipulation of resources. Early twentieth-century management writer Mary Parker Follett defined management as "the art of getting things done through people."
Production	The creation of finished goods and services using the factors of production: land, labor, capital, entrepreneurship, and knowledge.
Innovation	Innovation refers to the first commercially successful introduction of a new product, the use of a new method of production, or the creation of a new form of business organization.
Policy	Similar to a script in that a policy can be a less than completely rational decision-making method. Involves the use of a pre-existing set of decision steps for any problem that presents itself.
Fraud	Tax fraud falls into two categories: civil and criminal. Under civil fraud, the IRS may impose as a penalty of an amount equal to as much as 75 percent of the underpayment.
Ford	Ford is an American company that manufactures and sells automobiles worldwide. Ford introduced methods for large-scale manufacturing of cars, and large-scale management of an industrial workforce, especially elaborately engineered manufacturing sequences typified by the moving assembly lines.

Go to **Cram101.com** for the Practice Tests for this Chapter.

25

Aid	Assistance provided by countries and by international institutions such as the World Bank to developing countries in the form of monetary grants, loans at low interest rates, in kind, or a combination of these is called aid. Aid can also refer to assistance of any type rendered to benefit some group or individual.
Competitor	Other organizations in the same industry or type of business that provide a good or service to the same set of customers is referred to as a competitor.
Interest	In finance and economics, interest is the price paid by a borrower for the use of a lender's money. In other words, interest is the amount of paid to "rent" money for a period of time.
Futures	Futures refer to contracts for the sale and future delivery of stocks or commodities, wherein either party may waive delivery, and receive or pay, as the case may be, the difference in market price at the time set for delivery.
Administrator	Administrator refers to the personal representative appointed by a probate court to settle the estate of a deceased person who died.
Market	A market is, as defined in economics, a social arrangement that allows buyers and sellers to discover information and carry out a voluntary exchange of goods or services.
Expense	In accounting, an expense represents an event in which an asset is used up or a liability is incurred. In terms of the accounting equation, expenses reduce owners' equity.
Conflict of interest	A conflict that occurs when a corporate officer or director enters into a transaction with the corporation in which he or she has a personal interest is a conflict of interest.
Advertising agency	A firm that specializes in the creation, production, and placement of advertising messages and may provide other services that facilitate the marketing communications process is an advertising agency.
Advertising	Advertising refers to paid, nonpersonal communication through various media by organizations and individuals who are in some way identified in the advertising message.
Consultant	A professional that provides expert advice in a particular field or area in which customers occassionaly require this type of knowledge is a consultant.
Buyer	A buyer refers to a role in the buying center with formal authority and responsibility to select the supplier and negotiate the terms of the contract.
Board of directors	The group of individuals elected by the stockholders of a corporation to oversee its operations is a board of directors.
Committee	A long-lasting, sometimes permanent team in the organization structure created to deal with tasks that recur regularly is the committee.
Gain	In finance, gain is a profit or an increase in value of an investment such as a stock or bond. Gain is calculated by fair market value or the proceeds from the sale of the investment minus the sum of the purchase price and all costs associated with it.
Fund	Independent accounting entity with a self-balancing set of accounts segregated for the purposes of carrying on specific activities is referred to as a fund.
Initial public offering	Firms in the process of becoming publicly traded companies will issue shares of stock using an initial public offering, which is merely the process of selling stock for the first time to interested investors.
Credibility	The extent to which a source is perceived as having knowledge, skill, or experience relevant to a communication topic and can be trusted to give an unbiased opinion or present objective information on the issue is called credibility.
Entrepreneurship	The assembling of resources to produce new or improved products and technologies is referred

Go to **Cram101.com** for the Practice Tests for this Chapter.

to as entrepreneurship.

Entrepreneur	The owner/operator. The person who organizes, manages, and assumes the risks of a firm, taking a new idea or a new product and turning it into a successful business is an entrepreneur.
Trust	An arrangement in which shareholders of independent firms agree to give up their stock in exchange for trust certificates that entitle them to a share of the trust's common profits.
Merger	Merger refers to the combination of two firms into a single firm.
Forbes	David Churbuck founded online Forbes in 1996. The site drew attention when it uncovered Stephen Glass' journalistic fraud in The New Republic in 1998, a scoop that gave credibility to internet journalism.
Loyalty	Marketers tend to define customer loyalty as making repeat purchases. Some argue that it should be defined attitudinally as a strongly positive feeling about the brand.
Texaco	Texaco is the name of an American oil company that was merged into Chevron Corporation in 2001. For many years, Texaco was the only company selling gasoline in all 50 states, but this is no longer true.
Channel	Channel, in communications (sometimes called communications channel), refers to the medium used to convey information from a sender (or transmitter) to a receiver.
Damages	The sum of money recoverable by a plaintiff who has received a judgment in a civil case is called damages.
Public good	A good that is provided for users collectively where use by one does not preclude use of the same units of the good by others is referred to as public good. Police protection is an example of a public good.
Disclosure	Disclosure means the giving out of information, either voluntarily or to be in compliance with legal regulations or workplace rules.
Authority	Authority in agency law, refers to an agent's ability to affect his principal's legal relations with third parties. Also used to refer to an actor's legal power or ability to do something. In addition, sometimes used to refer to a statute, case, or other legal source that justifies a particular result.
Industry	A group of firms that produce identical or similar products is an industry. It is also used specifically to refer to an area of economic production focused on manufacturing which involves large amounts of capital investment before any profit can be realized, also called "heavy industry".
Corporate culture	The whole collection of beliefs, values, and behaviors of a firm that send messages to those within and outside the company about how business is done is the corporate culture.
Foundation	A Foundation is a type of philanthropic organization set up by either individuals or institutions as a legal entity (either as a corporation or trust) with the purpose of distributing grants to support causes in line with the goals of the foundation.
Core	A core is the set of feasible allocations in an economy that cannot be improved upon by subset of the set of the economy's consumers (a coalition). In construction, when the force in an element is within a certain center section, the core, the element will only be under compression.
Shareholder	A shareholder is an individual or company (including a corporation) that legally owns one or more shares of stock in a joined stock company.
Asset	An item of property, such as land, capital, money, a share in ownership, or a claim on others

29

	for future payment, such as a bond or a bank deposit is an asset.
Option	A contract that gives the purchaser the option to buy or sell the underlying financial instrument at a specified price, called the exercise price or strike price, within a specific period of time.
Ethics training	Training programs to help employees deal with ethical questions and values are called ethics training.
Lockheed Martin	Lockheed Martin is the world's largest defense contractor (by defense revenue). As of 2005, 95% of revenues came from the U.S. Department of Defense, other U.S. federal government agencies, and foreign military customers.
Instrument	Instrument refers to an economic variable that is controlled by policy makers and can be used to influence other variables, called targets. Examples are monetary and fiscal policies used to achieve external and internal balance.
Supervisor	A Supervisor is an employee of an organization with some of the powers and responsibilities of management, occupying a role between true manager and a regular employee. A Supervisor position is typically the first step towards being promoted into a management role.
Leadership	Management merely consists of leadership applied to business situations; or in other words: management forms a sub-set of the broader process of leadership.
Corporation	A legal entity chartered by a state or the Federal government that is distinct and separate from the individuals who own it is a corporation. This separation gives the corporation unique powers which other legal entities lack.
Stakeholder	A stakeholder is an individual or group with a vested interest in or expectation for organizational performance. Usually stakeholders can either have an effect on or are affected by an organization.
Controlling	A management function that involves determining whether or not an organization is progressing toward its goals and objectives, and taking corrective action if it is not is called controlling.
Administration	Administration refers to the management and direction of the affairs of governments and institutions; a collective term for all policymaking officials of a government; the execution and implementation of public policy.
Firestone Tire	The Firestone Tire and Rubber Company was founded to supply pneumatic tires for wagons, buggies, and other forms of wheeled transportation common in the era. They soon saw the huge potential for marketing tires for automobiles and befriended Henry Ford, the first industrialist to produce them using the techniques of mass production. This relationship was used to become the original equipment supplier of Ford Motor Company automobiles, and was also active in the replacement market.
Complaint	The pleading in a civil case in which the plaintiff states his claim and requests relief is called complaint. In the common law, it is a formal legal document that sets out the basic facts and legal reasons that the filing party (the plaintiffs) believes are sufficient to support a claim against another person, persons, entity or entities (the defendants) that entitles the plaintiff(s) to a remedy (either money damages or injunctive relief).
Utility	Utility refers to the want-satisfying power of a good or service; the satisfaction or pleasure a consumer obtains from the consumption of a good or service.
Openness	Openness refers to the extent to which an economy is open, often measured by the ratio of its trade to GDP.
Bottom line	The bottom line is net income on the last line of a income statement.

Dealer	People who link buyers with sellers by buying and selling securities at stated prices are referred to as a dealer.
Consumer protection	Consumer protection is government regulation to protect the interests of consumers, for example by requiring businesses to disclose detailed information about products, particularly in areas where safety or public health is an issue, such as food.
Deregulation	The lessening or complete removal of government regulations on an industry, especially concerning the price that firms are allowed to charge and leaving price to be determined by market forces a deregulation.
Economy	The income, expenditures, and resources that affect the cost of running a business and household are called an economy.
Enterprise	Enterprise refers to another name for a business organization. Other similar terms are business firm, sometimes simply business, sometimes simply firm, as well as company, and entity.
Federal government	Federal government refers to the government of the United States, as distinct from the state and local governments.
Contribution	In business organization law, the cash or property contributed to a business by its owners is referred to as contribution.
Wage	The payment for the service of a unit of labor, per unit time. In trade theory, it is the only payment to labor, usually unskilled labor. In empirical work, wage data may exclude other compenzation, which must be added to get the total cost of employment.
Variable	A variable is something measured by a number; it is used to analyze what happens to other things when the size of that number changes.
Equal employment opportunity	The government's attempt to ensure that all individuals have an equal opportunity for employment, regardless of race, color, religion, sex, age, disability, or national origin is equal employment opportunity.
Assessment	Collecting information and providing feedback to employees about their behavior, communication style, or skills is an assessment.
Charitable contributions	Charitable contributions refers to contributions that are tax deductible if made to qualified nonprofit charitable organizations. A cash basis taxpayer is entitled to a deduction solely in the year of payment.
Annual report	An annual report is prepared by corporate management that presents financial information including financial statements, footnotes, and the management discussion and analysis.
Patent	The legal right to the proceeds from and control over the use of an invented product or process, granted for a fixed period of time, usually 20 years. Patent is one form of intellectual property that is subject of the TRIPS agreement.
Revenue	Revenue is a U.S. business term for the amount of money that a company receives from its activities, mostly from sales of products and/or services to customers.
Audit	An examination of the financial reports to ensure that they represent what they claim and conform with generally accepted accounting principles is referred to as audit.
Strategic plan	The formal document that presents the ways and means by which a strategic goal will be achieved is a strategic plan. A long-term flexible plan that does not regulate activities but rather outlines the means to achieve certain results, and provides the means to alter the course of action should the desired ends change.
Philanthropy	Philanthropy is the voluntary act of donating money or goods or providing some other support

Go to **Cram101.com** for the Practice Tests for this Chapter.

to a charitable cause, usually over an extended period of time. In a more fundamental sense, philanthropy may encompass any activity which is intended to enhance the common good or improve human well being.

Evaluation	The consumer's appraisal of the product or brand on important attributes is called evaluation.
Public interest	The universal label that political actors wrap around the policies and programs that they advocate is referred to as public interest.
Investment	Investment refers to spending for the production and accumulation of capital and additions to inventories. In a financial sense, buying an asset with the expectation of making a return.
Contract	A contract is a "promise" or an "agreement" that is enforced or recognized by the law. In the civil law, a contract is considered to be part of the general law of obligations.
Boycott	To protest by refusing to purchase from someone, or otherwise do business with them. In international trade, a boycott most often takes the form of refusal to import a country's goods.
Receiver	A person that is appointed as a custodian of other people's property by a court of law or a creditor of the owner, pending a lawsuit or reorganization is called a receiver.
Marketing	Promoting and selling products or services to customers, or prospective customers, is referred to as marketing.
Corporate philanthropy	Dimension of social responsibility that includes charitable donations is called corporate philanthropy.
Valuing diversity	Valuing diversity refers to putting an end to the assumption that everyone who is not a member of the dominant group must assimilate. The first step is to recognize that diversity exists in organizations so that we can begin to manage it.
Green marketing	Green marketing refers to marketing efforts to produce, promote, and reclaim environmentally sensitive products.
Consideration	Consideration in contract law, a basic requirement for an enforceable agreement under traditional contract principles, defined in this text as legal value, bargained for and given in exchange for an act or promise. In corporation law, cash or property contributed to a corporation in exchange for shares, or a promise to contribute such cash or property.
Bribery	When one person gives another person money, property, favors, or anything else of value for a favor in return, we have bribery. Often referred to as a payoff or 'kickback.'
Trend	Trend refers to the long-term movement of an economic variable, such as its average rate of increase or decrease over enough years to encompass several business cycles.
Commerce	Commerce is the exchange of something of value between two entities. It is the central mechanism from which capitalism is derived.
Sexual harassment	Unwelcome sexual advances, requests for sexual favors, and other conduct of a sexual nature is called sexual harassment.
Code of ethics	A formal statement of ethical principles and rules of conduct is a code of ethics. Some may have the force of law; these are often promulgated by the (quasi-)governmental agency responsible for licensing a profession. Violations of these codes may be subject to administrative (e.g., loss of license), civil or penal remedies.
Better Business Bureau	An organization established and funded by businesses that operates primarily at the local level to monitor activities of companies and promote fair advertising and selling practices is a better business bureau.

Human resources	Human resources refers to the individuals within the firm, and to the portion of the firm's organization that deals with hiring, firing, training, and other personnel issues.
Premium	Premium refers to the fee charged by an insurance company for an insurance policy. The rate of losses must be relatively predictable: In order to set the premium (prices) insurers must be able to estimate them accurately.
Health insurance	Health insurance is a type of insurance whereby the insurer pays the medical costs of the insured if the insured becomes sick due to covered causes, or due to accidents. The insurer may be a private organization or a government agency.
Insurance	Insurance refers to a system by which individuals can reduce their exposure to risk of large losses by spreading the risks among a large number of persons.
Points	Loan origination fees that may be deductible as interest by a buyer of property. A seller of property who pays points reduces the selling price by the amount of the points paid for the buyer.
Budget	Budget refers to an account, usually for a year, of the planned expenditures and the expected receipts of an entity. For a government, the receipts are tax revenues.
Quality assurance	Those activities associated with assuring the quality of a product or service is called quality assurance.
Target audience	That group that composes the present and potential prospects for a product or service is called the target audience.
Brief	Brief refers to a statement of a party's case or legal arguments, usually prepared by an attorney. Also used to make legal arguments before appellate courts.
Dow Chemical	Dow Chemical is the world's largest producer of plastics, including polystyrene, polyurethanes, polyethylene, polypropylene, and synthetic rubbers. It is also a major producer of the chemicals calcium chloride, ethylene oxide, and various acrylates, surfactants, and cellulose resins. It produces many agricultural chemicals.
Microsoft	Microsoft is a multinational computer technology corporation with 2004 global annual sales of US$39.79 billion and 71,553 employees in 102 countries and regions as of July 2006. It develops, manufactures, licenses, and supports a wide range of software products for computing devices.
Napster	Napster is an online music service which was originally a file sharing service created by Shawn Fanning. Napster was the first widely-used peer-to-peer (or P2P) music sharing service, and it made a major impact on how people, especially university students, used the Internet.
Users	Users refer to people in the organization who actually use the product or service purchased by the buying center.
Exchange	The trade of things of value between buyer and seller so that each is better off after the trade is called the exchange.
Sony	Sony is a multinational corporation and one of the world's largest media conglomerates founded in Tokyo, Japan. One of its divisions Sony Electronics is one of the leading manufacturers of electronics, video, communications, and information technology products for the consumer and professional markets.
Intellectual property	In law, intellectual property is an umbrella term for various legal entitlements which attach to certain types of information, ideas, or other intangibles in their expressed form. The holder of this legal entitlement is generally entitled to exercise various exclusive rights in relation to its subject matter.
Property	Assets defined in the broadest legal sense. Property includes the unrealized receivables of a

cash basis taxpayer, but not services rendered.

Cooperative   A business owned and controlled by the people who use it, producers, consumers, or workers with similar needs who pool their resources for mutual gain is called cooperative.

Go to **Cram101.com** for the Practice Tests for this Chapter.

Supply	Supply is the aggregate amount of any material good that can be called into being at a certain price point; it comprises one half of the equation of supply and demand. In classical economic theory, a curve representing supply is one of the factors that produce price.
Market	A market is, as defined in economics, a social arrangement that allows buyers and sellers to discover information and carry out a voluntary exchange of goods or services.
Market structure	Market structure refers to the way that suppliers and demanders in an industry interact to determine price and quantity. Market structures range from perfect competition to monopoly.
Economic system	Economic system refers to a particular set of institutional arrangements and a coordinating mechanism for solving the economizing problem; a method of organizing an economy, of which the market system and the command system are the two general types.
Enterprise	Enterprise refers to another name for a business organization. Other similar terms are business firm, sometimes simply business, sometimes simply firm, as well as company, and entity.
Economy	The income, expenditures, and resources that affect the cost of running a business and household are called an economy.
Evaluation	The consumer's appraisal of the product or brand on important attributes is called evaluation.
International Business	International business refers to any firm that engages in international trade or investment.
Comparative advantage	The ability to produce a good at lower cost, relative to other goods, compared to another country is a comparative advantage.
International trade	The export of goods and services from a country and the import of goods and services into a country is referred to as the international trade.
Exchange rate	Exchange rate refers to the price at which one country's currency trades for another, typically on the exchange market.
Exchange	The trade of things of value between buyer and seller so that each is better off after the trade is called the exchange.
Business strategy	Business strategy, which refers to the aggregated operational strategies of single business firm or that of an SBU in a diversified corporation refers to the way in which a firm competes in its chosen arenas.
Chief executive officer	A chief executive officer is the highest-ranking corporate officer or executive officer of a corporation, or agency. In closely held corporations, it is general business culture that the office chief executive officer is also the chairman of the board.
Competitor	Other organizations in the same industry or type of business that provide a good or service to the same set of customers is referred to as a competitor.
Expatriate	Employee sent by his or her company to live and manage operations in a different country is called an expatriate.
Management	Management characterizes the process of leading and directing all or part of an organization, often a business, through the deployment and manipulation of resources. Early twentieth-century management writer Mary Parker Follett defined management as "the art of getting things done through people."
Regulation	Regulation refers to restrictions state and federal laws place on business with regard to the conduct of its activities.
Interest	In finance and economics, interest is the price paid by a borrower for the use of a lender's

money. In other words, interest is the amount of paid to "rent" money for a period of time.

Channel	Channel, in communications (sometimes called communications channel), refers to the medium used to convey information from a sender (or transmitter) to a receiver.
Federal government	Federal government refers to the government of the United States, as distinct from the state and local governments.
Partnership	In the common law, a partnership is a type of business entity in which partners share with each other the profits or losses of the business undertaking in which they have all invested.
Household	An economic unit that provides the economy with resources and uses the income received to purchase goods and services that satisfy economic wants is called household.
Mistake	In contract law a mistake is incorrect understanding by one or more parties to a contract and may be used as grounds to invalidate the agreement. Common law has identified three different types of mistake in contract: unilateral mistake, mutual mistake, and common mistake.
Logo	Logo refers to device or other brand name that cannot be spoken.
Appeal	Appeal refers to the act of asking an appellate court to overturn a decision after the trial court's final judgment has been entered.
Balance	In banking and accountancy, the outstanding balance is the amount of money owned, (or due), that remains in a deposit account (or a loan account) at a given date, after all past remittances, payments and withdrawal have been accounted for. It can be positive (then, in the balance sheet of a firm, it is an asset) or negative (a liability).
Unlimited wants	The insatiable desire of consumers for goods and services that will give them satisfaction or utility are called unlimited wants. Unlimited wants and needs are one half of the fundamental problem of scarcity that has plagued humanity since the beginning of time. The other half of the scarcity problem is limited resources.
Economics	The social science dealing with the use of scarce resources to obtain the maximum satisfaction of society's virtually unlimited economic wants is an economics.
Compromise	Compromise occurs when the interaction is moderately important to meeting goals and the goals are neither completely compatible nor completely incompatible.
Service	Service refers to a "non tangible product" that is not embodied in a physical good and that typically effects some change in another product, person, or institution. Contrasts with good.
Buyer	A buyer refers to a role in the buying center with formal authority and responsibility to select the supplier and negotiate the terms of the contract.
Demand curve	Demand curve refers to the graph of quantity demanded as a function of price, normally downward sloping, straight or curved, and drawn with quantity on the horizontal axis and price on the vertical axis.
Slope	The slope of a line in the plane containing the x and y axes is generally represented by the letter m, and is defined as the change in the y coordinate divided by the corresponding change in the x coordinate, between two distinct points on the line.
Ford	Ford is an American company that manufactures and sells automobiles worldwide. Ford introduced methods for large-scale manufacturing of cars, and large-scale management of an industrial workforce, especially elaborately engineered manufacturing sequences typified by the moving assembly lines.
Quantity demanded	The amount of a good or service that buyers desire to purchase at a particular price during some period is a quantity demanded.

Go to **Cram101.com** for the Practice Tests for this Chapter.

Time magazine	Time magazine was co-founded in 1923 by Briton Hadden and Henry Luce, making it the first weekly news magazine in the United States.
Developing country	Developing country refers to a country whose per capita income is low by world standards. Same as LDC. As usually used, it does not necessarily connote that the country's income is rising.
Movement along a demand curve	The change in quantity demanded brought about by a change in price is a movement along a demand curve.
Firm	An organization that employs resources to produce a good or service for profit and owns and operates one or more plants is referred to as a firm.
Complementary good	A complementary good refers to a product or service that is used together with another good. When the price of one falls, the demand for the other increases. Cameras and film are considered complementary goods.
Variable	A variable is something measured by a number; it is used to analyze what happens to other things when the size of that number changes.
Advertising	Advertising refers to paid, nonpersonal communication through various media by organizations and individuals who are in some way identified in the advertising message.
Marketing	Promoting and selling products or services to customers, or prospective customers, is referred to as marketing.
Profit	Profit refers to the return to the resource entrepreneurial ability; total revenue minus total cost.
Supply curve	Supply curve refers to the graph of quantity supplied as a function of price, normally upward sloping, straight or curved, and drawn with quantity on the horizontal axis and price on the vertical axis.
Quantity supplied	The amount of a good or service that producers offer to sell at a particular price during a given time period is called quantity supplied.
Inputs	The inputs used by a firm or an economy are the labor, raw materials, electricity and other resources it uses to produce its outputs.
Labor	People's physical and mental talents and efforts that are used to help produce goods and services are called labor.
Human resources	Human resources refers to the individuals within the firm, and to the portion of the firm's organization that deals with hiring, firing, training, and other personnel issues.
Capital	Capital generally refers to financial wealth, especially that used to start or maintain a business. In classical economics, capital is one of four factors of production, the others being land and labor and entrepreneurship.
Technology	The body of knowledge and techniques that can be used to combine economic resources to produce goods and services is called technology.
Factors of production	Economic resources: land, capital, labor, and entrepreneurial ability are called factors of production.
Production	The creation of finished goods and services using the factors of production: land, labor, capital, entrepreneurship, and knowledge.
Exporting	Selling products to another country is called exporting.
Supply and demand	The partial equilibrium supply and demand economic model originally developed by Alfred Marshall attempts to describe, explain, and predict changes in the price and quantity of

Go to **Cram101.com** for the Practice Tests for this Chapter.

goods sold in competitive markets.

Equilibrium price	Equilibrium price refers to the price in a competitive market at which the quantity demanded and the quantity supplied are equal, there is neither a shortage nor a surplus, and there is no tendency for price to rise or fall.
Market price	Market price is an economic concept with commonplace familiarity; it is the price that a good or service is offered at, or will fetch, in the marketplace; it is of interest mainly in the study of microeconomics.
Sony	Sony is a multinational corporation and one of the world's largest media conglomerates founded in Tokyo, Japan. One of its divisions Sony Electronics is one of the leading manufacturers of electronics, video, communications, and information technology products for the consumer and professional markets.
Export	In economics, an export is any good or commodity, shipped or otherwise transported out of a country, province, town to another part of the world in a legitimate fashion, typically for use in trade or sale.
Industry	A group of firms that produce identical or similar products is an industry. It is also used specifically to refer to an area of economic production focused on manufacturing which involves large amounts of capital investment before any profit can be realized, also called "heavy industry".
DaimlerChrysler	In 2002, the merged company, DaimlerChrysler, appeared to run two independent product lines, with few signs of corporate integration. In 2003, however, it was alleged by the Detroit News that the "merger of equals" was, in fact, a takeover.
Dealer	People who link buyers with sellers by buying and selling securities at stated prices are referred to as a dealer.
Markup	Markup is a term used in marketing to indicate how much the price of a product is above the cost of producing and distributing the product.
Law of supply	The principle that, other things equal, an increase in the price of a product will increase the quantity of it supplied, and conversely for a price decrease is the law of supply.
Economic environment	The economic environment represents the external conditions under which people are engaged in, and benefit from, economic activity. It includes aspects of economic status, paid employment, and finances.
Macroeconomics	Macroeconomics refers to the part of economics concerned with the economy as a whole; with such major aggregates as the household, business, and government sectors; and with measures of the total economy.
Goodwill	Goodwill is an important accounting concept that describes the value of a business entity not directly attributable to its tangible assets and liabilities.
Globalization	The increasing world-wide integration of markets for goods, services and capital that attracted special attention in the late 1990s is called globalization.
Lease	A contract for the possession and use of land or other property, including goods, on one side, and a recompense of rent or other income on the other is the lease.
Policy	Similar to a script in that a policy can be a less than completely rational decision-making method. Involves the use of a pre-existing set of decision steps for any problem that presents itself.
Mixed economy	An economy in which some production is done by the private sector and some by the state, in state-owned enterprises is called mixed economy.

Go to **Cram101.com** for the Practice Tests for this Chapter.

Market economy	A market economy is an economic system in which the production and distribution of goods and services takes place through the mechanism of free markets guided by a free price system rather than by the state in a planned economy.
Capitalism	Capitalism refers to an economic system in which capital is mostly owned by private individuals and corporations. Contrasts with communism.
Controlling	A management function that involves determining whether or not an organization is progressing toward its goals and objectives, and taking corrective action if it is not is called controlling.
Competitiveness	Competitiveness usually refers to characteristics that permit a firm to compete effectively with other firms due to low cost or superior technology, perhaps internationally.
Consideration	Consideration in contract law, a basic requirement for an enforceable agreement under traditional contract principles, defined in this text as legal value, bargained for and given in exchange for an act or promise. In corporation law, cash or property contributed to a corporation in exchange for shares, or a promise to contribute such cash or property.
Monopolistic competition	Monopolistic competition refers to a market structure in which there are many sellers each producing a differentiated product.
Pure competition	A market structure in which a very large number of firms sells a standardized product, into which entry is very easy, in which the individual seller has no control over the product price, and in which there is no non-price competition is pure competition.
Oligopoly	A market structure in which there are a small number of sellers, at least some of whose individual decisions about price or quantity matter to the others is an oligopoly.
Monopoly	A monopoly is defined as a persistent market situation where there is only one provider of a kind of product or service.
Homogeneous Product	Homogeneous product refers to the product of an industry in which the outputs of different firms are indistinguishable. Contrasts with differentiated product.
Homogeneous	In the context of procurement/purchasing, homogeneous is used to describe goods that do not vary in their essential characteristic irrespective of the source of supply.
Competitive market	A market in which no buyer or seller has market power is called a competitive market.
Retailing	All activities involved in selling, renting, and providing goods and services to ultimate consumers for personal, family, or household use is referred to as retailing.
Investment	Investment refers to spending for the production and accumulation of capital and additions to inventories. In a financial sense, buying an asset with the expectation of making a return.
Price competition	Price competition is where a company tries to distinguish its product or service from competing products on the basis of low price.
Pure monopoly	A market structure in which one firm sells a unique product, into which entry is blocked, in which the single firm has considerable control over product price, and in which non-price competition may or may not be found is called pure monopoly.
Pfizer	Pfizer is the world's largest pharmaceutical company based in New York City. It produces the number-one selling drug Lipitor (atorvastatin, used to lower blood cholesterol).
Research and development	The use of resources for the deliberate discovery of new information and ways of doing things, together with the application of that information in inventing new products or processes is referred to as research and development.
Patent	The legal right to the proceeds from and control over the use of an invented product or

49

process, granted for a fixed period of time, usually 20 years. Patent is one form of intellectual property that is subject of the TRIPS agreement.

Antitrust legislation	Antitrust legislation refers to laws prohibiting monopolization, restraints of trade, and collusion among firms to raise prices or inhibit competition.
Sherman Act	Federal antitrust act of 1890 that makes monopoly and conspiracies to restrain trade criminal offenses is the Sherman Act.
Clayton act	The Clayton act is a federal antitrust act of 1914 that strengthened the Sherman Act by making it illegal for firms to engage in certain specified practices.
Antitrust	Government intervention to alter market structure or prevent abuse of market power is called antitrust.
Grant	Grant refers to an intergovernmental transfer of funds . Since the New Deal, state and local governments have become increasingly dependent upon federal grants for an almost infinite variety of programs.
Authority	Authority in agency law, refers to an agent's ability to affect his principal's legal relations with third parties. Also used to refer to an actor's legal power or ability to do something. In addition, sometimes used to refer to a statute, case, or other legal source that justifies a particular result.
Petition	A petition is a request to an authority, most commonly a government official or public entity. In the colloquial sense, a petition is a document addressed to some official and signed by numerous individuals.
Option	A contract that gives the purchaser the option to buy or sell the underlying financial instrument at a specified price, called the exercise price or strike price, within a specific period of time.
Revenue	Revenue is a U.S. business term for the amount of money that a company receives from its activities, mostly from sales of products and/or services to customers.
Food and Drug Administration	The Food and Drug Administration is an agency of the United States Department of Health and Human Services and is responsible for regulating food (human and animal), dietary supplements, drugs (human and animal), cosmetics, medical devices (human and animal) and radiation emitting devices (including non-medical devices), biologics, and blood products in the United States.
Administration	Administration refers to the management and direction of the affairs of governments and institutions; a collective term for all policymaking officials of a government; the execution and implementation of public policy.
Fund	Independent accounting entity with a self-balancing set of accounts segregated for the purposes of carrying on specific activities is referred to as a fund.
Free market	A free market is a market where price is determined by the unregulated interchange of supply and demand rather than set by artificial means.
Insurance	Insurance refers to a system by which individuals can reduce their exposure to risk of large losses by spreading the risks among a large number of persons.
Trend	Trend refers to the long-term movement of an economic variable, such as its average rate of increase or decrease over enough years to encompass several business cycles.
Deregulation	The lessening or complete removal of government regulations on an industry, especially concerning the price that firms are allowed to charge and leaving price to be determined by market forces a deregulation.

Utility	Utility refers to the want-satisfying power of a good or service; the satisfaction or pleasure a consumer obtains from the consumption of a good or service.
Amway	Amway is a multi-level marketing company founded in 1959 by Jay Van Andel and Rich DeVos. The company's name is a portmanteau of "American Way." .
Resource allocation	Resource allocation refers to the manner in which an economy distributes its resources among the potential uses so as to produce a particular set of final goods.
Socialism	An economic system under which the state owns the resources and makes the economic decisions is called socialism.
Communism	Communism refers to an economic system in which capital is owned by private government. Contrasts with capitalism.
Karl Marx	Karl Marx (May 5, 1818, Trier, Germany – March 14, 1883, London) was an immensely influential German philosopher, political economist, and socialist revolutionary. He is most famous for his analysis of history in terms of class struggles, summed up in the opening line of the introduction to the Communist Manifesto: "The history of all hitherto existing society is the history of class struggles."
Private property	The right of private persons and firms to obtain, own, control, employ, dispose of, and bequeath land, capital, and other property is referred to as private property.
Property	Assets defined in the broadest legal sense. Property includes the unrealized receivables of a cash basis taxpayer, but not services rendered.
Incentive	An incentive is any factor (financial or non-financial) that provides a motive for a particular course of action, or counts as a reason for preferring one choice to the alternatives.
Union	A worker association that bargains with employers over wages and working conditions is called a union.
Prime minister	The Prime Minister of the United Kingdom of Great Britain and Northern Ireland is the head of government and so exercises many of the executive functions nominally vested in the Sovereign, who is head of state. According to custom, the Prime Minister and the Cabinet (which he or she heads) are accountable for their actions to Parliament, of which they are members by (modern) convention.
Boot	Boot is any type of personal property received in a real property transaction that is not like kind, such as cash, mortgage notes, a boat or stock. The exchanger pays taxes on the boot to the extent of recognized capital gain. In an exchange if any funds are not used in purchasing the replacement property, that also will be called boot.
Consignment	Consignment refers to a bailment for sale. The consignee does not undertake the absolute obligation to sell or pay for the goods.
Forbes	David Churbuck founded online Forbes in 1996. The site drew attention when it uncovered Stephen Glass' journalistic fraud in The New Republic in 1998, a scoop that gave credibility to internet journalism.
Gross domestic product	Gross domestic product refers to the total value of new goods and services produced in a given year within the borders of a country, regardless of by whom.
Operation	A standardized method or technique that is performed repetitively, often on different materials resulting in different finished goods is called an operation.
Domestic	From or in one's own country. A domestic producer is one that produces inside the home country. A domestic price is the price inside the home country. Opposite of 'foreign' or 'world.'.

Free enterprise	Free enterprise refers to a system in which economic agents are free to own property and engage in commercial transactions.
Privatization	A process in which investment bankers take companies that were previously owned by the government to the public markets is referred to as privatization.
Private corporation	Private corporation refers to a corporation formed to conduct privately owned business. A Corporation whose shares are not publicly traded on any exchange.
Government units	The federal, state, and local agencies that buy goods and services for the constituents they serve is a government units.
Corporation	A legal entity chartered by a state or the Federal government that is distinct and separate from the individuals who own it is a corporation. This separation gives the corporation unique powers which other legal entities lack.
Leadership	Management merely consists of leadership applied to business situations; or in other words: management forms a sub-set of the broader process of leadership.
Monetary policy	The use of the money supply and/or the interest rate to influence the level of economic activity and other policy objectives including the balance of payments or the exchange rate is called monetary policy.
Inflation	An increase in the overall price level of an economy, usually as measured by the CPI or by the implicit price deflator is called inflation.
Private sector	The households and business firms of the economy are referred to as private sector.
Labor union	A group of workers organized to advance the interests of the group is called a labor union.
Interest rate	The rate of return on bonds, loans, or deposits. When one speaks of 'the' interest rate, it is usually in a model where there is only one.
Money supply	There are several formal definitions, but all include the quantity of currency in circulation plus the amount of demand deposits. The money supply, together with the amount of real economic activity in a country, is an important determinant of price.
Expansionary monetary policy	Increases aggregate demand by increasing the money supply are referred to as expansionary monetary policy.
Economic growth	Economic growth refers to the increase over time in the capacity of an economy to produce goods and services and to improve the well-being of its citizens.
Downturn	A decline in a stock market or economic cycle is a downturn.
Federal reserve system	The central banking authority responsible for monetary policy in the United States is called federal reserve system or the Fed.
Federal Reserve	The Federal Reserve System was created via the Federal Reserve Act of December 23rd, 1913. All national banks were required to join the system and other banks could join. The Reserve Banks opened for business on November 16th, 1914. Federal Reserve Notes were created as part of the legislation, to provide an elastic supply of currency.
National debt	National debt refers to total of outstanding federal government bonds on which the federal government must pay interest.
Board of Governors	A board of governors is usually the governing board of a public entity; the Board of Governors of the Federal Reserve System; the Federal Reserve Board.
Welfare	Welfare refers to the economic well being of an individual, group, or economy. For individuals, it is conceptualized by a utility function. For groups, including countries and the world, it is a tricky philosophical concept, since individuals fare differently.

Go to **Cram101.com** for the Practice Tests for this Chapter.

Fiscal policy	Fiscal policy refers to any macroeconomic policy involving the levels of government purchases, transfers, or taxes, usually implicitly focused on domestic goods, residents, or firms.
Government spending	Government spending refers to spending by all levels of government on goods and services.
Economic expansion	The upward phase of the business cycle, in which GDP is rising and unemployment is falling over time is called economic expansion.
Unemployment rate	The unemployment rate is the number of unemployed workers divided by the total civilian labor force, which includes both the unemployed and those with jobs (all those willing and able to work for pay).
Budget	Budget refers to an account, usually for a year, of the planned expenditures and the expected receipts of an entity. For a government, the receipts are tax revenues.
Federal budget	The annual statement of the expenditures and tax revenues of the government of the United States together with the laws and regulations that approve and support those expenditures and taxes is the federal budget.
Interest payment	The payment to holders of bonds payable, calculated by multiplying the stated rate on the face of the bond by the par, or face, value of the bond. If bonds are issued at a discount or premium, the interest payment does not equal the interest expense.
Social Security	Social security primarily refers to a field of social welfare concerned with social protection, or protection against socially recognized conditions, including poverty, old age, disability, unemployment, families with children and others.
Security	Security refers to a claim on the borrower future income that is sold by the borrower to the lender. A security is a type of transferable interest representing financial value.
Recession	A significant decline in economic activity. In the U.S., recession is approximately defined as two successive quarters of falling GDP, as judged by NBER.
Deficit	The deficit is the amount by which expenditure exceed revenue.
Bond	Bond refers to a debt instrument, issued by a borrower and promising a specified stream of payments to the purchaser, usually regular interest payments plus a final repayment of principal.
Treasury notes	Intermediate-term obligations of the federal government with maturities from 1 to 10 years are called treasury notes.
Treasury bills	Short-term obligations of the federal government are treasury bills. They are like zero coupon bonds in that they do not pay interest prior to maturity; instead they are sold at a discount of the par value to create a positive yield to maturity.
Compaq	Compaq was founded in February 1982 by Rod Canion, Jim Harris and Bill Murto, three senior managers from semiconductor manufacturer Texas Instruments. Each invested $1,000 to form the company. Their first venture capital came from Ben Rosen and Sevin-Rosen partners. It is often told that the architecture of the original PC was first sketched out on a placemat by the founders while dining in the Houston restaurant, House of Pies.
Volkswagen	Volkswagen or VW is an automobile manufacturer based in Wolfsburg, Germany in the state of Lower Saxony. It forms the core of this Group, one of the world's four largest car producers. Its German tagline is "Aus Liebe zum Automobil", which is translated as "For the love of the car" - or, For Love of the People's Cars,".
Economic interdependence	Economic interdependence describes countries/nation-states and/or supranational states such as the European Union (EU) or North American Free Trade Agreement (NAFTA) that are

	interdependent for any (or all) of the following: food , energy, minerals,manufactured goods, multinational/transnational corporations , financial institutions and foreign debt.
Interdependence	The extent to which departments depend on each other for resources or materials to accomplish their tasks is referred to as interdependence.
Manufacturing	Production of goods primarily by the application of labor and capital to raw materials and other intermediate inputs, in contrast to agriculture, mining, forestry, fishing, and services a manufacturing.
Nike	Because Nike creates goods for a wide range of sports, they have competition from every sports and sports fashion brand there is. Nike has no direct competitors because there is no single brand which can compete directly with their range of sports and non-sports oriented gear, except for Reebok.
Entrepreneurship	The assembling of resources to produce new or improved products and technologies is referred to as entrepreneurship.
Openness	Openness refers to the extent to which an economy is open, often measured by the ratio of its trade to GDP.
Immigration	Immigration refers to the migration of people into a country.
Nokia	Nokia Corporation is the world's largest manufacturer of mobile telephones (as of June 2006), with a global market share of approximately 34% in Q2 of 2006. It produces mobile phones for every major market and protocol, including GSM, CDMA, and W-CDMA (UMTS).
Innovation	Innovation refers to the first commercially successful introduction of a new product, the use of a new method of production, or the creation of a new form of business organization.
Bureaucracy	Bureaucracy refers to an organization with many layers of managers who set rules and regulations and oversee all decisions.
Business cycle	Business cycle refers to the pattern followed by macroeconommic variables, such as GDP and unemployment that rise and fall irregularly over time, relative to trend.
Purchasing	Purchasing refers to the function in a firm that searches for quality material resources, finds the best suppliers, and negotiates the best price for goods and services.
Per capita income	The per capita income for a group of people may be defined as their total personal income, divided by the total population. Per capita income is usually reported in units of currency per year.
Per capita	Per capita refers to per person. Usually used to indicate the average per person of any given statistic, commonly income.
Disney	Disney is one of the largest media and entertainment corporations in the world. Founded on October 16, 1923 by brothers Walt and Roy Disney as a small animation studio, today it is one of the largest Hollywood studios and also owns nine theme parks and several television networks, including the American Broadcasting Company (ABC).
General Electric	In 1876, Thomas Alva Edison opened a new laboratory in Menlo Park, New Jersey. Out of the laboratory was to come perhaps the most famous invention of all—a successful development of the incandescent electric lamp. By 1890, Edison had organized his various businesses into the Edison General Electric Company.
Economic development	Increase in the economic standard of living of a country's population, normally accomplished by increasing its stocks of physical and human capital and improving its technology is an economic development.
Maquiladora	A maquiladora is a factory that imports materials and equipment on a duty-free and tariff-

Go to **Cram101.com** for the Practice Tests for this Chapter.

	free basis for assembly or manufacturing and then re-exports the assembled product usually back to the originating country.
Domestic output	Domestic output refers to gross domestic product; the total output of final goods and services produced in the economy.
Absolute advantage	A country has an absolute advantage economically over another when it can produce something more cheaply. This term is often used to differentiate between comparative advantage.
Emerging markets	The term emerging markets is commonly used to describe business and market activity in industrializing or emerging regions of the world. It is sometimes loosely used as a replacement for emerging economies, but really signifies a business phenomenon that is not fully described by or constrained to geography or economic strength; such countries are considered to be in a transitional phase between developing and developed status.
Emerging market	The term emerging market is commonly used to describe business and market activity in industrializing or emerging regions of the world.
Extension	Extension refers to an out-of-court settlement in which creditors agree to allow the firm more time to meet its financial obligations. A new repayment schedule will be developed, subject to the acceptance of creditors.
Competitive advantage	A business is said to have a competitive advantage when its unique strengths, often based on cost, quality, time, and innovation, offer consumers a greater percieved value and there by diffentiating it from its competitors.
Balance of payments	Balance of payments refers to a list, or accounting, of all of a country's international transactions for a given time period, usually one year.
Balance of trade	Balance of trade refers to the sum of the money gained by a given economy by selling exports, minus the cost of buying imports. They form part of the balance of payments, which also includes other transactions such as the international investment position.
Currency exchange rate	The rate between two currencies that specifies how much one country's currency is worth expressed in terms of the other country's currency is the currency exchange rate.
Trade surplus	A positive balance of trade is known as a trade surplus and consists of exporting more (in financial capital terms) than one imports.
Trade deficit	The amount by which imports exceed exports of goods and services is referred to as trade deficit.
Exporter	A firm that sells its product in another country is an exporter.
Trade balance	Balance of trade in terms of exports versus imports is called trade balance.
Economic forces	Forces that affect the availability, production, and distribution of a society's resources among competing users are referred to as economic forces.
Balance of payments surplus	Balance of payments surplus refers to a number summarizing the state of a country's international transactions, usually equal to the excess on the current account plus the balance on capital account.
Gap	In December of 1995, Gap became the first major North American retailer to accept independent monitoring of the working conditions in a contract factory producing its garments. Gap is the largest specialty retailer in the United States.
American Airlines	American Airlines developed from a conglomeration of about 82 small airlines through a series of corporate acquisitions and reorganizations: initially, the name American Airways was used as a common brand by a number of independent air carriers. American Airlines is the largest airline in the world in terms of total passengers transported and fleet size, and the second-

Go to **Cram101.com** for the Practice Tests for this Chapter.

	largest airline in the world.
American Express	From the early 1980s until the late 1990s, American Express was known for cutting its merchant fees (also known as a "discount rate") to fine merchants and restaurants if they only accepted American Express and no other credit or charge cards. This prompted competitors such as Visa and MasterCard to cry foul for a while, as the tactics "locked" restaurants into American Express.
Federal Express	The company officially began operations on April 17, 1973, utilizing a network of 14 Dassault Falcon 20s which connected 25 U.S. cities. FedEx, the first cargo airline to use jet aircraft for its services, expanded greatly after the deregulation of the cargo airlines sector. Federal Express use of the hub-spoke distribution paradigm in air freight enabled it to become a world leader in its field.
Walt Disney	As the co-founder of Walt Disney Productions, Walt became one of the most well-known motion picture producers in the world. The corporation he co-founded, now known as The Walt Disney Company, today has annual revenues of approximately US $30 billion.
Time Warner	Time Warner is the world's largest media company with major Internet, publishing, film, telecommunications and television divisions.
Allstate	Allstate was the first insurance company to use a computer program called "Colossus". The program was created by the Computer Sciences Corporation, CSC, based in El Segundo, California. Based on prefigured statistical information to aid adjusters with claims, the program has been the cause of class action lawsuits. One trial case cited the program has been manipulated to "drive down fair claims."
Advertising campaign	A comprehensive advertising plan that consists of a series of messages in a variety of media that center on a single theme or idea is referred to as an advertising campaign.
Euro	The common currency of a subset of the countries of the EU, adopted January 1, 1999 is called euro.
Devaluation	Lowering the value of a nation's currency relative to other currencies is called devaluation.
Pillsbury	Pillsbury the company was the first in the United States to use steam rollers for processing grain. The finished product required transportation, so the Pillsburys assisted in funding railroad development in Minnesota.
Barter	Barter is a type of trade where goods or services are exchanged for a certain amount of other goods or services; no money is involved in the transaction.
Commodity	Could refer to any good, but in trade a commodity is usually a raw material or primary product that enters into international trade, such as metals or basic agricultural products.
Customs	Customs is an authority or agency in a country responsible for collecting customs duties and for controlling the flow of people, animals and goods (including personal effects and hazardous items) in and out of the country.
Body language	Body language is a broad term for forms of communication using body movements or gestures instead of, or in addition to, sounds, verbal language, or other forms of communication.
Closing	The finalization of a real estate sales transaction that passes title to the property from the seller to the buyer is referred to as a closing. Closing is a sales term which refers to the process of making a sale. It refers to reaching the final step, which may be an exchange of money or acquiring a signature.
Users	Users refer to people in the organization who actually use the product or service purchased by the buying center.
Points	Loan origination fees that may be deductible as interest by a buyer of property. A seller of

Go to **Cram101.com** for the Practice Tests for this Chapter.

property who pays points reduces the selling price by the amount of the points paid for the buyer.

Accenture	In October 2002, the Congressional General Accounting Office (GAO) identified Accenture as one of four publicly-traded federal contractors that were incorporated in a tax haven country. Accenture is a global management consulting, technology services and outsourcing company. Its organizational structure includes divisions based on client industry types and employee workforces.
Trade show	A type of exhibition or forum where manufacturers can display their products to current as well as prospective buyers is referred to as trade show.
Business opportunity	A business opportunity involves the sale or lease of any product, service, equipment, etc. that will enable the purchaser-licensee to begin a business
Wireless communication	Wireless communication refers to a method of communication that uses low-powered radio waves to transmit data between devices. The term refers to communication without cables or cords, chiefly using radio frequency and infrared waves. Common uses include the various communications defined by the IrDA, the wireless networking of computers and cellular mobile phones.
Auction	A preexisting business model that operates successfully on the Internet by announcing an item for sale and permitting multiple purchasers to bid on them under specified rules and condition is an auction.
Bid	A bid price is a price offered by a buyer when he/she buys a good. In the context of stock trading on a stock exchange, the bid price is the highest price a buyer of a stock is willing to pay for a share of that given stock.
Debit	Debit refers to recording as negative in the balance of payments, any transaction that gives rise to a payment out of the country, such as an import, the purchase of an asset, or lending to foreigners. Opposite of credit.
Credit	Credit refers to a recording as positive in the balance of payments, any transaction that gives rise to a payment into the country, such as an export, the sale of an asset, or borrowing from abroad.
Commerce	Commerce is the exchange of something of value between two entities. It is the central mechanism from which capitalism is derived.
Host country	The country in which the parent-country organization seeks to locate or has already located a facility is a host country.
Stock	In financial terminology, stock is the capital raized by a corporation, through the issuance and sale of shares.
Stock exchange	A stock exchange is a corporation or mutual organization which provides facilities for stock brokers and traders, to trade company stocks and other securities.
Antitrust laws	Legislation that prohibits anticompetitive business activities such as price fixing, bid rigging, monopolization, and tying contracts is referred to as antitrust laws.
Brand	A name, symbol, or design that identifies the goods or services of one seller or group of sellers and distinguishes them from the goods and services of competitors is a brand.
Acquisition	A company's purchase of the property and obligations of another company is an acquisition.
Expense	In accounting, an expense represents an event in which an asset is used up or a liability is incurred. In terms of the accounting equation, expenses reduce owners' equity.
Bribery	When one person gives another person money, property, favors, or anything else of value for a

Go to **Cram101.com** for the Practice Tests for this Chapter.

favor in return, we have bribery. Often referred to as a payoff or 'kickback.'

Foreign Corrupt Practices Act	The Foreign Corrupt Practices Act of 1977 is a United States federal law requiring any company that has publicly-traded stock to maintain records that accurately and fairly represent the company's transactions; additionally, requires any publicly-traded company to have an adequate system of internal accounting controls.
Corruption	The unauthorized use of public office for private gain. The most common forms of corruption are bribery, extortion, and the misuse of inside information.
Prohibition	Prohibition refers to denial of the right to import or export, applying to particular products and/or particular countries. Includes embargo.
Treaties	The first source of international law, consisting of agreements or contracts between two or more nations that are formally signed by an authorized representative and ratified by the supreme power of each nation are called treaties.
Subsidy	Subsidy refers to government financial assistance to a domestic producer.
Trade barrier	An artificial disincentive to export and/or import, such as a tariff, quota, or other NTB is called a trade barrier.
Tariff	A tax imposed by a nation on an imported good is called a tariff.
Fixed price	Fixed price is a phrase used to mean that no bargaining is allowed over the price of a good or, less commonly, a service.
Discount	The difference between the face value of a bond and its selling price, when a bond is sold for less than its face value it's referred to as a discount.
Asset	An item of property, such as land, capital, money, a share in ownership, or a claim on others for future payment, such as a bond or a bank deposit is an asset.
Trade sanction	Use of a trade policy as a sanction, most commonly an embargo imposed against a country for violating human rights is referred to as trade sanction.
Protective tariff	A tariff designed to shield domestic producers of a good or service from the competition of foreign producers is referred to as a protective tariff.
Revenue tariff	A tariff designed to produce income for the Federal government is a revenue tariff.
Nontariff barrier	Any policy that interferes with exports or imports other than a simple tariff, prominently including quotas and vers is referred to as nontariff barrier.
Quota	A government-imposed restriction on quantity, or sometimes on total value, used to restrict the import of something to a specific quantity is called a quota.
Postal Service	The postal service was created in Philadelphia under Benjamin Franklin on July 26, 1775 by decree of the Second Continental Congress. Based on a clause in the United States Constitution empowering Congress "To establish Post Offices and post Roads."
Medicare	Medicare refers to federal program that is financed by payroll taxes and provides for compulsory hospital insurance for senior citizens and low-cost voluntary insurance to help older Americans pay physicians' fees.
Fortune magazine	Fortune magazine is America's longest-running business magazine. Currently owned by media conglomerate Time Warner, it was founded in 1930 by Henry Luce. It is known for its regular features ranking companies by revenue.
Organizational structure	Organizational structure is the way in which the interrelated groups of an organization are constructed. From a managerial point of view the main concerns are ensuring effective communication and coordination.

Go to **Cram101.com** for the Practice Tests for this Chapter.

| **Business Week** | Business Week is a business magazine published by McGraw-Hill. It was first published in 1929 under the direction of Malcolm Muir, who was serving as president of the McGraw-Hill Publishing company at the time. It is considered to be the standard both in industry and among students. |

Entrepreneur	The owner/operator. The person who organizes, manages, and assumes the risks of a firm, taking a new idea or a new product and turning it into a successful business is an entrepreneur.
Economy	The income, expenditures, and resources that affect the cost of running a business and household are called an economy.
Management	Management characterizes the process of leading and directing all or part of an organization, often a business, through the deployment and manipulation of resources. Early twentieth-century management writer Mary Parker Follett defined management as "the art of getting things done through people."
Merger	Merger refers to the combination of two firms into a single firm.
Trend	Trend refers to the long-term movement of an economic variable, such as its average rate of increase or decrease over enough years to encompass several business cycles.
Mergers and acquisitions	The phrase mergers and acquisitions refers to the aspect of corporate finance strategy and management dealing with the merging and acquiring of different companies as well as other assets. Usually mergers occur in a friendly setting where executives from the respective companies participate in a due diligence process to ensure a successful combination of all parts.
Acquisition	A company's purchase of the property and obligations of another company is an acquisition.
Public ownership	Public ownership is government ownership of any asset, industry, or corporation at any level, national, regional or local (municipal). The process of bringing an asset into public ownership is called nationalization or municipalization.
Cooperative	A business owned and controlled by the people who use it, producers, consumers, or workers with similar needs who pool their resources for mutual gain is called cooperative.
Brand	A name, symbol, or design that identifies the goods or services of one seller or group of sellers and distinguishes them from the goods and services of competitors is a brand.
Industry	A group of firms that produce identical or similar products is an industry. It is also used specifically to refer to an area of economic production focused on manufacturing which involves large amounts of capital investment before any profit can be realized, also called "heavy industry".
Stock	In financial terminology, stock is the capital raized by a corporation, through the issuance and sale of shares.
Business plan	A detailed written statement that describes the nature of the business, the target market, the advantages the business will have in relation to competition, and the resources and qualifications of the owner is referred to as a business plan.
Niche	In industry, a niche is a situation or an activity perfectly suited to a person. A niche can imply a working position or an area suited to a person who occupies it. Basically, a job where a person is able to succeed and thrive.
Mobil	Mobil is a major oil company which merged with the Exxon Corporation in 1999. Today Mobil continues as a major brand name within the combined company.
Exxon	Exxon formally replaced the Esso, Enco, and Humble brands on January 1, 1973, in the USA. The name Esso, pronounced S-O, attracted protests from other Standard Oil spinoffs because of its similarity to the name of the parent company, Standard Oil.
Firm	An organization that employs resources to produce a good or service for profit and owns and operates one or more plants is referred to as a firm.

Go to **Cram101.com** for the Practice Tests for this Chapter.

General Electric	In 1876, Thomas Alva Edison opened a new laboratory in Menlo Park, New Jersey. Out of the laboratory was to come perhaps the most famous invention of all—a successful development of the incandescent electric lamp. By 1890, Edison had organized his various businesses into the Edison General Electric Company.
Exxon Mobil	Exxon Mobil is the largest publicly traded integrated oil and gas company in the world, formed on November 30, 1999, by the merger of Exxon and Mobil. It is the sixth-largest company in the world as ranked by the Forbes Global 2000 and the largest company in the world (by revenue) as ranked by the Fortune Global 500.
Small business	Small business refers to a business that is independently owned and operated, is not dominant in its field of operation, and meets certain standards of size in terms of employees or annual receipts.
Service	Service refers to a "non tangible product" that is not embodied in a physical good and that typically effects some change in another product, person, or institution. Contrasts with good.
Purchasing	Purchasing refers to the function in a firm that searches for quality material resources, finds the best suppliers, and negotiates the best price for goods and services.
Competitor	Other organizations in the same industry or type of business that provide a good or service to the same set of customers is referred to as a competitor.
Advertising	Advertising refers to paid, nonpersonal communication through various media by organizations and individuals who are in some way identified in the advertising message.
Wholesale	According to the United Nations Statistics Division Wholesale is the resale of new and used goods to retailers, to industrial, commercial, institutional or professional users, or to other wholesalers, or involves acting as an agent or broker in buying merchandise for, or selling merchandise, to such persons or companies.
Technology	The body of knowledge and techniques that can be used to combine economic resources to produce goods and services is called technology.
Administration	Administration refers to the management and direction of the affairs of governments and institutions; a collective term for all policymaking officials of a government; the execution and implementation of public policy.
Business strategy	Business strategy, which refers to the aggregated operational strategies of single business firm or that of an SBU in a diversified corporation refers to the way in which a firm competes in its chosen arenas.
Profit	Profit refers to the return to the resource entrepreneurial ability; total revenue minus total cost.
Business Week	Business Week is a business magazine published by McGraw-Hill. It was first published in 1929 under the direction of Malcolm Muir, who was serving as president of the McGraw-Hill Publishing company at the time. It is considered to be the standard both in industry and among students.
Retailing	All activities involved in selling, renting, and providing goods and services to ultimate consumers for personal, family, or household use is referred to as retailing.
Sears	Before the Sears catalog, farmers typically bought supplies (often at very high prices) from local general stores. Sears took advantage of this by publishing his catalog with clearly stated prices, so that consumers could know what he was selling and at what price, and order and obtain them conveniently. The catalog business soon grew quickly.
Merchandising	Merchandising refers to the business of acquiring finished goods for resale, either in a

	wholesale or a retail operation.
Supply	Supply is the aggregate amount of any material good that can be called into being at a certain price point; it comprises one half of the equation of supply and demand. In classical economic theory, a curve representing supply is one of the factors that produce price.
Fund	Independent accounting entity with a self-balancing set of accounts segregated for the purposes of carrying on specific activities is referred to as a fund.
Shareholder	A shareholder is an individual or company (including a corporation) that legally owns one or more shares of stock in a joined stock company.
Operation	A standardized method or technique that is performed repetitively, often on different materials resulting in different finished goods is called an operation.
Labor	People's physical and mental talents and efforts that are used to help produce goods and services are called labor.
Adoption	In corporation law, a corporation's acceptance of a pre-incorporation contract by action of its board of directors, by which the corporation becomes liable on the contract, is referred to as adoption.
Drawback	Drawback refers to rebate of import duties when the imported good is re-exported or used as input to the production of an exported good.
Core	A core is the set of feasible allocations in an economy that cannot be improved upon by subset of the set of the economy's consumers (a coalition). In construction, when the force in an element is within a certain center section, the core, the element will only be under compression.
Gross domestic product	Gross domestic product refers to the total value of new goods and services produced in a given year within the borders of a country, regardless of by whom.
Domestic	From or in one's own country. A domestic producer is one that produces inside the home country. A domestic price is the price inside the home country. Opposite of 'foreign' or 'world.'.
Contribution	In business organization law, the cash or property contributed to a business by its owners is referred to as contribution.
Corporation	A legal entity chartered by a state or the Federal government that is distinct and separate from the individuals who own it is a corporation. This separation gives the corporation unique powers which other legal entities lack.
Customer service	The ability of logistics management to satisfy users in terms of time, dependability, communication, and convenience is called the customer service.
Innovation	Innovation refers to the first commercially successful introduction of a new product, the use of a new method of production, or the creation of a new form of business organization.
Product innovations	Innovations that introduce new goods or services to better meet customer needs are product innovations.
Product innovation	The development and sale of a new or improved product is a product innovation. Production of a new product on a commercial basis.
Product line	A group of products that are physically similar or are intended for a similar market are called the product line.
Auction	A preexisting business model that operates successfully on the Internet by announcing an item for sale and permitting multiple purchasers to bid on them under specified rules and condition is an auction.

EBay	eBay manages an online auction and shopping website, where people buy and sell goods and services worldwide.
Exchange	The trade of things of value between buyer and seller so that each is better off after the trade is called the exchange.
Overhead cost	An expenses of operating a business over and above the direct costs of producing a product is an overhead cost. They can include utilities (eg, electricity, telephone), advertizing and marketing, and any other costs not billed directly to the client or included in the price of the product.
Utility	Utility refers to the want-satisfying power of a good or service; the satisfaction or pleasure a consumer obtains from the consumption of a good or service.
Expense	In accounting, an expense represents an event in which an asset is used up or a liability is incurred. In terms of the accounting equation, expenses reduce owners' equity.
Inventory	Tangible property held for sale in the normal course of business or used in producing goods or services for sale is an inventory.
Personnel	A collective term for all of the employees of an organization. Personnel is also commonly used to refer to the personnel management function or the organizational unit responsible for administering personnel programs.
Overtime	Overtime is the amount of time someone works beyond normal working hours.
Production	The creation of finished goods and services using the factors of production: land, labor, capital, entrepreneurship, and knowledge.
Market	A market is, as defined in economics, a social arrangement that allows buyers and sellers to discover information and carry out a voluntary exchange of goods or services.
Market niche	A market niche or niche market is a focused, targetable portion of a market. By definition, then, a business that focuses on a niche market is addressing a need for a product or service that is not being addressed by mainstream providers.
Welfare	Welfare refers to the economic well being of an individual, group, or economy. For individuals, it is conceptualized by a utility function. For groups, including countries and the world, it is a tricky philosophical concept, since individuals fare differently.
Points	Loan origination fees that may be deductible as interest by a buyer of property. A seller of property who pays points reduces the selling price by the amount of the points paid for the buyer.
Competitive market	A market in which no buyer or seller has market power is called a competitive market.
Downturn	A decline in a stock market or economic cycle is a downturn.
Buyer	A buyer refers to a role in the buying center with formal authority and responsibility to select the supplier and negotiate the terms of the contract.
Marketing	Promoting and selling products or services to customers, or prospective customers, is referred to as marketing.
Specialist	A specialist is a trader who makes a market in one or several stocks and holds the limit order book for those stocks.
Bankruptcy	Bankruptcy is a legally declared inability or impairment of ability of an individual or organization to pay their creditors.
Consultant	A professional that provides expert advice in a particular field or area in which customers

occassionaly require this type of knowledge is a consultant.

Marketing research	Marketing research refers to the analysis of markets to determine opportunities and challenges, and to find the information needed to make good decisions.
Capital	Capital generally refers to financial wealth, especially that used to start or maintain a business. In classical economics, capital is one of four factors of production, the others being land and labor and entrepreneurship.
Benetton	Benetton has been known in the United States for producing a long-running series of controversial, sometimes offensive, advertisements that have caused a number of media critics to accuse the company of deliberately creating controversy in order to sell its products. This publicity campaign originated when photographer Oliviero Toscani was given carte blanche by the Benetton management.
Competitiveness	Competitiveness usually refers to characteristics that permit a firm to compete effectively with other firms due to low cost or superior technology, perhaps internationally.
Cash flow	In finance, cash flow refers to the amounts of cash being received and spent by a business during a defined period of time, sometimes tied to a specific project. Most of the time they are being used to determine gaps in the liquid position of a company.
Revenue	Revenue is a U.S. business term for the amount of money that a company receives from its activities, mostly from sales of products and/or services to customers.
Lender	Suppliers and financial institutions that lend money to companies is referred to as a lender.
Balance	In banking and accountancy, the outstanding balance is the amount of money owned, (or due), that remains in a deposit account (or a loan account) at a given date, after all past remittances, payments and withdrawal have been accounted for. It can be positive (then, in the balance sheet of a firm, it is an asset) or negative (a liability).
Pledge	In law a pledge (also pawn) is a bailment of personal property as a security for some debt or engagement.
Equity	Equity is the name given to the set of legal principles, in countries following the English common law tradition, which supplement strict rules of law where their application would operate harshly, so as to achieve what is sometimes referred to as "natural justice."
Asset	An item of property, such as land, capital, money, a share in ownership, or a claim on others for future payment, such as a bond or a bank deposit is an asset.
Equity financing	Financing that consists of funds that are invested in exchange for ownership in the company is called equity financing.
Collateral	Property that is pledged to the lender to guarantee payment in the event that the borrower is unable to make debt payments is called collateral.
Holding	The holding is a court's determination of a matter of law based on the issue presented in the particular case. In other words: under this law, with these facts, this result.
Personal saving	Personal saving refers to the personal income of households less personal taxes and personal consumption expenditures; disposable income not spent for consumer goods.
Credit	Credit refers to a recording as positive in the balance of payments, any transaction that gives rise to a payment into the country, such as an export, the sale of an asset, or borrowing from abroad.
Investment banks	Investment banks, assist public and private corporations in raising funds in the capital markets (both equity and debt), as well as in providing strategic advisory services for mergers, acquisitions and other types of financial transactions. They also act as

Go to **Cram101.com** for the Practice Tests for this Chapter.

	intermediaries in trading for clients. Investment banks differ from commercial banks, which take deposits and make commercial and retail loans.
Investment	Investment refers to spending for the production and accumulation of capital and additions to inventories. In a financial sense, buying an asset with the expectation of making a return.
Interest	In finance and economics, interest is the price paid by a borrower for the use of a lender's money. In other words, interest is the amount of paid to "rent" money for a period of time.
Mistake	In contract law a mistake is incorrect understanding by one or more parties to a contract and may be used as grounds to invalidate the agreement. Common law has identified three different types of mistake in contract: unilateral mistake, mutual mistake, and common mistake.
Debt financing	Obtaining financing by borrowing money is debt financing.
Interest rate	The rate of return on bonds, loans, or deposits. When one speaks of 'the' interest rate, it is usually in a model where there is only one.
Users	Users refer to people in the organization who actually use the product or service purchased by the buying center.
A share	In finance the term A share has two distinct meanings, both relating to securities. The first is a designation for a 'class' of common or preferred stock. A share of common or preferred stock typically has enhanced voting rights or other benefits compared to the other forms of shares that may have been created. The equity structure, or how many types of shares are offered, is determined by the corporate charter.
Line of credit	Line of credit refers to a given amount of unsecured short-term funds a bank will lend to a business, provided the funds are readily available.
Venture capital firm	A financial intermediary that pools the resources of its partners and uses the funds to help entrepreneurs start up new businesses is referred to as a venture capital firm.
Venture capital	Venture capital is capital provided by outside investors for financing of new, growing or struggling businesses. Venture capital investments generally are high risk investments but offer the potential for above average returns.
Partnership	In the common law, a partnership is a type of business entity in which partners share with each other the profits or losses of the business undertaking in which they have all invested.
Boot	Boot is any type of personal property received in a real property transaction that is not like kind, such as cash, mortgage notes, a boat or stock. The exchanger pays taxes on the boot to the extent of recognized capital gain. In an exchange if any funds are not used in purchasing the replacement property, that also will be called boot.
Venture capitalists	Venture capitalists refer to individuals or companies that invest in new businesses in exchange for partial ownership of those businesses.
Budget	Budget refers to an account, usually for a year, of the planned expenditures and the expected receipts of an entity. For a government, the receipts are tax revenues.
Exempt	Employees who are not covered by the Fair Labor Standards Act are exempt. Exempt employees are not eligible for overtime pay.
Regulation	Regulation refers to restrictions state and federal laws place on business with regard to the conduct of its activities.
Occupational Safety and Health Administration	The United States Occupational Safety and Health Administration is an agency of the United States Department of Labor. It was created by Congress under the Occupational Safety and Health Act, signed by President Richard M. Nixon, on December 29, 1970.

Compliance	A type of influence process where a receiver accepts the position advocated by a source to obtain favorable outcomes or to avoid punishment is the compliance.
Social Security	Social security primarily refers to a field of social welfare concerned with social protection, or protection against socially recognized conditions, including poverty, old age, disability, unemployment, families with children and others.
Insurance	Insurance refers to a system by which individuals can reduce their exposure to risk of large losses by spreading the risks among a large number of persons.
Security	Security refers to a claim on the borrower future income that is sold by the borrower to the lender. A security is a type of transferable interest representing financial value.
Business incubator	An innovation that provides shared office space, management support services, and management advice to entrepreneurs is a business incubator.
Market share	That fraction of an industry's output accounted for by an individual firm or group of firms is called market share.
Entrepreneurship	The assembling of resources to produce new or improved products and technologies is referred to as entrepreneurship.
Journal	Book of original entry, in which transactions are recorded in a general ledger system, is referred to as a journal.
Business development	Business development emcompasses a number of techniques designed to grow an economic enterprise. Such techniques include, but are not limited to, assessments of marketing opportunities and target markets, intelligence gathering on customers and competitors, generating leads for possible sales, followup sales activity, and formal proposal writing.
Commerce	Commerce is the exchange of something of value between two entities. It is the central mechanism from which capitalism is derived.
Target market	One or more specific groups of potential consumers toward which an organization directs its marketing program are a target market.
Distribution	Distribution in economics, the manner in which total output and income is distributed among individuals or factors.
Demographic	A demographic is a term used in marketing and broadcasting, to describe a demographic grouping or a market segment.
Breakeven point	Breakeven point refers to quantity of output sold at which total revenues equal total costs, that is where the economic profit is zero.
Liability	A liability is a present obligation of the enterprise arizing from past events, the settlement of which is expected to result in an outflow from the enterprise of resources embodying economic benefits.
Principal	In agency law, one under whose direction an agent acts and for whose benefit that agent acts is a principal.
Sole proprietorship	A sole proprietorship is a business which legally has no separate existence from its owner. Hence, the limitations of liability enjoyed by a corporation do not apply.
Appeal	Appeal refers to the act of asking an appellate court to overturn a decision after the trial court's final judgment has been entered.
Chief executive officer	A chief executive officer is the highest-ranking corporate officer or executive officer of a corporation, or agency. In closely held corporations, it is general business culture that the office chief executive officer is also the chairman of the board.

Go to **Cram101.com** for the Practice Tests for this Chapter.

Variable	A variable is something measured by a number; it is used to analyze what happens to other things when the size of that number changes.
Credibility	The extent to which a source is perceived as having knowledge, skill, or experience relevant to a communication topic and can be trusted to give an unbiased opinion or present objective information on the issue is called credibility.
Government procurement	Government procurement refers to purchase of goods and services by government and by state-owned enterprises.
Procurement	Procurement is the acquisition of goods or services at the best possible total cost of ownership, in the right quantity, at the right time, in the right place for the direct benefit or use of the governments, corporations, or individuals generally via, but not limited to a contract.
Recovery	Characterized by rizing output, falling unemployment, rizing profits, and increasing economic activity following a decline is a recovery.
Total cost	The sum of fixed cost and variable cost is referred to as total cost.
Applicant	In many tribunal and administrative law suits, the person who initiates the claim is called the applicant.
Estate	An estate is the totality of the legal rights, interests, entitlements and obligations attaching to property. In the context of wills and probate, it refers to the totality of the property which the deceased owned or in which some interest was held.
Enterprise	Enterprise refers to another name for a business organization. Other similar terms are business firm, sometimes simply business, sometimes simply firm, as well as company, and entity.
Intel	Intel Corporation, founded in 1968 and based in Santa Clara, California, USA, is the world's largest semiconductor company. Intel is best known for its PC microprocessors, where it maintains roughly 80% market share.
Sun Microsystems	Sun Microsystems is most well known for its Unix systems, which have a reputation for system stability and a consistent design philosophy.
Federal Express	The company officially began operations on April 17, 1973, utilizing a network of 14 Dassault Falcon 20s which connected 25 U.S. cities. FedEx, the first cargo airline to use jet aircraft for its services, expanded greatly after the deregulation of the cargo airlines sector. Federal Express use of the hub-spoke distribution paradigm in air freight enabled it to become a world leader in its field.
America Online	In 2000 America Online and Time Warner announced plans to merge, and the deal was approved by the Federal Trade Commission on January 11, 2001. This merger was primarily a product of the Internet mania of the late-1990s, known as the Internet bubble. The deal is known as one of the worst corporate mergers in history, destroying over $200 billion in shareholder value.
Apple Computer	Apple Computer has been a major player in the evolution of personal computing since its founding in 1976. The Apple II microcomputer, introduced in 1977, was a hit with home users.
Contract	A contract is a "promise" or an "agreement" that is enforced or recognized by the law. In the civil law, a contract is considered to be part of the general law of obligations.
Authority	Authority in agency law, refers to an agent's ability to affect his principal's legal relations with third parties. Also used to refer to an actor's legal power or ability to do something. In addition, sometimes used to refer to a statute, case, or other legal source that justifies a particular result.
Business	A business opportunity involves the sale or lease of any product, service, equipment, etc.

Go to **Cram101.com** for the Practice Tests for this Chapter.

opportunity	that will enable the purchaser-licensee to begin a business
Tenant	The party to whom the leasehold is transferred is a tenant. A leasehold estate is an ownership interest in land in which a lessee or a tenant holds real property by some form of title from a lessor or landlord.
Remainder	A remainder in property law is a future interest created in a transferee that is capable of becoming possessory upon the natural termination of a prior estate created by the same instrument.
Logistics	Those activities that focus on getting the right amount of the right products to the right place at the right time at the lowest possible cost is referred to as logistics.
Merchant	Under the Uniform Commercial Code, one who regularly deals in goods of the kind sold in the contract at issue, or holds himself out as having special knowledge or skill relevant to such goods, or who makes the sale through an agent who regularly deals in such goods or claims such knowledge or skill is referred to as merchant.
Devise	In a will, a gift of real property is called a devise.
Manufacturing business	A business firm that makes the products it sells is called a manufacturing business.
Manufacturing	Production of goods primarily by the application of labor and capital to raw materials and other intermediate inputs, in contrast to agriculture, mining, forestry, fishing, and services a manufacturing.
Publicity	Publicity refers to any information about an individual, product, or organization that's distributed to the public through the media and that's not paid for or controlled by the seller.
Federal government	Federal government refers to the government of the United States, as distinct from the state and local governments.
Mentor	An experienced employee who supervises, coaches, and guides lower-level employees by introducing them to the right people and generally being their organizational sponsor is a mentor.
Foundation	A Foundation is a type of philanthropic organization set up by either individuals or institutions as a legal entity (either as a corporation or trust) with the purpose of distributing grants to support causes in line with the goals of the foundation.
Immigration	Immigration refers to the migration of people into a country.
Shares	Shares refer to an equity security, representing a shareholder's ownership of a corporation. Shares are one of a finite number of equal portions in the capital of a company, entitling the owner to a proportion of distributed, non-reinvested profits known as dividends and to a portion of the value of the company in case of liquidation.
Agent	A person who makes economic decisions for another economic actor. A hired manager operates as an agent for a firm's owner.
Change agent	A change agent is someone who engages either deliberately or whose behavior results in social, cultural or behavioral change. This can be studied scientifically and effective techniques can be discovered and employed.
Intrapreneur	Creative person who works as an entrepreneur within corporations is referred to as an intrapreneur.
Allocate	Allocate refers to the assignment of income for various tax purposes. A multistate corporation's nonbusiness income usually is distributed to the state where the nonbusiness

	assets are located; it is not apportioned with the rest of the entity's income.
Policy	Similar to a script in that a policy can be a less than completely rational decision-making method. Involves the use of a pre-existing set of decision steps for any problem that presents itself.
Marketing Plan	Marketing plan refers to a road map for the marketing activities of an organization for a specified future period of time, such as one year or five years.
Sponsorship	When the advertiser assumes responsibility for the production and usually the content of a television program as well as the advertising that appears within it, we have sponsorship.
Chief financial officer	Chief financial officer refers to executive responsible for overseeing the financial operations of an organization.
Evaluation	The consumer's appraisal of the product or brand on important attributes is called evaluation.
Bill Gates	Bill Gates is the co-founder, chairman, former chief software architect, and former CEO of Microsoft Corporation. He is one of the best-known entrepreneurs of the personal computer revolution and he is widely respected for his foresight and ambition.
Steve Case	Steve Case is a businessman best known as the co-founder and former chief executive officer and chairman of America Online (AOL). He reached his highest profile when he played an instrumental role in AOL's merger with Time Warner in 2000.
Microsoft	Microsoft is a multinational computer technology corporation with 2004 global annual sales of US$39.79 billion and 71,553 employees in 102 countries and regions as of July 2006. It develops, manufactures, licenses, and supports a wide range of software products for computing devices.
Downsizing	The process of eliminating managerial and non-managerial positions are called downsizing.
Browser	A program that allows a user to connect to the World Wide Web by simply typing in a URL is a browser.
Status quo	Status quo is a Latin term meaning the present, current, existing state of affairs.
Public relations firm	An organization that develops and implements programs to manage a company's publicity, image, and affairs with consumers and other relevant publics is referred to as a public relations firm.
Public relations	Public relations refers to the management function that evaluates public attitudes, changes policies and procedures in response to the public's requests, and executes a program of action and information to earn public understanding and acceptance.
Subcontract	A subcontract is a contract that assigns part of an existing contract to a different party.
Toyota	Toyota is a Japanese multinational corporation that manufactures automobiles, trucks and buses. Toyota is the world's second largest automaker by sales. Toyota also provides financial services through its subsidiary, Toyota Financial Services, and participates in other lines of business.
Supplier Diversity	Supplier Diversity is a business program that encourages the use of previously underutilized minority owned vendors as suppliers. It is not directly correlated with supply chain diversification, although utilizing more vendors may enhance supply chain diversification.
United airlines	United Airlines is a major airline of the United States headquartered in unincorporated Elk Grove Township, Illinois, near Chicago's O'Hare International Airport, the airline's largest traffic hub, with 650 daily departures. On February 1, 2006, it emerged from Chapter 11 bankruptcy protection under which it had operated since December 9, 2002, the largest and

	longest airline bankruptcy case in history.
General Motors	General Motors is the world's largest automaker. Founded in 1908, today it employs about 327,000 people around the world. With global headquarters in Detroit, it manufactures its cars and trucks in 33 countries.
Eastman Kodak	Eastman Kodak Company is an American multinational public company producing photographic materials and equipment. Long known for its wide range of photographic film products, it has focused in recent years on three main businesses: digital photography, health imaging, and printing. This company remains the largest supplier of films in the world, both for the amateur and professional markets.
Paul Allen	Paul Allen (born January 21, 1953) is an American entrepreneur whose fortune was founded when he formed Microsoft with Bill Gates.
Technological change	The introduction of new methods of production or new products intended to increase the productivity of existing inputs or to raise marginal products is a technological change.
Aid	Assistance provided by countries and by international institutions such as the World Bank to developing countries in the form of monetary grants, loans at low interest rates, in kind, or a combination of these is called aid. Aid can also refer to assistance of any type rendered to benefit some group or individual.
Rite Aid	Rite Aid is a United States retailer and pharmacy chain, operating nearly 3,400 stores in 28 states and the District of Columbia. Rite Aid is a major contributor to the Children's Miracle Network. It was named the third largest drugstore in the United States by 1981; shortly thereafter, 1983 marked a sales milestone of $1 billion.
Broker	In commerce, a broker is a party that mediates between a buyer and a seller. A broker who also acts as a seller or as a buyer becomes a principal party to the deal.
Billboard	The most common form of outdoor advertising is called a billboard.
Private sector	The households and business firms of the economy are referred to as private sector.
Screening	Screening in economics refers to a strategy of combating adverse selection, one of the potential decision-making complications in cases of asymmetric information.
Gain	In finance, gain is a profit or an increase in value of an investment such as a stock or bond. Gain is calculated by fair market value or the proceeds from the sale of the investment minus the sum of the purchase price and all costs associated with it.
Internal locus of control	People tend to ascribe their chances of future successes or failures either to internal or external causes. Persons with an internal locus of control see themselves as responsible for the outcomes of their own actions.
Forbes	David Churbuck founded online Forbes in 1996. The site drew attention when it uncovered Stephen Glass' journalistic fraud in The New Republic in 1998, a scoop that gave credibility to internet journalism.
Franchising	Franchising is a method of doing business wherein a franchisor licenses trademarks and tried and proven methods of doing business to a franchisee in exchange for a recurring payment, and usually a percentage piece of gross sales or gross profits as well as the annual fees. The term " franchising " is used to describe a wide variety of business systems which may or may not fall into the legal definition provided above.
Dealer	People who link buyers with sellers by buying and selling securities at stated prices are referred to as a dealer.
Franchise	A contractual right to sell certain products or services, use certain trademarks, or perform activities in a geographical region is called a franchise.

91

Franchisor	A company that develops a product concept and sells others the rights to make and sell the products is referred to as a franchisor.
Preparation	Preparation refers to usually the first stage in the creative process. It includes education and formal training.
Accounting	A system that collects and processes financial information about an organization and reports that information to decision makers is referred to as accounting.
Royalties	Remuneration paid to the owners of technology, patents, or trade names for the use of same name are called royalties.
Intangible assets	Assets that have special rights but not physical substance are referred to as intangible assets.
Intangible asset	An intangible assets is defined as an asset that is not physical in nature. The most common types are trade secrets (e.g., customer lists and know-how), copyrights, patents, trademarks, and goodwill.
Tangible	Having a physical existence is referred to as the tangible. Personal property other than real estate, such as cars, boats, stocks, or other assets.
Franchise agreement	An arrangement whereby someone with a good idea for a business sells the rights to use the business name and sell a product or service to others in a given territory is a franchise agreement.
Service business	A business firm that provides services to consumers, such as accounting and legal services, is referred to as a service business.
Kroger	As well as stocking a variety of national brand products, Kroger also employs one of the largest networks of private label manufacturing in the country. Forty-two plants (either wholly owned or used with operating agreements) in seventeen states create about half of the nearly eight thousand private label products. A three-tiered marketing strategy divides the brand names for shoppers' simplicity and understanding.
Property	Assets defined in the broadest legal sense. Property includes the unrealized receivables of a cash basis taxpayer, but not services rendered.
Quality control	The measurement of products and services against set standards is referred to as quality control.
Independent business	In business, an independent business as a term of distinction generally refers to privately-owned companies (as opposed to those companies owned publicly through a distribution of shares on the market).
Recruitment	Recruitment refers to the set of activities used to obtain a sufficient number of the right people at the right time; its purpose is to select those who best meet the needs of the organization.
License	A license in the sphere of Intellectual Property Rights (IPR) is a document, contract or agreement giving permission or the 'right' to a legally-definable entity to do something (such as manufacture a product or to use a service), or to apply something (such as a trademark), with the objective of achieving commercial gain.
Federal trade commission	The commission of five members established by the Federal Trade Commission Act of 1914 to investigate unfair competitive practices of firms, to hold hearings on the complaints of such practices, and to issue cease-and-desist orders when firms were found guilty of unfair practices.
Better Business Bureau	An organization established and funded by businesses that operates primarily at the local level to monitor activities of companies and promote fair advertising and selling practices

	is a better business bureau.
Consumer protection	Consumer protection is government regulation to protect the interests of consumers, for example by requiring businesses to disclose detailed information about products, particularly in areas where safety or public health is an issue, such as food.
Complaint	The pleading in a civil case in which the plaintiff states his claim and requests relief is called complaint. In the common law, it is a formal legal document that sets out the basic facts and legal reasons that the filing party (the plaintiffs) believes are sufficient to support a claim against another person, persons, entity or entities (the defendants) that entitles the plaintiff(s) to a remedy (either money damages or injunctive relief).
Incentive	An incentive is any factor (financial or non-financial) that provides a motive for a particular course of action, or counts as a reason for preferring one choice to the alternatives.
Trade name	A commercial legal name under which a company does business is referred to as the trade name.
Trade secret	Trade secret refers to a secret formula, pattern, process, program, device, method, technique, or compilation of information that is used in its owner's business and affords that owner a competitive advantage. Trade secrets are protected by state law.
Financial liability	A financial liability is something that is owed to another party. This is typically contrasted with an asset which is something of value that is owned.
Option	A contract that gives the purchaser the option to buy or sell the underlying financial instrument at a specified price, called the exercise price or strike price, within a specific period of time.
Form of ownership	Distinguishes retail outlets based on whether individuals, corporate chains, or contractual systems own the outlet is called form of ownership.
Limited liability partnership	Limited liability partnership refers to a form of business organization allowed by many of the states, where partners have a form of limited liability, similar to that of the shareholders of a corporation.
Limited liability	Limited liability is a liability that is limited to a partner or investor's investment. Shareholders in a corporation or in a limited liability company cannot lose more money than the value of their shares if the corporation runs into debt, as they are not personally responsible for the corporation's obligations.
Heir	In common law jurisdictions an heir is a person who is entitled to receive a share of the decedent's property via the rules of inheritance in the jurisdiction where the decedent died or owned property at the time of his death.
C corporation	C corporation refers to a separate taxable entity, subject to the rules of Subchapter C of the Code. This business form may create a double taxation effect relative to its shareholders.
Discount	The difference between the face value of a bond and its selling price, when a bond is sold for less than its face value it's referred to as a discount.
Double taxation	The taxation of both corporate net income and the dividends paid from this net income when they become the personal income of households a double taxation.
Stockholder	A stockholder is an individual or company (including a corporation) that legally owns one or more shares of stock in a joined stock company. The shareholders are the owners of a corporation. Companies listed at the stock market strive to enhance shareholder value.
Motorola	The Six Sigma quality system was developed at Motorola even though it became most well known because of its use by General Electric. It was created by engineer Bill Smith, under the

direction of Bob Galvin (son of founder Paul Galvin) when he was running the company.

Proprietary	Proprietary indicates that a party, or proprietor, exercises private ownership, control or use over an item of property, usually to the exclusion of other parties. Where a party, holds or claims proprietary interests in relation to certain types of property (eg. a creative literary work, or software), that property may also be the subject of intellectual property law (eg. copyright or patents).
Stock dividend	Stock dividend refers to pro rata distributions of stock or stock rights on common stock. They are usually issued in proportion to shares owned.
Dividend	Amount of corporate profits paid out for each share of stock is referred to as dividend.
Legal entity	A legal entity is a legal construct through which the law allows a group of natural persons to act as if it were an individual for certain purposes. The most common purposes are lawsuits, property ownership, and contracts.
S corporation	One designation for a small business corporation is a S corporation.
Limited liability company	Limited liability company refers to a form of entity allowed by all of the states. The entity is taxed as a partnership in which all members or owners of the limited liability company are treated much like limited partners.
Partnership agreement	A document that defines the specific terms of a partnership or business relationship, such as how much work each partner will do and how the profits are divided is a partnership agreement.
Operating agreement	Operating agreement refers to an agreement entered into among members that governs the affairs and business of the LLC and the relations among members, managers, and the LLC.
Forming	The first stage of team development, where the team is formed and the objectives for the team are set is referred to as forming.
Alien corporation	A corporation incorporated in one country that is doing business in another country is called alien corporation.
Domestic corporation	A corporation in the state in which it was formed is a domestic corporation.
Foreign corporation	Foreign corporation refers to a corporation incorporated in one state doing business in another state. A corporation doing business in a jurisdiction in which it was not formed.
Incorporation	Incorporation is the forming of a new corporation. The corporation may be a business, a non-profit organization or even a government of a new city or town.
Leadership	Management merely consists of leadership applied to business situations; or in other words: management forms a sub-set of the broader process of leadership.
Board of directors	The group of individuals elected by the stockholders of a corporation to oversee its operations is a board of directors.
Fortune magazine	Fortune magazine is America's longest-running business magazine. Currently owned by media conglomerate Time Warner, it was founded in 1930 by Henry Luce. It is known for its regular features ranking companies by revenue.
Grant	Grant refers to an intergovernmental transfer of funds . Since the New Deal, state and local governments have become increasingly dependent upon federal grants for an almost infinite variety of programs.
Charter	Charter refers to an instrument or authority from the sovereign power bestowing the right or power to do business under the corporate form of organization. Also, the organic law of a city or town, and representing a portion of the statute law of the state.

Articles of incorporation	Items on an application filed with a state agency for the formation of a corporation that contain such information as the corporation's name, its purpose, its location, its expected life, provisions for its capital stock, and a list of the members of its board of directors are referred to as articles of incorporation.
Bylaw	In corporation law, a document that supplements the articles of incorporation and contains less important rights, powers, and responsibilities of a corporation and its shareholders, officers, and directors is referred to as a bylaw.
Closely held corporation	Closely held corporation refers to a corporation where stock ownership is not widely dispersed. Rather, a few shareholders are in control of corporate policy and are in a position to benefit personally from that policy.
Publicly held corporation	Publicly held corporation refers to a corporation that may have thousands of stockholders and whose stock is regularly traded on a national securities market.
Financial capital	Common stock, preferred stock, bonds, and retained earnings are financial capital. Financial capital appears on the corporate balance sheet under long-term liabilities and equity.
Consideration	Consideration in contract law, a basic requirement for an enforceable agreement under traditional contract principles, defined in this text as legal value, bargained for and given in exchange for an act or promise. In corporation law, cash or property contributed to a corporation in exchange for shares, or a promise to contribute such cash or property.
Preferred stock	Stock that has specified rights over common stock is a preferred stock.
Holder	A person in possession of a document of title or an instrument payable or indorsed to him, his order, or to bearer is a holder.
Income distribution	A description of the fractions of a population that are at various levels of income. The larger these differences in income, the 'worse' the income distribution is usually said to be, the smaller the 'better.'
Common stock	Common stock refers to the basic, normal, voting stock issued by a corporation; called residual equity because it ranks after preferred stock for dividend and liquidation distributions.
Residual	Residual payments can refer to an ongoing stream of payments in respect of the completion of past achievements.
Outside director	A member of the board of directors who is not an officer of the corporation is called outside director.
Inside director	A member of the board of directors who is either an employee or stakeholder in the company is an inside director.
Chief information officer	The chief information officer is a job title for the head of information technology group within an organization. They often report to the chief executive officer or chief financial officer.
Chief operating officer	A chief operating officer is a corporate officer responsible for managing the day-to-day activities of the corporation. The chief operating officer is one of the highest ranking members of an organization, monitoring the daily operations of the company and reporting to the chief executive officer directly.
Middle management	Middle management refers to the level of management that includes general managers, division managers, and branch and plant managers who are responsible for tactical planning and controlling.
Hierarchy	A system of grouping people in an organization according to rank from the top down in which all subordinate managers must report to one person is called a hierarchy.

Stock option	A stock option is a specific type of option that uses the stock itself as an underlying instrument to determine the option's pay-off and therefore its value.
Market price	Market price is an economic concept with commonplace familiarity; it is the price that a good or service is offered at, or will fetch, in the marketplace; it is of interest mainly in the study of microeconomics.
Human resources	Human resources refers to the individuals within the firm, and to the portion of the firm's organization that deals with hiring, firing, training, and other personnel issues.
Organization structure	The system of task, reporting, and authority relationships within which the organization does its work is referred to as the organization structure.
Union	A worker association that bargains with employers over wages and working conditions is called a union.
Joint venture	Joint venture refers to an undertaking by two parties for a specific purpose and duration, taking any of several legal forms.
Keebler	The Keebler Company is the second-largest cookie and cracker manufacturer in the United States. Founded in 1853, it has produced numerous baked snacks and has been the leading supplier of baked goods to the Girl Scouts for their annual cookie drives.
Viacom	Viacom is an American-based media conglomerate with various worldwide interests in cable and satellite television networks (MTV Networks and BET), video gaming (part of Sega of America), and movie production and distribution (the Paramount Pictures movie studio and DreamWorks).
Subsidiary	A company that is controlled by another company or corporation is a subsidiary.
Conglomerate	A conglomerate is a large company that consists of divisions of often seemingly unrelated businesses.
Raw material	Raw material refers to a good that has not been transformed by production; a primary product.
Time Warner	Time Warner is the world's largest media company with major Internet, publishing, film, telecommunications and television divisions.
Horizontal merger	Horizontal merger refers to the merger into a single firm of two firms producing the same product and selling it in the same geographic market.
Conglomerate merger	A conglomerate merger is whereby two companies or organizations which have no common interest and nor competitors or have or could have the same supplier or customers merger.
Takeover	A takeover in business refers to one company (the acquirer) purchasing another (the target). Such events resemble mergers, but without the formation of a new company.
Argument	The discussion by counsel for the respective parties of their contentions on the law and the facts of the case being tried in order to aid the jury in arriving at a correct and just conclusion is called argument.
Warehouse	Warehouse refers to a location, often decentralized, that a firm uses to store, consolidate, age, or mix stock; house product-recall programs; or ease tax burdens.
Privatization	A process in which investment bankers take companies that were previously owned by the government to the public markets is referred to as privatization.
Enabling	Enabling refers to giving workers the education and tools they need to assume their new decision-making powers.
Distribution center	Designed to facilitate the timely movement of goods and represent a very important part of a supply chain is a distribution center.
Intellectual	In law, intellectual property is an umbrella term for various legal entitlements which

property	attach to certain types of information, ideas, or other intangibles in their expressed form. The holder of this legal entitlement is generally entitled to exercise various exclusive rights in relation to its subject matter.
Honeywell	Honeywell is a major American multinational corporation that produces electronic control systems and automation equipment. It is a major supplier of engineering services and avionics for NASA, Boeing and the United States Department of Defense.
Blockbuster Video	The standard business model for video rental stores was that they would pay a large flat fee per video, approximately US$65, and have unlimited rentals for the lifetime of the cassette itself. It was Sumner Redstone, whose Viacom conglomerate then owned Blockbuster Video, who personally pioneered a new revenue-sharing arrangement for video, in the mid-1990s. Blockbuster obtained videos for little or no cost and kept 60 percent rental fee, paying the other 40 percent to the studio
Assignment	A transfer of property or some right or interest is referred to as assignment.

Go to **Cram101.com** for the Practice Tests for this Chapter.

Corporation	A legal entity chartered by a state or the Federal government that is distinct and separate from the individuals who own it is a corporation. This separation gives the corporation unique powers which other legal entities lack.
Advertising	Advertising refers to paid, nonpersonal communication through various media by organizations and individuals who are in some way identified in the advertising message.
Brand	A name, symbol, or design that identifies the goods or services of one seller or group of sellers and distinguishes them from the goods and services of competitors is a brand.
Market	A market is, as defined in economics, a social arrangement that allows buyers and sellers to discover information and carry out a voluntary exchange of goods or services.
Users	Users refer to people in the organization who actually use the product or service purchased by the buying center.
Operation	A standardized method or technique that is performed repetitively, often on different materials resulting in different finished goods is called an operation.
Interest	In finance and economics, interest is the price paid by a borrower for the use of a lender's money. In other words, interest is the amount of paid to "rent" money for a period of time.
Broker	In commerce, a broker is a party that mediates between a buyer and a seller. A broker who also acts as a seller or as a buyer becomes a principal party to the deal.
Firm	An organization that employs resources to produce a good or service for profit and owns and operates one or more plants is referred to as a firm.
Brokerage firm	A company that conducts various aspects of securities trading, analysis and advisory services is a brokerage firm.
Charles Schwab	Charles Schwab is the world's second-largest discount broker. Besides discount brokerage, the firm offers mutual funds, annuities, bond trading, and now mortgages through its Charles Schwab Bank.
Competitor	Other organizations in the same industry or type of business that provide a good or service to the same set of customers is referred to as a competitor.
Channel	Channel, in communications (sometimes called communications channel), refers to the medium used to convey information from a sender (or transmitter) to a receiver.
British Aerospace	British Aerospace was a UK aircraft and defence systems manufacturer, now part of BAE Systems. The company was formed as a statutory corporation on April 29, 1977 as a result the Aircraft and Shipbuilding Industries Act.
Service	Service refers to a "non tangible product" that is not embodied in a physical good and that typically effects some change in another product, person, or institution. Contrasts with good.
Industry	A group of firms that produce identical or similar products is an industry. It is also used specifically to refer to an area of economic production focused on manufacturing which involves large amounts of capital investment before any profit can be realized, also called "heavy industry".
Mistake	In contract law a mistake is incorrect understanding by one or more parties to a contract and may be used as grounds to invalidate the agreement. Common law has identified three different types of mistake in contract: unilateral mistake, mutual mistake, and common mistake.
Electronic commerce	Electronic commerce or e-commerce, refers to any activity that uses some form of electronic communication in the inventory, exchange, advertisement, distribution, and payment of goods and services.

Go to **Cram101.com** for the Practice Tests for this Chapter.

Commerce	Commerce is the exchange of something of value between two entities. It is the central mechanism from which capitalism is derived.
Globalization	The increasing world-wide integration of markets for goods, services and capital that attracted special attention in the late 1990s is called globalization.
Technology	The body of knowledge and techniques that can be used to combine economic resources to produce goods and services is called technology.
Browser	A program that allows a user to connect to the World Wide Web by simply typing in a URL is a browser.
Microsoft	Microsoft is a multinational computer technology corporation with 2004 global annual sales of US$39.79 billion and 71,553 employees in 102 countries and regions as of July 2006. It develops, manufactures, licenses, and supports a wide range of software products for computing devices.
Scope	Scope of a project is the sum total of all projects products and their requirements or features.
Revenue	Revenue is a U.S. business term for the amount of money that a company receives from its activities, mostly from sales of products and/or services to customers.
Supply	Supply is the aggregate amount of any material good that can be called into being at a certain price point; it comprises one half of the equation of supply and demand. In classical economic theory, a curve representing supply is one of the factors that produce price.
Proprietary	Proprietary indicates that a party, or proprietor, exercises private ownership, control or use over an item of property, usually to the exclusion of other parties. Where a party, holds or claims proprietary interests in relation to certain types of property (eg. a creative literary work, or software), that property may also be the subject of intellectual property law (eg. copyright or patents).
Trend	Trend refers to the long-term movement of an economic variable, such as its average rate of increase or decrease over enough years to encompass several business cycles.
Gap	In December of 1995, Gap became the first major North American retailer to accept independent monitoring of the working conditions in a contract factory producing its garments. Gap is the largest specialty retailer in the United States.
Receiver	A person that is appointed as a custodian of other people's property by a court of law or a creditor of the owner, pending a lawsuit or reorganization is called a receiver.
Manufacturing	Production of goods primarily by the application of labor and capital to raw materials and other intermediate inputs, in contrast to agriculture, mining, forestry, fishing, and services a manufacturing.
Customer service	The ability of logistics management to satisfy users in terms of time, dependability, communication, and convenience is called the customer service.
Product line	A group of products that are physically similar or are intended for a similar market are called the product line.
Advertisement	Advertisement is the promotion of goods, services, companies and ideas, usually by an identified sponsor. Marketers see advertising as part of an overall promotional strategy.
Sweepstakes	Sales promotions consisting of a game of chance requiring no analytical or creative effort by the consumer is a sweepstakes.
Sweepstake	A sweepstake is technically a lottery in which the prize is financed through the tickets sold. In the United States the word has become associated with promotions where prizes are

given away for free.

Journal	Book of original entry, in which transactions are recorded in a general ledger system, is referred to as a journal.
Wall Street Journal	Dow Jones & Company was founded in 1882 by reporters Charles Dow, Edward Jones and Charles Bergstresser. Jones converted the small Customers' Afternoon Letter into The Wall Street Journal, first published in 1889, and began delivery of the Dow Jones News Service via telegraph. The Journal featured the Jones 'Average', the first of several indexes of stock and bond prices on the New York Stock Exchange.
Public domain	The public domain comprises the body of knowledge and innovation in relation to which no person or other legal entity can establish or maintain proprietary interests within a particular legal jurisdiction.
Chief executive officer	A chief executive officer is the highest-ranking corporate officer or executive officer of a corporation, or agency. In closely held corporations, it is general business culture that the office chief executive officer is also the chairman of the board.
Cisco Systems	While Cisco Systems was not the first company to develop and sell a router (a device that forwards computer traffic from one network to another), it did create the first commercially successful multi-protocol router to allow previously incompatible computers to communicate using different network protocols.
Investment	Investment refers to spending for the production and accumulation of capital and additions to inventories. In a financial sense, buying an asset with the expectation of making a return.
Financial report	Financial report refers to a written statement-also called an accountant's certificate, accountant's opinion, or audit report-prepared by an independent accountant or auditor after an audit.
Yahoo	Yahoo is an American computer services company. It operates an Internet portal, the Yahoo Directory and a host of other services including the popular Yahoo Mail. Yahoo is the most visited website on the Internet today with more than 400 million unique users. The global network of Yahoo! websites received 3.4 billion page views per day on average as of October 2005.
BMW	BMW is an independent German company and manufacturer of automobiles and motorcycles. BMW is the world's largest premium carmaker and is the parent company of the BMW MINI and Rolls-Royce car brands, and, formerly, Rover.
Stock	In financial terminology, stock is the capital raized by a corporation, through the issuance and sale of shares.
Coupon	In finance, a coupon is "attached" to a bond, either physically (as with old bonds) or electronically. Each coupon represents a predetermined payment promized to the bond-holder in return for his or her loan of money to the bond-issuer. .
Electronic business	Electronic business is any business process that is empowered by an information system. Today, this is mostly done with Web-based technologies.
Multinational corporations	Firms that own production facilities in two or more countries and produce and sell their products globally are referred to as multinational corporations.
Multinational corporation	An organization that manufactures and markets products in many different countries and has multinational stock ownership and multinational management is referred to as multinational corporation.
Entrepreneur	The owner/operator. The person who organizes, manages, and assumes the risks of a firm, taking a new idea or a new product and turning it into a successful business is an

Go to **Cram101.com** for the Practice Tests for this Chapter.

	entrepreneur.
Business plan	A detailed written statement that describes the nature of the business, the target market, the advantages the business will have in relation to competition, and the resources and qualifications of the owner is referred to as a business plan.
Ticketmaster	One of the first ticketing companies to sell tickets on the Internet, Ticketmaster now sells a large percentage of its tickets online. On April 28, 1997, Ticketmaster sued Microsoft over its Sidewalk service for allegedly deep linking into Ticketmaster's site.
Oracle	In 2004, sales at Oracle grew at a rate of 14.5% to $6.2 billion, giving it 41.3% and the top share of the relational-database market. Their main competitors in the database arena are IBM DB2 and Microsoft SQL Server, and to a lesser extent Sybase, Teradata, Informix, and MySQL. In the applications arena, their main competitor is SAP.
Layout	Layout refers to the physical arrangement of the various parts of an advertisement including the headline, subheads, illustrations, body copy, and any identifying marks.
Buyer	A buyer refers to a role in the buying center with formal authority and responsibility to select the supplier and negotiate the terms of the contract.
Marketing	Promoting and selling products or services to customers, or prospective customers, is referred to as marketing.
Vendor	A person who sells property to a vendee is a vendor. The words vendor and vendee are more commonly applied to the seller and purchaser of real estate, and the words seller and buyer are more commonly applied to the seller and purchaser of personal property.
Gain	In finance, gain is a profit or an increase in value of an investment such as a stock or bond. Gain is calculated by fair market value or the proceeds from the sale of the investment minus the sum of the purchase price and all costs associated with it.
Innovation	Innovation refers to the first commercially successful introduction of a new product, the use of a new method of production, or the creation of a new form of business organization.
Credit	Credit refers to a recording as positive in the balance of payments, any transaction that gives rise to a payment into the country, such as an export, the sale of an asset, or borrowing from abroad.
Security	Security refers to a claim on the borrower future income that is sold by the borrower to the lender. A security is a type of transferable interest representing financial value.
Broadband technology	Technology that delivers voice, video, and data through the internet is broadband technology.
Consultant	A professional that provides expert advice in a particular field or area in which customers occassionaly require this type of knowledge is a consultant.
Profit	Profit refers to the return to the resource entrepreneurial ability; total revenue minus total cost.
Inbound telemarketing	The use of toll-free telephone numbers that customers can call to obtain information about products or services and make purchases is called inbound telemarketing.
Personnel	A collective term for all of the employees of an organization. Personnel is also commonly used to refer to the personnel management function or the organizational unit responsible for administering personnel programs.
Intermediaries	Intermediaries specialize in information either to bring together two parties to a transaction or to buy in order to sell again.
Invoice	The itemized bill for a transaction, stating the nature of the transaction and its cost. In

Go to **Cram101.com** for the Practice Tests for this Chapter.

international trade, the invoice price is often the preferred basis for levying an ad valorem tariff.

Electronic data interchange

Electronic data interchange refers to the direct exchange between organizations of data via a computer-to-computer interface.

Purchase order

A form on which items or services needed by a business firm are specified and then communicated to the vendor is a purchase order.

Exchange

The trade of things of value between buyer and seller so that each is better off after the trade is called the exchange.

Production

The creation of finished goods and services using the factors of production: land, labor, capital, entrepreneurship, and knowledge.

Inventory

Tangible property held for sale in the normal course of business or used in producing goods or services for sale is an inventory.

Market leader

The market leader is dominant in its industry. It has substantial market share and often extensive distribution arrangements with retailers. It typically is the industry leader in developing innovative new business models and new products (although not always).

Quick response

An inventory management system designed to reduce the retailer's lead-time, thereby lowering its inventory investment, improving customer service levels, and reducing logistics expense is referred to as quick response.

Intel

Intel Corporation, founded in 1968 and based in Santa Clara, California, USA, is the world's largest semiconductor company. Intel is best known for its PC microprocessors, where it maintains roughly 80% market share.

Expense

In accounting, an expense represents an event in which an asset is used up or a liability is incurred. In terms of the accounting equation, expenses reduce owners' equity.

Private exchange

A marketplace that is sponsored by a single enterprise for the benefit of its suppliers or customers or both is the private exchange.

Principal

In agency law, one under whose direction an agent acts and for whose benefit that agent acts is a principal.

Extranet

An extension of the Internet that connects suppliers, customers, and other organizations via secure websites is an extranet.

Discount

The difference between the face value of a bond and its selling price, when a bond is sold for less than its face value it's referred to as a discount.

Nissan

Nissan is Japan's second largest car company after Toyota. Nissan is among the top three Asian rivals of the "big three" in the US.

Ford

Ford is an American company that manufactures and sells automobiles worldwide. Ford introduced methods for large-scale manufacturing of cars, and large-scale management of an industrial workforce, especially elaborately engineered manufacturing sequences typified by the moving assembly lines.

DaimlerChrysler

In 2002, the merged company, DaimlerChrysler, appeared to run two independent product lines, with few signs of corporate integration. In 2003, however, it was alleged by the Detroit News that the "merger of equals" was, in fact, a takeover.

General Motors

General Motors is the world's largest automaker. Founded in 1908, today it employs about 327,000 people around the world. With global headquarters in Detroit, it manufactures its cars and trucks in 33 countries.

Subcontractor

A subcontractor is an individual or in many cases a business that signs a contract to perform

part or all of the obligations of another's contract. A subcontractor is hired by a general or prime contractor to perform a specific task as part of the overall project.

Auction	A preexisting business model that operates successfully on the Internet by announcing an item for sale and permitting multiple purchasers to bid on them under specified rules and condition is an auction.
Kmart	Kmart is an international chain of discount department stores in the United States, Australia, and New Zealand. Kmart merged with Sears in early 2005, creating the Sears Holdings Corporation.
Safeway	On April 18, 2005, Safeway began a 100 million dollar brand re-positioning campaign labeled "Ingredients for life". This was done in an attempt to differentiate itself from its competitors, and to increase brand involvement. Steve Burd described it as "branding the shopping experience".
Purchasing	Purchasing refers to the function in a firm that searches for quality material resources, finds the best suppliers, and negotiates the best price for goods and services.
Management	Management characterizes the process of leading and directing all or part of an organization, often a business, through the deployment and manipulation of resources. Early twentieth-century management writer Mary Parker Follett defined management as "the art of getting things done through people."
Enterprise	Enterprise refers to another name for a business organization. Other similar terms are business firm, sometimes simply business, sometimes simply firm, as well as company, and entity.
General Electric	In 1876, Thomas Alva Edison opened a new laboratory in Menlo Park, New Jersey. Out of the laboratory was to come perhaps the most famous invention of all—a successful development of the incandescent electric lamp. By 1890, Edison had organized his various businesses into the Edison General Electric Company.
Strike	The withholding of labor services by an organized group of workers is referred to as a strike.
Bid	A bid price is a price offered by a buyer when he/she buys a good. In the context of stock trading on a stock exchange, the bid price is the highest price a buyer of a stock is willing to pay for a share of that given stock.
Raytheon	Since nearly all of Raytheon's revenues are obtained from defense contracts, there is necessarily a tight cooperation between Raytheon and the U.S. Department of Defense. This, along with heavy lobbying, has led to perennial charges of influence peddling. Raytheon contributed nearly a million dollars to various defense-related political campaigns in 2004, spending much more than that on lobbying expenses. And there are many tight ties between the company and all levels of government.
Product design	Product Design is defined as the idea generation, concept development, testing and manufacturing or implementation of a physical object or service. It is possibly the evolution of former discipline name - Industrial Design.
Intranet	Intranet refers to a companywide network, closed to public access, that uses Internet-type technology. A set of communications links within one company that travel over the Internet but are closed to public access.
Retail sale	The sale of goods and services to consumers for their own use is a retail sale.
Retailing	All activities involved in selling, renting, and providing goods and services to ultimate consumers for personal, family, or household use is referred to as retailing.

Sears	Before the Sears catalog, farmers typically bought supplies (often at very high prices) from local general stores. Sears took advantage of this by publishing his catalog with clearly stated prices, so that consumers could know what he was selling and at what price, and order and obtain them conveniently. The catalog business soon grew quickly.
Marketing research	Marketing research refers to the analysis of markets to determine opportunities and challenges, and to find the information needed to make good decisions.
Smart card	A stored-value card that contains a computer chip that allows it to be loaded with digital cash from the owner's bank account whenever needed is called a smart card.
Expedia	Founded as a division of Microsoft in 1996, Expedia was spun off in 1999, and was purchased by USA Networks in 2001 (USA changed its name to InterActiveCorp in 2003). IAC spun off its travel group of businesses under the Expedia name in August 2005.
Discount rate	Discount rate refers to the rate, per year, at which future values are diminished to make them comparable to values in the present. Can be either subjective or objective .
Financial institution	A financial institution acts as an agent that provides financial services for its clients. Financial institutions generally fall under financial regulation from a government authority.
Merchant	Under the Uniform Commercial Code, one who regularly deals in goods of the kind sold in the contract at issue, or holds himself out as having special knowledge or skill relevant to such goods, or who makes the sale through an agent who regularly deals in such goods or claims such knowledge or skill is referred to as merchant.
License	A license in the sphere of Intellectual Property Rights (IPR) is a document, contract or agreement giving permission or the 'right' to a legally-definable entity to do something (such as manufacture a product or to use a service), or to apply something (such as a trademark), with the objective of achieving commercial gain.
Fraud	Tax fraud falls into two categories: civil and criminal. Under civil fraud, the IRS may impose as a penalty of an amount equal to as much as 75 percent of the underpayment.
Promotion	Promotion refers to all the techniques sellers use to motivate people to buy products or services. An attempt by marketers to inform people about products and to persuade them to participate in an exchange.
Trademark	A distinctive word, name, symbol, device, or combination thereof, which enables consumers to identify favored products or services and which may find protection under state or federal law is a trademark.
Copyright	The legal right to the proceeds from and control over the use of a created product, such a written work, audio, video, film, or software is a copyright. This right generally extends over the life of the author plus fifty years.
Fair use	Fair use is a doctrine in United States copyright law that allows limited use of copyrighted material without requiring permission from the rights holders, such as use for scholarship or review.
Sales tax	A sales tax is a tax on consumption. It is normally a certain percentage that is added onto the price of a good or service that is purchased.
Authentication	Such official attestation of a written instrument as will render it legally admissible in evidence is called authentication.
Policy	Similar to a script in that a policy can be a less than completely rational decision-making method. Involves the use of a pre-existing set of decision steps for any problem that presents itself.
Electronic	Uses digital signature technology to make the person's signature part of a document in such a

Go to **Cram101.com** for the Practice Tests for this Chapter.

signature	way that any alteration can be detected are referred to as electronic signature.
Insurance	Insurance refers to a system by which individuals can reduce their exposure to risk of large losses by spreading the risks among a large number of persons.
Contract	A contract is a "promise" or an "agreement" that is enforced or recognized by the law. In the civil law, a contract is considered to be part of the general law of obligations.
Mortgage	Mortgage refers to a note payable issued for property, such as a house, usually repaid in equal installments consisting of part principle and part interest, over a specified period.
Property	Assets defined in the broadest legal sense. Property includes the unrealized receivables of a cash basis taxpayer, but not services rendered.
Distribution	Distribution in economics, the manner in which total output and income is distributed among individuals or factors.
Level playing field	The objective of those who advocate protection on the grounds the foreign firms have an unfair advantage. A level playing field would remove such advantages, although it is not usually clear what sorts of advantage would be permitted to remain.
Customer database	Customer database refers to a computer database specifically designed for storage, retrieval, and analysis of customer data by marketers.
Trust	An arrangement in which shareholders of independent firms agree to give up their stock in exchange for trust certificates that entitle them to a share of the trust's common profits.
Targeting	In advertizing, targeting is to select a demographic or other group of people to advertise to, and create advertisements appropriately.
Tacit knowledge	Knowledge that has not been articulated. Tacit knowledge is often subconscious and relatively difficult to communicate to other people. Tacit knowledge consists often of habits and culture that we do not recognize in ourselves.
Federal Bureau of Investigation	The Federal Bureau of Investigation is a federal criminal investigative, intelligence agency, and the primary investigative arm of the United States Department of Justice (DOJ). At present, the it has investigative jurisdiction over violations of more than 200 categories of federal crimes and thus has the broadest investigative authority of any U.S. federal law enforcement agency. The motto of the bureau is "Fidelity, Bravery, Integrity."
Analyst	Analyst refers to a person or tool with a primary function of information analysis, generally with a more limited, practical and short term set of goals than a researcher.
Default	In finance, default occurs when a debtor has not met its legal obligations according to the debt contract, e.g. it has not made a scheduled payment, or violated a covenant (condition) of the debt contract.
Dealer	People who link buyers with sellers by buying and selling securities at stated prices are referred to as a dealer.
Customs	Customs is an authority or agency in a country responsible for collecting customs duties and for controlling the flow of people, animals and goods (including personal effects and hazardous items) in and out of the country.
Technological change	The introduction of new methods of production or new products intended to increase the productivity of existing inputs or to raise marginal products is a technological change.
Small business	Small business refers to a business that is independently owned and operated, is not dominant in its field of operation, and meets certain standards of size in terms of employees or annual receipts.
Intellectual	In law, intellectual property is an umbrella term for various legal entitlements which

Go to **Cram101.com** for the Practice Tests for this Chapter.

property	attach to certain types of information, ideas, or other intangibles in their expressed form. The holder of this legal entitlement is generally entitled to exercise various exclusive rights in relation to its subject matter.
Fund	Independent accounting entity with a self-balancing set of accounts segregated for the purposes of carrying on specific activities is referred to as a fund.
International Business	International business refers to any firm that engages in international trade or investment.
Trade barrier	An artificial disincentive to export and/or import, such as a tariff, quota, or other NTB is called a trade barrier.
Regulation	Regulation refers to restrictions state and federal laws place on business with regard to the conduct of its activities.
External customers	Dealers, who buy products to sell to others, and ultimate customers, who buy products for their own personal use are referred to as external customers.
Banner ad	A banner ad is a form of advertising on the World Wide Web. This form of online advertising entails embedding an advertisement into a web page.
Brief	Brief refers to a statement of a party's case or legal arguments, usually prepared by an attorney. Also used to make legal arguments before appellate courts.
Case study	A case study is a particular method of qualitative research. Rather than using large samples and following a rigid protocol to examine a limited number of variables, case study methods involve an in-depth, longitudinal examination of a single instance or event: a case. They provide a systematic way of looking at events, collecting data, analyzing information, and reporting the results.
Authority	Authority in agency law, refers to an agent's ability to affect his principal's legal relations with third parties. Also used to refer to an actor's legal power or ability to do something. In addition, sometimes used to refer to a statute, case, or other legal source that justifies a particular result.
Warehouse	Warehouse refers to a location, often decentralized, that a firm uses to store, consolidate, age, or mix stock; house product-recall programs; or ease tax burdens.

Leadership	Management merely consists of leadership applied to business situations; or in other words: management forms a sub-set of the broader process of leadership.
Corporate culture	The whole collection of beliefs, values, and behaviors of a firm that send messages to those within and outside the company about how business is done is the corporate culture.
Organization structure	The system of task, reporting, and authority relationships within which the organization does its work is referred to as the organization structure.
Departmental- zation	The dividing of organizational functions into separate units is called departmentalization.
Firm	An organization that employs resources to produce a good or service for profit and owns and operates one or more plants is referred to as a firm.
Strategic planning	The process of determining the major goals of the organization and the policies and strategies for obtaining and using resources to achieve those goals is called strategic planning.
Nokia	Nokia Corporation is the world's largest manufacturer of mobile telephones (as of June 2006), with a global market share of approximately 34% in Q2 of 2006. It produces mobile phones for every major market and protocol, including GSM, CDMA, and W-CDMA (UMTS).
Manufacturing	Production of goods primarily by the application of labor and capital to raw materials and other intermediate inputs, in contrast to agriculture, mining, forestry, fishing, and services a manufacturing.
Conglomerate	A conglomerate is a large company that consists of divisions of often seemingly unrelated businesses.
Empathy	Empathy refers to dimension of service quality-caring individualized attention provided to customers.
Chief executive officer	A chief executive officer is the highest-ranking corporate officer or executive officer of a corporation, or agency. In closely held corporations, it is general business culture that the office chief executive officer is also the chairman of the board.
Profit	Profit refers to the return to the resource entrepreneurial ability; total revenue minus total cost.
Siemens	Siemens is the world's largest conglomerate company. Worldwide, Siemens and its subsidiaries employs 461,000 people (2005) in 190 countries and reported global sales of €75.4 billion in fiscal year 2005.
Technology	The body of knowledge and techniques that can be used to combine economic resources to produce goods and services is called technology.
Market	A market is, as defined in economics, a social arrangement that allows buyers and sellers to discover information and carry out a voluntary exchange of goods or services.
Scope	Scope of a project is the sum total of all projects products and their requirements or features.
Gatekeeper	Gatekeeper refers to an individual who has a strategic position in the network that allows him or her to control information moving in either direction through a channel.
Chief financial officer	Chief financial officer refers to executive responsible for overseeing the financial operations of an organization.
Operation	A standardized method or technique that is performed repetitively, often on different materials resulting in different finished goods is called an operation.

Logistics	Those activities that focus on getting the right amount of the right products to the right place at the right time at the lowest possible cost is referred to as logistics.
Management team	A management team is directly responsible for managing the day-to-day operations (and profitability) of a company.
Management	Management characterizes the process of leading and directing all or part of an organization, often a business, through the deployment and manipulation of resources. Early twentieth-century management writer Mary Parker Follett defined management as "the art of getting things done through people."
Brand	A name, symbol, or design that identifies the goods or services of one seller or group of sellers and distinguishes them from the goods and services of competitors is a brand.
Effective manager	Leader of a team that consistently achieves high performance goals is an effective manager.
Appeal	Appeal refers to the act of asking an appellate court to overturn a decision after the trial court's final judgment has been entered.
Production	The creation of finished goods and services using the factors of production: land, labor, capital, entrepreneurship, and knowledge.
Stock	In financial terminology, stock is the capital raized by a corporation, through the issuance and sale of shares.
Stock exchange	A stock exchange is a corporation or mutual organization which provides facilities for stock brokers and traders, to trade company stocks and other securities.
Starbucks	Although it has endured much criticism for its purported monopoly on the global coffee-bean market, Starbucks purchases only 3% of the coffee beans grown worldwide. In 2000 the company introduced a line of fair trade products and now offers three options for socially conscious coffee drinkers. According to Starbucks, they purchased 4.8 million pounds of Certified Fair Trade coffee in fiscal year 2004 and 11.5 million pounds in 2005.
Exchange	The trade of things of value between buyer and seller so that each is better off after the trade is called the exchange.
Hierarchy	A system of grouping people in an organization according to rank from the top down in which all subordinate managers must report to one person is called a hierarchy.
Ford	Ford is an American company that manufactures and sells automobiles worldwide. Ford introduced methods for large-scale manufacturing of cars, and large-scale management of an industrial workforce, especially elaborately engineered manufacturing sequences typified by the moving assembly lines.
Ford Motor Company	Ford Motor Company introduced methods for large-scale manufacturing of cars, and large-scale management of an industrial workforce, especially elaborately engineered manufacturing sequences typified by the moving assembly lines. Henry Ford's combination of highly efficient factories, highly paid workers, and low prices revolutionized manufacturing and came to be known around the world as Fordism by 1914.
Supervisor	A Supervisor is an employee of an organization with some of the powers and responsibilities of management, occupying a role between true manager and a regular employee. A Supervisor position is typically the first step towards being promoted into a management role.
AlliedSignal	AlliedSignal was created through a 1985 merger of Allied Chemical & Dye Corportation and Signal Oil, the company renamed to AlliedSignal on September 19, 1985. The company's involvement in aerospace stems from a previous merger between Signal Oil and the Garrett Corporation in 1968. After that merger, aviation became the company's largest division. In

Go to **Cram101.com** for the Practice Tests for this Chapter.

	1999. AlliedSignal acquired Honeywell and took its more-recognizable name.
Honeywell	Honeywell is a major American multinational corporation that produces electronic control systems and automation equipment. It is a major supplier of engineering services and avionics for NASA, Boeing and the United States Department of Defense.
Service	Service refers to a "non tangible product" that is not embodied in a physical good and that typically effects some change in another product, person, or institution. Contrasts with good.
Customer service	The ability of logistics management to satisfy users in terms of time, dependability, communication, and convenience is called the customer service.
Labor	People's physical and mental talents and efforts that are used to help produce goods and services are called labor.
Glass ceiling	Glass ceiling refers to a term that refers to the many barriers that can exist to thwart a woman's rise to the top of an organization; one that provides a view of the top, but a ceiling on how far a woman can go.
Dow Chemical	Dow Chemical is the world's largest producer of plastics, including polystyrene, polyurethanes, polyethylene, polypropylene, and synthetic rubbers. It is also a major producer of the chemicals calcium chloride, ethylene oxide, and various acrylates, surfactants, and cellulose resins. It produces many agricultural chemicals.
Middle management	Middle management refers to the level of management that includes general managers, division managers, and branch and plant managers who are responsible for tactical planning and controlling.
General manager	A manager who is responsible for several departments that perform different functions is called general manager.
Distribution	Distribution in economics, the manner in which total output and income is distributed among individuals or factors.
Total quality management	The broad set of management and control processes designed to focus an entire organization and all of its employees on providing products or services that do the best possible job of satisfying the customer is called total quality management.
Customer satisfaction	Customer satisfaction is a business term which is used to capture the idea of measuring how satisfied an enterprise's customers are with the organization's efforts in a marketplace.
Quality management	Quality management is a method for ensuring that all the activities necessary to design, develop and implement a product or service are effective and efficient with respect to the system and its performance.
Quality control	The measurement of products and services against set standards is referred to as quality control.
Budget	Budget refers to an account, usually for a year, of the planned expenditures and the expected receipts of an entity. For a government, the receipts are tax revenues.
Product development	In business and engineering, new product development is the complete process of bringing a new product to market. There are two parallel aspects to this process : one involves product engineering ; the other marketing analysis. Marketers see new product development as the first stage in product life cycle management, engineers as part of Product Lifecycle Management.
Journal	Book of original entry, in which transactions are recorded in a general ledger system, is referred to as a journal.

Conceptual skill	The ability to analyze and solve complex problems is called conceptual skill. Conceptual skill involves the formulation of ideas.
Accounting	A system that collects and processes financial information about an organization and reports that information to decision makers is referred to as accounting.
Purchasing	Purchasing refers to the function in a firm that searches for quality material resources, finds the best suppliers, and negotiates the best price for goods and services.
Analyst	Analyst refers to a person or tool with a primary function of information analysis, generally with a more limited, practical and short term set of goals than a researcher.
Information system	An information system is a system whether automated or manual, that comprises people, machines, and/or methods organized to collect, process, transmit, and disseminate data that represent user information.
Marketing	Promoting and selling products or services to customers, or prospective customers, is referred to as marketing.
Bill Gates	Bill Gates is the co-founder, chairman, former chief software architect, and former CEO of Microsoft Corporation. He is one of the best-known entrepreneurs of the personal computer revolution and he is widely respected for his foresight and ambition.
Microsoft	Microsoft is a multinational computer technology corporation with 2004 global annual sales of US$39.79 billion and 71,553 employees in 102 countries and regions as of July 2006. It develops, manufactures, licenses, and supports a wide range of software products for computing devices.
Interpersonal skills	Interpersonal skills are used to communicate with, understand, and motivate individuals and groups.
Workplace diversity	A workplace diversity program is designed to create an equitable employment system for all employees. Such a program includes both policies and practices.
Conflict resolution	Conflict resolution is the process of resolving a dispute or a conflict. Successful conflict resolution occurs by providing each side's needs, and adequately addressing their interests so that they are each satisfied with the outcome. Conflict resolution aims to end conflicts before they start or lead to physical fighting.
Assessment	Collecting information and providing feedback to employees about their behavior, communication style, or skills is an assessment.
Personnel	A collective term for all of the employees of an organization. Personnel is also commonly used to refer to the personnel management function or the organizational unit responsible for administering personnel programs.
Points	Loan origination fees that may be deductible as interest by a buyer of property. A seller of property who pays points reduces the selling price by the amount of the points paid for the buyer.
Tactic	A short-term immediate decision that, in its totality, leads to the achievement of strategic goals is called a tactic.
Business strategy	Business strategy, which refers to the aggregated operational strategies of single business firm or that of an SBU in a diversified corporation refers to the way in which a firm competes in its chosen arenas.
Trust	An arrangement in which shareholders of independent firms agree to give up their stock in exchange for trust certificates that entitle them to a share of the trust's common profits.
Assignment	A transfer of property or some right or interest is referred to as assignment.

Go to **Cram101.com** for the Practice Tests for this Chapter.

Philip Morris	Philip Morris, is the world's largest commercial tobacco company by sales. Philip Morris was begun by a London tobacconist of the same name. He was one of the first people to sell hand-rolled cigarettes in the 1860s, selling them under the brand names Oxford and Cambridge Blues, following the adoption of cigarette smoking by British soldiers returning from the Crimean War.
Nissan	Nissan is Japan's second largest car company after Toyota. Nissan is among the top three Asian rivals of the "big three" in the US.
Chief operating officer	A chief operating officer is a corporate officer responsible for managing the day-to-day activities of the corporation. The chief operating officer is one of the highest ranking members of an organization, monitoring the daily operations of the company and reporting to the chief executive officer directly.
Administration	Administration refers to the management and direction of the affairs of governments and institutions; a collective term for all policymaking officials of a government; the execution and implementation of public policy.
Contribution	In business organization law, the cash or property contributed to a business by its owners is referred to as contribution.
Culture shock	Feelings of confusion, disorientation, and anxiety that result from being immersed in a foreign culture are referred to as culture shock.
Controlling	A management function that involves determining whether or not an organization is progressing toward its goals and objectives, and taking corrective action if it is not is called controlling.
Authority	Authority in agency law, refers to an agent's ability to affect his principal's legal relations with third parties. Also used to refer to an actor's legal power or ability to do something. In addition, sometimes used to refer to a statute, case, or other legal source that justifies a particular result.
Southwest airlines	Southwest Airlines is a low-fare airline in the United States. It is the third-largest airline in the world, by number of passengers carried, and the largest in the United States by number of passengers carried domestically.
Shareholder	A shareholder is an individual or company (including a corporation) that legally owns one or more shares of stock in a joined stock company.
Fortune magazine	Fortune magazine is America's longest-running business magazine. Currently owned by media conglomerate Time Warner, it was founded in 1930 by Henry Luce. It is known for its regular features ranking companies by revenue.
Mistake	In contract law a mistake is incorrect understanding by one or more parties to a contract and may be used as grounds to invalidate the agreement. Common law has identified three different types of mistake in contract: unilateral mistake, mutual mistake, and common mistake.
Competitor	Other organizations in the same industry or type of business that provide a good or service to the same set of customers is referred to as a competitor.
Michael Dell	Michael Dell is the founder of Dell, Inc., the world's largest computer manufacturer which revolutionized the home computer industry.
Industry	A group of firms that produce identical or similar products is an industry. It is also used specifically to refer to an area of economic production focused on manufacturing which involves large amounts of capital investment before any profit can be realized, also called "heavy industry".
Enabling	Enabling refers to giving workers the education and tools they need to assume their new

Go to **Cram101.com** for the Practice Tests for this Chapter.

	decision-making powers.
PepsiCo	In many ways, PepsiCo differs from its main competitor, having three times as many employees, larger revenues, but a smaller net profit.
Market share	That fraction of an industry's output accounted for by an individual firm or group of firms is called market share.
Enterprise	Enterprise refers to another name for a business organization. Other similar terms are business firm, sometimes simply business, sometimes simply firm, as well as company, and entity.
Kraft Foods	Kraft Foods is the largest food and beverage company headquartered in North America and the second largest in the world. In 1993 the Kraft Foods plant in Boston was hit with a $250,000 fine for violating the Clean Air Act of 1970.
Evaluation	The consumer's appraisal of the product or brand on important attributes is called evaluation.
Business plan	A detailed written statement that describes the nature of the business, the target market, the advantages the business will have in relation to competition, and the resources and qualifications of the owner is referred to as a business plan.
Quota	A government-imposed restriction on quantity, or sometimes on total value, used to restrict the import of something to a specific quantity is called a quota.
Utility	Utility refers to the want-satisfying power of a good or service; the satisfaction or pleasure a consumer obtains from the consumption of a good or service.
Resource allocation	Resource allocation refers to the manner in which an economy distributes its resources among the potential uses so as to produce a particular set of final goods.
America Online	In 2000 America Online and Time Warner announced plans to merge, and the deal was approved by the Federal Trade Commission on January 11, 2001. This merger was primarily a product of the Internet mania of the late-1990s, known as the Internet bubble. The deal is known as one of the worst corporate mergers in history, destroying over $200 billion in shareholder value.
Preparation	Preparation refers to usually the first stage in the creative process. It includes education and formal training.
Mission statement	Mission statement refers to an outline of the fundamental purposes of an organization.
Comprehensive	A comprehensive refers to a layout accurate in size, color, scheme, and other necessary details to show how a final ad will look. For presentation only, never for reproduction.
Tactical planning	The process of developing detailed, short-term decisions about what is to be done, who is to do it, and how it is to be done is called tactical planning.
Strategic plan	The formal document that presents the ways and means by which a strategic goal will be achieved is a strategic plan. A long-term flexible plan that does not regulate activities but rather outlines the means to achieve certain results, and provides the means to alter the course of action should the desired ends change.
Operational planning	The process of setting work standards and schedules necessary to implement the tactical objectives is operational planning.
Human resources	Human resources refers to the individuals within the firm, and to the portion of the firm's organization that deals with hiring, firing, training, and other personnel issues.
Autocratic leader	A leader who tends to centralize authority and rely on legitimate, reward, and coercive power to manage subordinates is an autocratic leader.

Go to **Cram101.com** for the Practice Tests for this Chapter.

133

Policy	Similar to a script in that a policy can be a less than completely rational decision-making method. Involves the use of a pre-existing set of decision steps for any problem that presents itself.
Insurance	Insurance refers to a system by which individuals can reduce their exposure to risk of large losses by spreading the risks among a large number of persons.
Broker	In commerce, a broker is a party that mediates between a buyer and a seller. A broker who also acts as a seller or as a buyer becomes a principal party to the deal.
Agent	A person who makes economic decisions for another economic actor. A hired manager operates as an agent for a firm's owner.
Management consulting	Management consulting refers to both the practice of helping companies to improve performance through analysis of existing business problems and development of future plans, as well as to the firms that specialize in this sort of consulting.
Econometrics	Econometrics refers to the application of statistical methods to the empirical estimation of economic relationships.
Contingency planning	The process of preparing alternative courses of action that may be used if the primary plans do not achieve the objectives of the organization is called contingency planning.
Communications management	Communications management is the systematic planning, implementing, monitoring, and revision of all the channels of communication within an organization and between organizations.
Quick response	An inventory management system designed to reduce the retailer's lead-time, thereby lowering its inventory investment, improving customer service levels, and reducing logistics expense is referred to as quick response.
Downturn	A decline in a stock market or economic cycle is a downturn.
Recovery	Characterized by rizing output, falling unemployment, rizing profits, and increasing economic activity following a decline is a recovery.
Crisis management	Crisis management involves identifying a crisis, planning a response to the crisis and confronting and resolving the crisis.
Chain of command	An unbroken line of authority that links all individuals in the organization and specifies who reports to whom is a chain of command. The concept of chain of command also implies that higher rank alone does not entitle a person to give commands.
Saks Fifth Avenue	Saks Fifth Avenue is a chain of upscale department stores that is a owned and operated by Saks Fifth Avenue Enterprises, a subsidiary of Saks Incorporated. It competes on a price level on par with Neiman Marcus, Bergdorf Goodman and above Bloomingdale's and Nordstrom. Saks Fifth Avenue is headquartered in New York City.
Continental Airlines	Continental Airlines is an airline of the United States. Based in Houston, Texas, it is the 6th largest airline in the U.S. and the 8th largest in the world. Continental's tagline, since 1998, has been Work Hard, Fly Right.
Frequency	Frequency refers to the speed of the up and down movements of a fluctuating economic variable; that is, the number of times per unit of time that the variable completes a cycle of up and down movement.
Financial management	The job of managing a firm's resources so it can meet its goals and objectives is called financial management.
Product innovation	The development and sale of a new or improved product is a product innovation. Production of a new product on a commercial basis.
Innovation	Innovation refers to the first commercially successful introduction of a new product, the use

of a new method of production, or the creation of a new form of business organization.

General Mills	In 2001, the General Mills purchased Pillsbury, although it was officially described as a "merger." While many of the Pillsbury-branded products are still manufactured by General Mills, some products had to be sold off to allow the merger since the new company would have held a very strong monopoly position.
Management system	A management system is the framework of processes and procedures used to ensure that an organization can fulfill all tasks required to achieve its objectives.
Dell Computer	Dell Computer, formerly PC's Limited, was founded on the principle that by selling personal computer systems directly to customers, PC's Limited could best understand their needs and provide the most effective computing solutions to meet those needs.
Corporation	A legal entity chartered by a state or the Federal government that is distinct and separate from the individuals who own it is a corporation. This separation gives the corporation unique powers which other legal entities lack.
Buyer	A buyer refers to a role in the buying center with formal authority and responsibility to select the supplier and negotiate the terms of the contract.
Expense	In accounting, an expense represents an event in which an asset is used up or a liability is incurred. In terms of the accounting equation, expenses reduce owners' equity.
Operating expense	In throughput accounting, the cost accounting aspect of Theory of Constraints (TOC), operating expense is the money spent turning inventory into throughput. In TOC, operating expense is limited to costs that vary strictly with the quantity produced, like raw materials and purchased components.
Pillsbury	Pillsbury the company was the first in the United States to use steam rollers for processing grain. The finished product required transportation, so the Pillsburys assisted in funding railroad development in Minnesota.
Promotion	Promotion refers to all the techniques sellers use to motivate people to buy products or services. An attempt by marketers to inform people about products and to persuade them to participate in an exchange.
Bond	Bond refers to a debt instrument, issued by a borrower and promising a specified stream of payments to the purchaser, usually regular interest payments plus a final repayment of principal.
Market share data	A comparative measure that determines relative positions of firms in the marketplace is called market share data.
Complaint	The pleading in a civil case in which the plaintiff states his claim and requests relief is called complaint. In the common law, it is a formal legal document that sets out the basic facts and legal reasons that the filing party (the plaintiffs) believes are sufficient to support a claim against another person, persons, entity or entities (the defendants) that entitles the plaintiff(s) to a remedy (either money damages or injunctive relief).
Raytheon	Since nearly all of Raytheon's revenues are obtained from defense contracts, there is necessarily a tight cooperation between Raytheon and the U.S. Department of Defense. This, along with heavy lobbying, has led to perennial charges of influence peddling. Raytheon contributed nearly a million dollars to various defense-related political campaigns in 2004, spending much more than that on lobbying expenses. And there are many tight ties between the company and all levels of government.
Strike	The withholding of labor services by an organized group of workers is referred to as a strike.

Go to **Cram101.com** for the Practice Tests for this Chapter.

Management functions	Management functions were set forth by Henri Fayol; they include planning, organizing, leading, and controling.
Nonprogrammed decision	Nonprogrammed decision refers to a decision that recurs infrequently and for which there is no previously established decision rule.
Advertising	Advertising refers to paid, nonpersonal communication through various media by organizations and individuals who are in some way identified in the advertising message.
Trial	An examination before a competent tribunal, according to the law of the land, of the facts or law put in issue in a cause, for the purpose of determining such issue is a trial. When the court hears and determines any issue of fact or law for the purpose of determining the rights of the parties, it may be considered a trial.
Product line	A group of products that are physically similar or are intended for a similar market are called the product line.
Chief information officer	The chief information officer is a job title for the head of information technology group within an organization. They often report to the chief executive officer or chief financial officer.
Interdependence	The extent to which departments depend on each other for resources or materials to accomplish their tasks is referred to as interdependence.
Loyalty	Marketers tend to define customer loyalty as making repeat purchases. Some argue that it should be defined attitudinally as a strongly positive feeling about the brand.
Autocratic leadership	Leadership style that involves making managerial decisions without consulting others is an autocratic leadership.
Warrant	A warrant is a security that entitles the holder to buy or sell a certain additional quantity of an underlying security at an agreed-upon price, at the holder's discretion.
Trend	Trend refers to the long-term movement of an economic variable, such as its average rate of increase or decrease over enough years to encompass several business cycles.
Empowerment	Giving employees the authority and responsibility to respond quickly to customer requests is called empowerment.
Grant	Grant refers to an intergovernmental transfer of funds . Since the New Deal, state and local governments have become increasingly dependent upon federal grants for an almost infinite variety of programs.
Intel	Intel Corporation, founded in 1968 and based in Santa Clara, California, USA, is the world's largest semiconductor company. Intel is best known for its PC microprocessors, where it maintains roughly 80% market share.
General Electric	In 1876, Thomas Alva Edison opened a new laboratory in Menlo Park, New Jersey. Out of the laboratory was to come perhaps the most famous invention of all—a successful development of the incandescent electric lamp. By 1890, Edison had organized his various businesses into the Edison General Electric Company.
DaimlerChrysler	In 2002, the merged company, DaimlerChrysler, appeared to run two independent product lines, with few signs of corporate integration. In 2003, however, it was alleged by the Detroit News that the "merger of equals" was, in fact, a takeover.
Core	A core is the set of feasible allocations in an economy that cannot be improved upon by subset of the set of the economy's consumers (a coalition). In construction, when the force in an element is within a certain center section, the core, the element will only be under compression.

Go to **Cram101.com** for the Practice Tests for this Chapter.

Core business	The core business of an organization is an idealized construct intended to express that organization's "main" or "essential" activity.
Home Depot	Home Depot has recently added self checkout registers at most of its stores in North America. These automated kiosks allow the customer to scan the barcode of the item they wish to purchase, then insert money to pay for the items, and receive any change automatically. The customer no longer needs to interact with a store employee during checkout.
Option	A contract that gives the purchaser the option to buy or sell the underlying financial instrument at a specified price, called the exercise price or strike price, within a specific period of time.
Stock option	A stock option is a specific type of option that uses the stock itself as an underlying instrument to determine the option's pay-off and therefore its value.
Bezos	Bezos founded Amazon.com in 1994, and became one of the most prominent dot-com billionaire entrepreneurs. In 2004, he started a human spaceflight start-up company called Blue Origin.
Turnover	Turnover in a financial context refers to the rate at which a provider of goods cycles through its average inventory. Turnover in a human resources context refers to the characteristic of a given company or industry, relative to rate at which an employer gains and loses staff.
Competitive Strategy	An outline of how a business intends to compete with other firms in the same industry is called competitive strategy.
Supply	Supply is the aggregate amount of any material good that can be called into being at a certain price point; it comprises one half of the equation of supply and demand. In classical economic theory, a curve representing supply is one of the factors that produce price.
Advertisement	Advertisement is the promotion of goods, services, companies and ideas, usually by an identified sponsor. Marketers see advertising as part of an overall promotional strategy.
Complexity	The technical sophistication of the product and hence the amount of understanding required to use it is referred to as complexity. It is the opposite of simplicity.
Organization chart	Organization chart refers to a visual device, which shows the relationship and divides the organization's work; it shows who is accountable for the completion of specific work and who reports to whom.
Public relations	Public relations refers to the management function that evaluates public attitudes, changes policies and procedures in response to the public's requests, and executes a program of action and information to earn public understanding and acceptance.
Labor relations	The field of labor relations looks at the relationship between management and workers, particularly groups of workers represented by a labor union.
Boeing	Boeing is the world's largest aircraft manufacturer by revenue. Headquartered in Chicago, Illinois, Boeing is the second-largest defense contractor in the world. In 2005, the company was the world's largest civil aircraft manufacturer in terms of value.
United airlines	United Airlines is a major airline of the United States headquartered in unincorporated Elk Grove Township, Illinois, near Chicago's O'Hare International Airport, the airline's largest traffic hub, with 650 daily departures. On February 1, 2006, it emerged from Chapter 11 bankruptcy protection under which it had operated since December 9, 2002, the largest and longest airline bankruptcy case in history.
Forming	The first stage of team development, where the team is formed and the objectives for the team are set is referred to as forming.
Knowledge worker	Employees who own the means of producing a product or service are called a knowledge worker.

Delegation	Delegation is the handing of a task over to another person, usually a subordinate. It is the assignment of authority and responsibility to another person to carry out specific activities.
Span of control	Span of control refers to the optimum number of subordinates a manager supervises or should supervise.
Organizational commitment	A person's identification with and attachment to an organization is called organizational commitment.
Wage	The payment for the service of a unit of labor, per unit time. In trade theory, it is the only payment to labor, usually unskilled labor. In empirical work, wage data may exclude other compenzation, which must be added to get the total cost of employment.
Investment	Investment refers to spending for the production and accumulation of capital and additions to inventories. In a financial sense, buying an asset with the expectation of making a return.
Holding	The holding is a court's determination of a matter of law based on the issue presented in the particular case. In other words: under this law, with these facts, this result.
Economy	The income, expenditures, and resources that affect the cost of running a business and household are called an economy.
New economy	New economy, this term was used in the late 1990's to suggest that globalization and/or innovations in information technology had changed the way that the world economy works.
Revenue	Revenue is a U.S. business term for the amount of money that a company receives from its activities, mostly from sales of products and/or services to customers.
Organizational culture	The mindset of employees, including their shared beliefs, values, and goals is called the organizational culture.
Golden Parachute	Highly attractive termination payments made to current management in the event of a takeover of the company is called a golden parachute.
Business Week	Business Week is a business magazine published by McGraw-Hill. It was first published in 1929 under the direction of Malcolm Muir, who was serving as president of the McGraw-Hill Publishing company at the time. It is considered to be the standard both in industry and among students.
Information technology	Information technology refers to technology that helps companies change business by allowing them to use new methods.
Centralization	A structural policy in which decision-making authority is concentrated at the top of the organizational hierarchy is referred to as centralization.
Decentralization	Decentralization is the process of redistributing decision-making closer to the point of service or action. This gives freedom to managers at lower levels of the organization to make decisions.
Matrix structure	An organizational structure which typically crosses a functional approach with a product or service-based design, often resulting in employees having two bosses is the matrix structure.
Committee	A long-lasting, sometimes permanent team in the organization structure created to deal with tasks that recur regularly is the committee.
Line organization	An organization that has direct two-way lines of responsibility, authority, and communication running from the top to the bottom of the organization, with all people reporting to only one supervisor is referred to as line organization.
Line authority	A form of authority in which individuals in management positions have the formal power to direct and control immediate subordinates is referred to as line authority.

Aid	Assistance provided by countries and by international institutions such as the World Bank to developing countries in the form of monetary grants, loans at low interest rates, in kind, or a combination of these is called aid. Aid can also refer to assistance of any type rendered to benefit some group or individual.
Specialist	A specialist is a trader who makes a market in one or several stocks and holds the limit order book for those stocks.
Interest	In finance and economics, interest is the price paid by a borrower for the use of a lender's money. In other words, interest is the amount of paid to "rent" money for a period of time.
Matrix organization	Matrix organization refers to an organization in which specialists from different parts of the organization are brought together to work on specific projects but still remain part of a traditional line-and-staff structure.
Project management	Project management is the discipline of organizing and managing resources in such a way that these resources deliver all the work required to complete a project within defined scope, time, and cost constraints.
Project manager	Project manager refers to a manager responsible for a temporary work project that involves the participation of other people from various functions and levels of the organization.
Multinational corporations	Firms that own production facilities in two or more countries and produce and sell their products globally are referred to as multinational corporations.
Multinational corporation	An organization that manufactures and markets products in many different countries and has multinational stock ownership and multinational management is referred to as multinational corporation.
Chase Manhattan	The Chase Manhattan Bank was formed by the merger of the Chase National Bank and the Bank of the Manhattan Company in 1955.
National Aeronautics and Space Administration	The National Aeronautics and Space Administration is an agency of the United States Government, responsible for the nation's public space program. Its annual funding amounts to $16 billion and is widely regarded as the forefront leader of space agencies worldwide. In addition to the space program, it is also responsible for long-term civilian and military aerospace research.
Small business	Small business refers to a business that is independently owned and operated, is not dominant in its field of operation, and meets certain standards of size in terms of employees or annual receipts.
SWOT	SWOT analysis refers to an acronym describing an organization's appraisal of its internal strengths and weaknesses and its external opportunities and threats.
Organizational goals	Objectives that management seeks to achieve in pursuing the firm's purpose are organizational goals.
Brief	Brief refers to a statement of a party's case or legal arguments, usually prepared by an attorney. Also used to make legal arguments before appellate courts.
Nike	Because Nike creates goods for a wide range of sports, they have competition from every sports and sports fashion brand there is. Nike has no direct competitors because there is no single brand which can compete directly with their range of sports and non-sports oriented gear, except for Reebok.
Charisma	A form of interpersonal attraction that inspires support and acceptance from others is charisma. It refers especially to a quality in certain people who easily draw the attention and admiration (or even hatred if the charisma is negative) of others due to a "magnetic" quality of personality and/or appearance.

Go to **Cram101.com** for the Practice Tests for this Chapter.

Leadership	Management merely consists of leadership applied to business situations; or in other words: management forms a sub-set of the broader process of leadership.
Enterprise	Enterprise refers to another name for a business organization. Other similar terms are business firm, sometimes simply business, sometimes simply firm, as well as company, and entity.
Market	A market is, as defined in economics, a social arrangement that allows buyers and sellers to discover information and carry out a voluntary exchange of goods or services.
Analyst	Analyst refers to a person or tool with a primary function of information analysis, generally with a more limited, practical and short term set of goals than a researcher.
Industry	A group of firms that produce identical or similar products is an industry. It is also used specifically to refer to an area of economic production focused on manufacturing which involves large amounts of capital investment before any profit can be realized, also called "heavy industry".
Advertising slogan	A advertising slogan is claimed to be, and often is proven to be, the most effective means of drawing attention to one or more aspects of a product or products. Typically they make claims about being the best quality, the tastiest, cheapest, most nutritious, providing an important benefit or solution, or being most suitable for the potential customer.
Advertising	Advertising refers to paid, nonpersonal communication through various media by organizations and individuals who are in some way identified in the advertising message.
Pizza Hut	Pizza Hut is the world's largest pizza restaurant chain with nearly 34,000 restaurants, delivery-carry out units, and kiosks in 100 countries
Appeal	Appeal refers to the act of asking an appellate court to overturn a decision after the trial court's final judgment has been entered.
Turnover	Turnover in a financial context refers to the rate at which a provider of goods cycles through its average inventory. Turnover in a human resources context refers to the characteristic of a given company or industry, relative to rate at which an employer gains and loses staff.
Recruitment	Recruitment refers to the set of activities used to obtain a sufficient number of the right people at the right time; its purpose is to select those who best meet the needs of the organization.
Evaluation	The consumer's appraisal of the product or brand on important attributes is called evaluation.
Outsourcing	Outsourcing refers to a production activity that was previously done inside a firm or plant that is now conducted outside that firm or plant.
Downsizing	The process of eliminating managerial and non-managerial positions are called downsizing.
Maslow	Maslow was an American psychologist. He is mostly noted today for his proposal of a hierarchy of human needs.
Job enrichment	A motivational strategy that emphasizes motivating the worker through the job itself is called job enrichment.
Hierarchy	A system of grouping people in an organization according to rank from the top down in which all subordinate managers must report to one person is called a hierarchy.
Theory X	Theory X refers to concept described by Douglas McGregor indicating an approach to management that takes a negative and pessimistic view of workers.
Theory Y	Theory Y refers to concept described by Douglas McGregor reflecting an approach to management

147

	that takes a positive and optimistic perspective on workers.
Tactic	A short-term immediate decision that, in its totality, leads to the achievement of strategic goals is called a tactic.
Labor	People's physical and mental talents and efforts that are used to help produce goods and services are called labor.
Management	Management characterizes the process of leading and directing all or part of an organization, often a business, through the deployment and manipulation of resources. Early twentieth-century management writer Mary Parker Follett defined management as "the art of getting things done through people."
Trend	Trend refers to the long-term movement of an economic variable, such as its average rate of increase or decrease over enough years to encompass several business cycles.
Inventory	Tangible property held for sale in the normal course of business or used in producing goods or services for sale is an inventory.
Lease	A contract for the possession and use of land or other property, including goods, on one side, and a recompense of rent or other income on the other is the lease.
Human resources	Human resources refers to the individuals within the firm, and to the portion of the firm's organization that deals with hiring, firing, training, and other personnel issues.
Profit	Profit refers to the return to the resource entrepreneurial ability; total revenue minus total cost.
Pension	A pension is a steady income given to a person (usually after retirement). Pensions are typically payments made in the form of a guaranteed annuity to a retired or disabled employee.
Wage	The payment for the service of a unit of labor, per unit time. In trade theory, it is the only payment to labor, usually unskilled labor. In empirical work, wage data may exclude other compenzation, which must be added to get the total cost of employment.
Profit sharing	A compenzation plan in which payments are based on a measure of organization performance and do not become part of the employees' base salary is profit sharing.
Chief executive officer	A chief executive officer is the highest-ranking corporate officer or executive officer of a corporation, or agency. In closely held corporations, it is general business culture that the office chief executive officer is also the chairman of the board.
Property	Assets defined in the broadest legal sense. Property includes the unrealized receivables of a cash basis taxpayer, but not services rendered.
Technology	The body of knowledge and techniques that can be used to combine economic resources to produce goods and services is called technology.
Corporation	A legal entity chartered by a state or the Federal government that is distinct and separate from the individuals who own it is a corporation. This separation gives the corporation unique powers which other legal entities lack.
Insurance	Insurance refers to a system by which individuals can reduce their exposure to risk of large losses by spreading the risks among a large number of persons.
Union	A worker association that bargains with employers over wages and working conditions is called a union.
Collective bargaining	Collective bargaining refers to the negotiation of labor contracts between labor unions and firms or government entities.

Go to **Cram101.com** for the Practice Tests for this Chapter.

Human resource management	The process of evaluating human resource needs, finding people to fill those needs, and getting the best work from each employee by providing the right incentives and job environment, all with the goal of meeting the needs of the firm are called human resource management.
Resource management	Resource management is the efficient and effective deployment of an organization's resources when they are needed. Such resources may include financial resources, inventory, human skills, production resources, or information technology.
Disney	Disney is one of the largest media and entertainment corporations in the world. Founded on October 16, 1923 by brothers Walt and Roy Disney as a small animation studio, today it is one of the largest Hollywood studios and also owns nine theme parks and several television networks, including the American Broadcasting Company (ABC).
Walt Disney	As the co-founder of Walt Disney Productions, Walt became one of the most well-known motion picture producers in the world. The corporation he co-founded, now known as The Walt Disney Company, today has annual revenues of approximately US $30 billion.
Authority	Authority in agency law, refers to an agent's ability to affect his principal's legal relations with third parties. Also used to refer to an actor's legal power or ability to do something. In addition, sometimes used to refer to a statute, case, or other legal source that justifies a particular result.
Complexity	The technical sophistication of the product and hence the amount of understanding required to use it is referred to as complexity. It is the opposite of simplicity.
Firm	An organization that employs resources to produce a good or service for profit and owns and operates one or more plants is referred to as a firm.
Balance	In banking and accountancy, the outstanding balance is the amount of money owned, (or due), that remains in a deposit account (or a loan account) at a given date, after all past remittances, payments and withdrawal have been accounted for. It can be positive (then, in the balance sheet of a firm, it is an asset) or negative (a liability).
Labor force	In economics the labor force is the group of people who have a potential for being employed.
Entrepreneur	The owner/operator. The person who organizes, manages, and assumes the risks of a firm, taking a new idea or a new product and turning it into a successful business is an entrepreneur.
Service	Service refers to a "non tangible product" that is not embodied in a physical good and that typically effects some change in another product, person, or institution. Contrasts with good.
Unemployment insurance	The social insurance program that in the United States is financed by state payroll taxes on employers and makes income available to workers who become unemployed and are unable to find jobs is unemployment insurance.
Compliance	A type of influence process where a receiver accepts the position advocated by a source to obtain favorable outcomes or to avoid punishment is the compliance.
Labor law	Labor law is the body of laws, administrative rulings, and precedents which addresses the legal rights of, and restrictions on, workers and their organizations.
Policy	Similar to a script in that a policy can be a less than completely rational decision-making method. Involves the use of a pre-existing set of decision steps for any problem that presents itself.
Committee	A long-lasting, sometimes permanent team in the organization structure created to deal with tasks that recur regularly is the committee.

General manager	A manager who is responsible for several departments that perform different functions is called general manager.
Supervisor	A Supervisor is an employee of an organization with some of the powers and responsibilities of management, occupying a role between true manager and a regular employee. A Supervisor position is typically the first step towards being promoted into a management role.
Organizational goals	Objectives that management seeks to achieve in pursuing the firm's purpose are organizational goals.
Competitive advantage	A business is said to have a competitive advantage when its unique strengths, often based on cost, quality, time, and innovation, offer consumers a greater percieved value and there by differtiating it from its competitors.
Core	A core is the set of feasible allocations in an economy that cannot be improved upon by subset of the set of the economy's consumers (a coalition). In construction, when the force in an element is within a certain center section, the core, the element will only be under compression.
Staffing	Staffing refers to a management function that includes hiring, motivating, and retaining the best people available to accomplish the company's objectives.
Job satisfaction	Job satisfaction describes how content an individual is with his or her job. It is a relatively recent term since in previous centuries the jobs available to a particular person were often predetermined by the occupation of that person's parent.
Human resource planning	Forecasting the organization's human resource needs, developing replacement charts for all levels of the organization, and preparing inventories of the skills and abilities individuals need to move within the organization is called human resource planning.
Marketing	Promoting and selling products or services to customers, or prospective customers, is referred to as marketing.
Cisco Systems	While Cisco Systems was not the first company to develop and sell a router (a device that forwards computer traffic from one network to another), it did create the first commercially successful multi-protocol router to allow previously incompatible computers to communicate using different network protocols.
Microsoft	Microsoft is a multinational computer technology corporation with 2004 global annual sales of US$39.79 billion and 71,553 employees in 102 countries and regions as of July 2006. It develops, manufactures, licenses, and supports a wide range of software products for computing devices.
Company culture	Company culture is the term given to the values and practices shared by the employees of a firm.
Asset	An item of property, such as land, capital, money, a share in ownership, or a claim on others for future payment, such as a bond or a bank deposit is an asset.
Complaint	The pleading in a civil case in which the plaintiff states his claim and requests relief is called complaint. In the common law, it is a formal legal document that sets out the basic facts and legal reasons that the filing party (the plaintiffs) believes are sufficient to support a claim against another person, persons, entity or entities (the defendants) that entitles the plaintiff(s) to a remedy (either money damages or injunctive relief).
Applicant	In many tribunal and administrative law suits, the person who initiates the claim is called the applicant.
Banner ad	A banner ad is a form of advertising on the World Wide Web. This form of online advertising entails embedding an advertisement into a web page.

Competitor	Other organizations in the same industry or type of business that provide a good or service to the same set of customers is referred to as a competitor.
Civil rights act of 1964	The Civil Rights Act of 1964 is a federal law that, in Title VII, outlaws discrimination based on race, color, religion, gender, or national origin in hiring, promoting, and compensating workers.
Americans with Disabilities Act	The Americans with Disabilities Act of 1990 is a wide-ranging civil rights law that prohibits discrimination based on disability.
Equal employment opportunity	The government's attempt to ensure that all individuals have an equal opportunity for employment, regardless of race, color, religion, sex, age, disability, or national origin is equal employment opportunity.
Trial	An examination before a competent tribunal, according to the law of the land, of the facts or law put in issue in a cause, for the purpose of determining such issue is a trial. When the court hears and determines any issue of fact or law for the purpose of determining the rights of the parties, it may be considered a trial.
Damages	The sum of money recoverable by a plaintiff who has received a judgment in a civil case is called damages.
Jury	A body of lay persons, selected by lot, or by some other fair and impartial means, to ascertain, under the guidance of the judge, the truth in questions of fact arising either in civil litigation or a criminal process is referred to as jury.
Employment discrimination	Inferior treatment in hiring, promotions, work assignments, and such for a particular group of employees, based on criteria that is not controllable, is referred to as employment discrimination.
Punitive damages	Damages received or paid by the taxpayer can be classified as compensatory damages or as punitive damages. Punitive damages are those awarded to punish the defendant for gross negligence or the intentional infliction of harm. Such damages are includible.
Punitive	Damages designed to punish flagrant wrongdoers and to deter them and others from engaging in similar conduct in the future are called punitive.
Publicity	Publicity refers to any information about an individual, product, or organization that's distributed to the public through the media and that's not paid for or controlled by the seller.
Preference	The act of a debtor in paying or securing one or more of his creditors in a manner more favorable to them than to other creditors or to the exclusion of such other creditors is a preference. In the absence of statute, a preference is perfectly good, but to be legal it must be bona fide, and not a mere subterfuge of the debtor to secure a future benefit to himself or to prevent the application of his property to his debts.
Xerox	Xerox was founded in 1906 as "The Haloid Company" manufacturing photographic paper and equipment. The company came to prominence in 1959 with the introduction of the first plain paper photocopier using the process of xerography (electrophotography) developed by Chester Carlson, the Xerox 914.
Employment law	Employment law is the body of laws, administrative rulings, and precedents which addresses the legal rights of, and restrictions on, workers and their organizations.
Personnel	A collective term for all of the employees of an organization. Personnel is also commonly used to refer to the personnel management function or the organizational unit responsible for administering personnel programs.

Go to **Cram101.com** for the Practice Tests for this Chapter.

Home Depot	Home Depot has recently added self checkout registers at most of its stores in North America. These automated kiosks allow the customer to scan the barcode of the item they wish to purchase, then insert money to pay for the items, and receive any change automatically. The customer no longer needs to interact with a store employee during checkout.
Promotion	Promotion refers to all the techniques sellers use to motivate people to buy products or services. An attempt by marketers to inform people about products and to persuade them to participate in an exchange.
Federal Bureau of Investigation	The Federal Bureau of Investigation is a federal criminal investigative, intelligence agency, and the primary investigative arm of the United States Department of Justice (DOJ). At present, the it has investigative jurisdiction over violations of more than 200 categories of federal crimes and thus has the broadest investigative authority of any U.S. federal law enforcement agency. The motto of the bureau is "Fidelity, Bravery, Integrity."
Exempt	Employees who are not covered by the Fair Labor Standards Act are exempt. Exempt employees are not eligible for overtime pay.
Central Intelligence Agency	The primary function of the Central Intelligence Agency is obtaining and analyzing information about foreign governments, corporations, and individuals, and reporting such information to the various branches of the Government. A second function is overtly and covertly disseminating information, both true and false, that influences others to make decisions favorable to the United States Government.
Contract	A contract is a "promise" or an "agreement" that is enforced or recognized by the law. In the civil law, a contract is considered to be part of the general law of obligations.
Security	Security refers to a claim on the borrower future income that is sold by the borrower to the lender. A security is a type of transferable interest representing financial value.
Employment test	A written or computerbased test designed to measure a particular attribute such as intelligence or aptitude is an employment test.
Mistake	In contract law a mistake is incorrect understanding by one or more parties to a contract and may be used as grounds to invalidate the agreement. Common law has identified three different types of mistake in contract: unilateral mistake, mutual mistake, and common mistake.
Basic skills	Basic skills refer to reading, writing, and communication skills needed to understand the content of a training program.
Employment at will	A rule stating that if an employment is not for a definite time period, either party may terminate the employment without liability at any time and for any reason is called employment at will.
Investment	Investment refers to spending for the production and accumulation of capital and additions to inventories. In a financial sense, buying an asset with the expectation of making a return.
Federal Express	The company officially began operations on April 17, 1973, utilizing a network of 14 Dassault Falcon 20s which connected 25 U.S. cities. FedEx, the first cargo airline to use jet aircraft for its services, expanded greatly after the deregulation of the cargo airlines sector. Federal Express use of the hub-spoke distribution paradigm in air freight enabled it to become a world leader in its field.
Expense	In accounting, an expense represents an event in which an asset is used up or a liability is incurred. In terms of the accounting equation, expenses reduce owners' equity.
Operation	A standardized method or technique that is performed repetitively, often on different materials resulting in different finished goods is called an operation.
Apprenticeship	A work-study training method with both on-the-job and classroom training is an

apprenticeship.Most of their training is on the job, working for an employer who helps the apprentices learn their trade, art or craft. Less formal, theoretical education is involved.

Users	Users refer to people in the organization who actually use the product or service purchased by the buying center.
Customer service	The ability of logistics management to satisfy users in terms of time, dependability, communication, and convenience is called the customer service.
Credit	Credit refers to a recording as positive in the balance of payments, any transaction that gives rise to a payment into the country, such as an export, the sale of an asset, or borrowing from abroad.
Aid	Assistance provided by countries and by international institutions such as the World Bank to developing countries in the form of monetary grants, loans at low interest rates, in kind, or a combination of these is called aid. Aid can also refer to assistance of any type rendered to benefit some group or individual.
Assignment	A transfer of property or some right or interest is referred to as assignment.
Management development	The process of training and educating employees to become good managers and then monitoring the progress of their managerial skills over time is management development.
Best practice	Best practice is a management idea which asserts that there is a technique, method, process, activity, incentive or reward that is more effective at delivering a particular outcome than any other technique, method, process, etc.
Interpersonal skills	Interpersonal skills are used to communicate with, understand, and motivate individuals and groups.
Chief information officer	The chief information officer is a job title for the head of information technology group within an organization. They often report to the chief executive officer or chief financial officer.
Information technology	Information technology refers to technology that helps companies change business by allowing them to use new methods.
Performance appraisal	An evaluation in which the performance level of employees is measured against established standards to make decisions about promotions, compenzation, additional training, or firing is referred to as performance appraisal.
Productivity	Productivity refers to the total output of goods and services in a given period of time divided by work hours.
United parcel service	United Parcel Service is the world's largest package delivery company, delivering more than 14 million packages a day to more than 200 countries around the world. It has recently expanded its operations to include logistics and other transportation-related areas.
Customer focus	Customer focus acknowledges that the more a company understands and meets the real needs of its consumers, the more likely it is to have happy customers who come back for more, and tell their friends.
Product cost	Product cost refers to sum of the costs assigned to a product for a specific purpose. A concept used in applying the cost plus approach to product pricing in which only the costs of manufacturing the product are included in the cost amount to which the markup is added.
Production	The creation of finished goods and services using the factors of production: land, labor, capital, entrepreneurship, and knowledge.
Adjusted for inflation	Adjusted for inflation refers to correcting for price changes to yield an equivalent real rate, or real non-inflationary number. The adjustment divides nominal amounts for different

159

years by price indices for those years -- eg the CPI or the implicit price deflator -- and multiplies by 100. This converts to real values, ie valued at the prices of the base year for the price index.

Cost of living	The amount of money it takes to buy the goods and services that a typical family consumes is the cost of living.
Minimum wage	The lowest wage employers may legally pay for an hour of work is the minimum wage.
Inflation	An increase in the overall price level of an economy, usually as measured by the CPI or by the implicit price deflator is called inflation.
Gain	In finance, gain is a profit or an increase in value of an investment such as a stock or bond. Gain is calculated by fair market value or the proceeds from the sale of the investment minus the sum of the purchase price and all costs associated with it.
Margin	A deposit by a buyer in stocks with a seller or a stockbroker, as security to cover fluctuations in the market in reference to stocks that the buyer has purchased but for which he has not paid is a margin. Commodities are also traded on margin.
Profit margin	Profit margin is a measure of profitability. It is calculated using a formula and written as a percentage or a number. Profit margin = Net income before tax and interest / Revenue.
Labor market	Any arrangement that brings buyers and sellers of labor services together to agree on conditions of work and pay is called a labor market.
Incentive	An incentive is any factor (financial or non-financial) that provides a motive for a particular course of action, or counts as a reason for preferring one choice to the alternatives.
Option	A contract that gives the purchaser the option to buy or sell the underlying financial instrument at a specified price, called the exercise price or strike price, within a specific period of time.
Stock	In financial terminology, stock is the capital raized by a corporation, through the issuance and sale of shares.
Gain sharing	Gain sharing refers to a pay system that links pay and performance by giving the workers the opportunity to share in productivity gains through increased earnings.
Stock option	A stock option is a specific type of option that uses the stock itself as an underlying instrument to determine the option's pay-off and therefore its value.
Variable	A variable is something measured by a number; it is used to analyze what happens to other things when the size of that number changes.
Social Security	Social security primarily refers to a field of social welfare concerned with social protection, or protection against socially recognized conditions, including poverty, old age, disability, unemployment, families with children and others.
Contribution	In business organization law, the cash or property contributed to a business by its owners is referred to as contribution.
Family and Medical Leave Act of 1993	The Family and Medical Leave Act of 1993 is a United States labor law allowing an employee to take unpaid leave due to illness or to care for a sick family member.
Health insurance	Health insurance is a type of insurance whereby the insurer pays the medical costs of the insured if the insured becomes sick due to covered causes, or due to accidents. The insurer may be a private organization or a government agency.
Department of	The United States Department of Labor is a Cabinet department of the United States government

Labor	responsible for occupational safety, wage and hour standards, unemployment insurance benefits, re-employment services, and some economic statistics.
Conversion	Conversion refers to any distinct act of dominion wrongfully exerted over another's personal property in denial of or inconsistent with his rights therein. That tort committed by a person who deals with chattels not belonging to him in a manner that is inconsistent with the ownership of the lawful owner.
Revenue	Revenue is a U.S. business term for the amount of money that a company receives from its activities, mostly from sales of products and/or services to customers.
Internal Revenue Service	In 1862, during the Civil War, President Lincoln and Congress created the office of Commissioner of Internal Revenue and enacted an income tax to pay war expenses. The position of Commissioner still exists today. The Commissioner is the head of the Internal Revenue Service.
Cafeteria plan	Cafeteria plan refers to an employee benefit plan under which an employee is allowed to select from among a variety of employer-provided fringe benefits. Some of the benefits may be taxable, and some may be statutory nontaxable benefits.
Allowance	Reduction in the selling price of goods extended to the buyer because the goods are defective or of lower quality than the buyer ordered and to encourage a buyer to keep merchandise that would otherwise be returned is the allowance.
Overtime	Overtime is the amount of time someone works beyond normal working hours.
Medicare	Medicare refers to federal program that is financed by payroll taxes and provides for compulsory hospital insurance for senior citizens and low-cost voluntary insurance to help older Americans pay physicians' fees.
Compressed workweek	A situation in which employees work a full forty-hour week in fewer than the traditional five days is referred to as compressed workweek.
Job sharing	Situation in which the duties and hours of one job position are carried out by two people is job sharing.
Flextime	A scheduling method that gives employees control over their work schedule is flextime; usually involves some 'core' times when employees must be at work, and a set of 'flextime' that can be adjustable for various employees.
Manufacturing	Production of goods primarily by the application of labor and capital to raw materials and other intermediate inputs, in contrast to agriculture, mining, forestry, fishing, and services a manufacturing.
Trust	An arrangement in which shareholders of independent firms agree to give up their stock in exchange for trust certificates that entitle them to a share of the trust's common profits.
Brief	Brief refers to a statement of a party's case or legal arguments, usually prepared by an attorney. Also used to make legal arguments before appellate courts.
Telecommuting	Telecommuting is a work arrangement in which employees enjoy limited flexibility in working location and hours.
Merrill Lynch	Merrill Lynch through its subsidiaries and affiliates, provides capital markets services, investment banking and advisory services, wealth management, asset management, insurance, banking and related products and services on a global basis. It is best known for its Global Private Client services and its strong sales force.
Exit interview	An interview conducted with departing employees to determine the reasons for their termination is called exit interview.

Go to **Cram101.com** for the Practice Tests for this Chapter.

Sexual harassment	Unwelcome sexual advances, requests for sexual favors, and other conduct of a sexual nature is called sexual harassment.
Organizational structure	Organizational structure is the way in which the interrelated groups of an organization are constructed. From a managerial point of view the main concerns are ensuring effective communication and coordination.
Overhead cost	An expenses of operating a business over and above the direct costs of producing a product is an overhead cost. They can include utilities (eg, electricity, telephone), advertizing and marketing, and any other costs not billed directly to the client or included in the price of the product.
Market share	That fraction of an industry's output accounted for by an individual firm or group of firms is called market share.
Chevron	Chevron Corporation is one of the world's largest global energy companies. Headquartered in San Ramon, California, USA and active in more than 180 countries, it is engaged in every aspect of the oil and gas industry, including exploration and production; refining, marketing and transport; chemicals manufacturing and sales; and power generation.
Consultant	A professional that provides expert advice in a particular field or area in which customers occasionaly require this type of knowledge is a consultant.
Domestic	From or in one's own country. A domestic producer is one that produces inside the home country. A domestic price is the price inside the home country. Opposite of 'foreign' or 'world.'.
Utility	Utility refers to the want-satisfying power of a good or service; the satisfaction or pleasure a consumer obtains from the consumption of a good or service.
Information technology management	Information technology management is a common business function within corporations. Strictly speaking, there are two incarnations to this definition. One implies the management of a collection of systems, infrastructure, and information that resides on them. Another implies the management of information technologies as a business function.
Product line	A group of products that are physically similar or are intended for a similar market are called the product line.
Accounting	A system that collects and processes financial information about an organization and reports that information to decision makers is referred to as accounting.
Economy	The income, expenditures, and resources that affect the cost of running a business and household are called an economy.
Gap	In December of 1995, Gap became the first major North American retailer to accept independent monitoring of the working conditions in a contract factory producing its garments. Gap is the largest specialty retailer in the United States.
Motorola	The Six Sigma quality system was developed at Motorola even though it became most well known because of its use by General Electric. It was created by engineer Bill Smith, under the direction of Bob Galvin (son of founder Paul Galvin) when he was running the company.
Knowledge worker	Employees who own the means of producing a product or service are called a knowledge worker.
Flexible factory	A manufacturing plant that has short production runs, is organized around products, and use decentralized scheduling are called a flexible factory.
Product design	Product Design is defined as the idea generation, concept development, testing and manufacturing or implementation of a physical object or service. It is possibly the evolution of former discipline name - Industrial Design.

Go to **Cram101.com** for the Practice Tests for this Chapter.

Competitiveness	Competitiveness usually refers to characteristics that permit a firm to compete effectively with other firms due to low cost or superior technology, perhaps internationally.
Complement	A good that is used in conjunction with another good is a complement. For example, cameras and film would complement eachother.
Bid	A bid price is a price offered by a buyer when he/she buys a good. In the context of stock trading on a stock exchange, the bid price is the highest price a buyer of a stock is willing to pay for a share of that given stock.
Principal	In agency law, one under whose direction an agent acts and for whose benefit that agent acts is a principal.
Partnership	In the common law, a partnership is a type of business entity in which partners share with each other the profits or losses of the business undertaking in which they have all invested.
Flexible work schedule	A flexible work schedule is a shedule in which an employee has a forty hour work week but can set their own schedule within the limits set by the employer.
Exchange	The trade of things of value between buyer and seller so that each is better off after the trade is called the exchange.
Strike	The withholding of labor services by an organized group of workers is referred to as a strike.
Grievance	A charge by employees that management is not abiding by the terms of the negotiated labormanagement agreement is the grievance.
Hierarchy of needs	Hierarchy of needs refers to Maslow's theory that human needs are arranged in an order or hierarchy based on their importance. The need hierarchy includes physiological, safety, social-love and belonging, esteem, and self-actualization needs.
Needs theory	Henry Murray (1893-1988), developed a personality theory during the 1930s up to the 1960s, which he called the Needs Theory. A need in this theory is defined as 'the potentiality or readiness to respond in a certain way under given circumstances'.
Occupational Safety and Health Administration	The United States Occupational Safety and Health Administration is an agency of the United States Department of Labor. It was created by Congress under the Occupational Safety and Health Act, signed by President Richard M. Nixon, on December 29, 1970.
Administration	Administration refers to the management and direction of the affairs of governments and institutions; a collective term for all policymaking officials of a government; the execution and implementation of public policy.
Appreciation	Appreciation refers to a rise in the value of a country's currency on the exchange market, relative either to a particular other currency or to a weighted average of other currencies. The currency is said to appreciate. Opposite of 'depreciation.' Appreciation can also refer to the increase in value of any asset.
Telecommute	To work at home and keep in touch with the company through telecommunications is referred to as telecommute.
Negotiation	Negotiation is the process whereby interested parties resolve disputes, agree upon courses of action, bargain for individual or collective advantage, and/or attempt to craft outcomes which serve their mutual interests.
Interest	In finance and economics, interest is the price paid by a borrower for the use of a lender's money. In other words, interest is the amount of paid to "rent" money for a period of time.
Hearing	A hearing is a proceeding before a court or other decision-making body or officer. A hearing

Go to **Cram101.com** for the Practice Tests for this Chapter.

	is generally distinguished from a trial in that it is usually shorter and often less formal.
Arbitration	Arbitration is a form of mediation or conciliation, where the mediating party is given power by the disputant parties to settle the dispute by making a finding. In practice arbitration is generally used as a substitute for judicial systems, particularly when the judicial processes are viewed as too slow, expensive or biased. Arbitration is also used by communities which lack formal law, as a substitute for formal law.
Open position	An obligation to take or make delivery of an asset or currency in the future without cover, that is, without a matching obligation in the other direction that protects them from effects of change in the price of the asset or currency is an open position.
Bureau of Labor Statistics	The Bureau of Labor Statistics is a unit of the United States Department of Labor, is the principal fact-finding agency for the U.S. government in the field of labor economics and statistics.
Labor relations	The field of labor relations looks at the relationship between management and workers, particularly groups of workers represented by a labor union.
Unemployment rate	The unemployment rate is the number of unemployed workers divided by the total civilian labor force, which includes both the unemployed and those with jobs (all those willing and able to work for pay).
Welfare	Welfare refers to the economic well being of an individual, group, or economy. For individuals, it is conceptualized by a utility function. For groups, including countries and the world, it is a tricky philosophical concept, since individuals fare differently.

169

Labor	People's physical and mental talents and efforts that are used to help produce goods and services are called labor.
Resource management	Resource management is the efficient and effective deployment of an organization's resources when they are needed. Such resources may include financial resources, inventory, human skills, production resources, or information technology.
Management	Management characterizes the process of leading and directing all or part of an organization, often a business, through the deployment and manipulation of resources. Early twentieth-century management writer Mary Parker Follett defined management as "the art of getting things done through people."
Promotion	Promotion refers to all the techniques sellers use to motivate people to buy products or services. An attempt by marketers to inform people about products and to persuade them to participate in an exchange.
Credit	Credit refers to a recording as positive in the balance of payments, any transaction that gives rise to a payment into the country, such as an export, the sale of an asset, or borrowing from abroad.
Tax credit	Allows a firm to reduce the taxes paid to the home government by the amount of taxes paid to the foreign government is referred to as tax credit.
Merrill Lynch	Merrill Lynch through its subsidiaries and affiliates, provides capital markets services, investment banking and advisory services, wealth management, asset management, insurance, banking and related products and services on a global basis. It is best known for its Global Private Client services and its strong sales force.
Telecommuting	Telecommuting is a work arrangement in which employees enjoy limited flexibility in working location and hours.
Recruitment	Recruitment refers to the set of activities used to obtain a sufficient number of the right people at the right time; its purpose is to select those who best meet the needs of the organization.
Profit	Profit refers to the return to the resource entrepreneurial ability; total revenue minus total cost.
Contract	A contract is a "promise" or an "agreement" that is enforced or recognized by the law. In the civil law, a contract is considered to be part of the general law of obligations.
Residual	Residual payments can refer to an ongoing stream of payments in respect of the completion of past achievements.
Trend	Trend refers to the long-term movement of an economic variable, such as its average rate of increase or decrease over enough years to encompass several business cycles.
Team cohesiveness	The extent to which team members are attracted to the team and motivated to remain in it is called team cohesiveness.
Effective communication	When the intended meaning equals the perceived meaning it is called effective communication.
Technology	The body of knowledge and techniques that can be used to combine economic resources to produce goods and services is called technology.
Preparation	Preparation refers to usually the first stage in the creative process. It includes education and formal training.
Interest	In finance and economics, interest is the price paid by a borrower for the use of a lender's money. In other words, interest is the amount of paid to "rent" money for a period of time.

171

Word of mouth	People influencing each other during their face-to-face converzations is called word of mouth.
Operation	A standardized method or technique that is performed repetitively, often on different materials resulting in different finished goods is called an operation.
Consultant	A professional that provides expert advice in a particular field or area in which customers occassionaly require this type of knowledge is a consultant.
Incentive	An incentive is any factor (financial or non-financial) that provides a motive for a particular course of action, or counts as a reason for preferring one choice to the alternatives.
Firm	An organization that employs resources to produce a good or service for profit and owns and operates one or more plants is referred to as a firm.
Organizational performance	Organizational performance comprises the actual output or results of an organization as measured against its intended outputs (or goals and objectives).
Empowerment	Giving employees the authority and responsibility to respond quickly to customer requests is called empowerment.
Teamwork	That which occurs when group members work together in ways that utilize their skills well to accomplish a purpose is called teamwork.
Information technology	Information technology refers to technology that helps companies change business by allowing them to use new methods.
Honda	With more than 14 million internal combustion engines built each year, Honda is the largest engine-maker in the world. In 2004, the company began to produce diesel motors, which were both very quiet whilst not requiring particulate filters to pass pollution standards. It is arguable, however, that the foundation of their success is the motorcycle division.
Adidas	Adidas is a German sports apparel manufacturer, part of the Adidas Group. The company was named after its founder, Adolf Dassler, who started producing shoes in the 1920s in Herzogenaurach near Nuremberg with the help of his brother Rudolf Dassler who later formed rival shoe company PUMA AG.
Total quality management	The broad set of management and control processes designed to focus an entire organization and all of its employees on providing products or services that do the best possible job of satisfying the customer is called total quality management.
Customer satisfaction	Customer satisfaction is a business term which is used to capture the idea of measuring how satisfied an enterprise's customers are with the organization's efforts in a marketplace.
Quality management	Quality management is a method for ensuring that all the activities necessary to design, develop and implement a product or service are effective and efficient with respect to the system and its performance.
Production	The creation of finished goods and services using the factors of production: land, labor, capital, entrepreneurship, and knowledge.
Information system	An information system is a system whether automated or manual, that comprises people, machines, and/or methods organized to collect, process, transmit, and disseminate data that represent user information.
Specialist	A specialist is a trader who makes a market in one or several stocks and holds the limit order book for those stocks.
Deming	Deming is widely credited with improving production in the United States during World War II, although he is perhaps best known for his work in Japan. There, from 1950 onward he taught

Go to **Cram101.com** for the Practice Tests for this Chapter.

top management how to improve design (and thus service), product quality, testing and sales (the latter through global markets).

Leadership	Management merely consists of leadership applied to business situations; or in other words: management forms a sub-set of the broader process of leadership.
Authority	Authority in agency law, refers to an agent's ability to affect his principal's legal relations with third parties. Also used to refer to an actor's legal power or ability to do something. In addition, sometimes used to refer to a statute, case, or other legal source that justifies a particular result.
Profit and loss statement	Profit and loss statement refers to another term for the income statement.
Policy	Similar to a script in that a policy can be a less than completely rational decision-making method. Involves the use of a pre-existing set of decision steps for any problem that presents itself.
Intranet	Intranet refers to a companywide network, closed to public access, that uses Internet-type technology. A set of communications links within one company that travel over the Internet but are closed to public access.
Accounts receivable	Accounts receivable is one of a series of accounting transactions dealing with the billing of customers which owe money to a person, company or organization for goods and services that have been provided to the customer. This is typically done in a one person organization by writing an invoice and mailing or delivering it to each customer.
Financial statement	Financial statement refers to a summary of all the transactions that have occurred over a particular period.
Enabling	Enabling refers to giving workers the education and tools they need to assume their new decision-making powers.
Industry	A group of firms that produce identical or similar products is an industry. It is also used specifically to refer to an area of economic production focused on manufacturing which involves large amounts of capital investment before any profit can be realized, also called "heavy industry".
Employee empowerment	Employee empowerment is a method of improving customer service in which workers have discretion to do what they believe is necessary, but within reason, to satisfy the customer, even if this means bending some company rules.
Hierarchy	A system of grouping people in an organization according to rank from the top down in which all subordinate managers must report to one person is called a hierarchy.
Browser	A program that allows a user to connect to the World Wide Web by simply typing in a URL is a browser.
Competitor	Other organizations in the same industry or type of business that provide a good or service to the same set of customers is referred to as a competitor.
Personnel	A collective term for all of the employees of an organization. Personnel is also commonly used to refer to the personnel management function or the organizational unit responsible for administering personnel programs.
Productivity	Productivity refers to the total output of goods and services in a given period of time divided by work hours.
Competitive Strategy	An outline of how a business intends to compete with other firms in the same industry is called competitive strategy.

Trust	An arrangement in which shareholders of independent firms agree to give up their stock in exchange for trust certificates that entitle them to a share of the trust's common profits.
Turnover	Turnover in a financial context refers to the rate at which a provider of goods cycles through its average inventory. Turnover in a human resources context refers to the characteristic of a given company or industry, relative to rate at which an employer gains and loses staff.
Disney	Disney is one of the largest media and entertainment corporations in the world. Founded on October 16, 1923 by brothers Walt and Roy Disney as a small animation studio, today it is one of the largest Hollywood studios and also owns nine theme parks and several television networks, including the American Broadcasting Company (ABC).
Walt Disney	As the co-founder of Walt Disney Productions, Walt became one of the most well-known motion picture producers in the world. The corporation he co-founded, now known as The Walt Disney Company, today has annual revenues of approximately US $30 billion.
Business plan	A detailed written statement that describes the nature of the business, the target market, the advantages the business will have in relation to competition, and the resources and qualifications of the owner is referred to as a business plan.
Board of directors	The group of individuals elected by the stockholders of a corporation to oversee its operations is a board of directors.
Supply	Supply is the aggregate amount of any material good that can be called into being at a certain price point; it comprises one half of the equation of supply and demand. In classical economic theory, a curve representing supply is one of the factors that produce price.
Purchasing	Purchasing refers to the function in a firm that searches for quality material resources, finds the best suppliers, and negotiates the best price for goods and services.
Gain	In finance, gain is a profit or an increase in value of an investment such as a stock or bond. Gain is calculated by fair market value or the proceeds from the sale of the investment minus the sum of the purchase price and all costs associated with it.
Pay for Performance	A one-time cash payment to an investment center manager as a reward for meeting a predetermined criterion on a specified performance measure is referred to as pay for performance.
Gain sharing	Gain sharing refers to a pay system that links pay and performance by giving the workers the opportunity to share in productivity gains through increased earnings.
Regular meeting	A meeting held by the board of directors that is held at regular intervals at the time and place established in the bylaws is called a regular meeting.
Employee Stock Ownership Plans	Like profit sharing, Employee Stock Ownership Plans are based on the total organization's performance, but are measured in terms of stock price.
Employee stock ownership plan	Employee Stock Ownership Plan is a qualified employee-benefit plan in which employees are entitled and encouraged to invest in shares of the company's stock and often at a favorable price. The employer's contributions are tax deductible for the employer and tax deferred for the employee.
Option	A contract that gives the purchaser the option to buy or sell the underlying financial instrument at a specified price, called the exercise price or strike price, within a specific period of time.
Stock	In financial terminology, stock is the capital raized by a corporation, through the issuance and sale of shares.
Stock option	A stock option is a specific type of option that uses the stock itself as an underlying

Go to **Cram101.com** for the Practice Tests for this Chapter.

	instrument to determine the option's pay-off and therefore its value.
Shares	Shares refer to an equity security, representing a shareholder's ownership of a corporation. Shares are one of a finite number of equal portions in the capital of a company, entitling the owner to a proportion of distributed, non-reinvested profits known as dividends and to a portion of the value of the company in case of liquidation.
Revenue	Revenue is a U.S. business term for the amount of money that a company receives from its activities, mostly from sales of products and/or services to customers.
Expense	In accounting, an expense represents an event in which an asset is used up or a liability is incurred. In terms of the accounting equation, expenses reduce owners' equity.
Pension	A pension is a steady income given to a person (usually after retirement). Pensions are typically payments made in the form of a guaranteed annuity to a retired or disabled employee.
Fund	Independent accounting entity with a self-balancing set of accounts segregated for the purposes of carrying on specific activities is referred to as a fund.
Regulation	Regulation refers to restrictions state and federal laws place on business with regard to the conduct of its activities.
Grant	Grant refers to an intergovernmental transfer of funds . Since the New Deal, state and local governments have become increasingly dependent upon federal grants for an almost infinite variety of programs.
Ford	Ford is an American company that manufactures and sells automobiles worldwide. Ford introduced methods for large-scale manufacturing of cars, and large-scale management of an industrial workforce, especially elaborately engineered manufacturing sequences typified by the moving assembly lines.
Motorola	The Six Sigma quality system was developed at Motorola even though it became most well known because of its use by General Electric. It was created by engineer Bill Smith, under the direction of Bob Galvin (son of founder Paul Galvin) when he was running the company.
Home Depot	Home Depot has recently added self checkout registers at most of its stores in North America. These automated kiosks allow the customer to scan the barcode of the item they wish to purchase, then insert money to pay for the items, and receive any change automatically. The customer no longer needs to interact with a store employee during checkout.
A share	In finance the term A share has two distinct meanings, both relating to securities. The first is a designation for a 'class' of common or preferred stock. A share of common or preferred stock typically has enhanced voting rights or other benefits compared to the other forms of shares that may have been created. The equity structure, or how many types of shares are offered, is determined by the corporate charter.
Evaluation	The consumer's appraisal of the product or brand on important attributes is called evaluation.
Applicant	In many tribunal and administrative law suits, the person who initiates the claim is called the applicant.
Consideration	Consideration in contract law, a basic requirement for an enforceable agreement under traditional contract principles, defined in this text as legal value, bargained for and given in exchange for an act or promise. In corporation law, cash or property contributed to a corporation in exchange for shares, or a promise to contribute such cash or property.
Xerox	Xerox was founded in 1906 as "The Haloid Company" manufacturing photographic paper and equipment. The company came to prominence in 1959 with the introduction of the first plain

Go to **Cram101.com** for the Practice Tests for this Chapter.

paper photocopier using the process of xerography (electrophotography) developed by Chester Carlson, the Xerox 914.

Service	Service refers to a "non tangible product" that is not embodied in a physical good and that typically effects some change in another product, person, or institution. Contrasts with good.
Asset	An item of property, such as land, capital, money, a share in ownership, or a claim on others for future payment, such as a bond or a bank deposit is an asset.
Asset management	Asset management is the method that a company uses to track fixed assets, for example factory equipment, desks and chairs, computers, even buildings. Although the exact details of the task varies widely from company to company, asset management often includes tracking the physical location of assets, managing demand for scarce resources, and accounting tasks such as amortization.
Continental Airlines	Continental Airlines is an airline of the United States. Based in Houston, Texas, it is the 6th largest airline in the U.S. and the 8th largest in the world. Continental's tagline, since 1998, has been Work Hard, Fly Right.
Customer service	The ability of logistics management to satisfy users in terms of time, dependability, communication, and convenience is called the customer service.
Quality circle	A quality circle is a volunteer group composed of workers who meet together to discuss workplace improvement, and make presentations to management with their ideas.
Scope	Scope of a project is the sum total of all projects products and their requirements or features.
International Business	International business refers to any firm that engages in international trade or investment.
Downsizing	The process of eliminating managerial and non-managerial positions are called downsizing.
Management team	A management team is directly responsible for managing the day-to-day operations (and profitability) of a company.
Virtual team	A group of physically dispersed people who work as a team via alternative communication modes is called virtual team.
Specie	Specie refers to coins, normally including only those made of precious metal.
Market	A market is, as defined in economics, a social arrangement that allows buyers and sellers to discover information and carry out a voluntary exchange of goods or services.
Intrapreneurship	Intrapreneurship is the practice of entrepreneurial skills and approaches by or within a company. Employees, perhaps engaged in a special project within a larger firm are supposed to behave as entrepreneurs, even though they have the resources and capabilities of the larger firm to draw upon.
Innovation	Innovation refers to the first commercially successful introduction of a new product, the use of a new method of production, or the creation of a new form of business organization.
DaimlerChrysler	In 2002, the merged company, DaimlerChrysler, appeared to run two independent product lines, with few signs of corporate integration. In 2003, however, it was alleged by the Detroit News that the "merger of equals" was, in fact, a takeover.
Marketing	Promoting and selling products or services to customers, or prospective customers, is referred to as marketing.
General Electric	In 1876, Thomas Alva Edison opened a new laboratory in Menlo Park, New Jersey. Out of the laboratory was to come perhaps the most famous invention of all—a successful development of

Go to **Cram101.com** for the Practice Tests for this Chapter.

181

the incandescent electric lamp. By 1890, Edison had organized his various businesses into the Edison General Electric Company.

Partnership	In the common law, a partnership is a type of business entity in which partners share with each other the profits or losses of the business undertaking in which they have all invested.
Time Warner	Time Warner is the world's largest media company with major Internet, publishing, film, telecommunications and television divisions.
Microsoft	Microsoft is a multinational computer technology corporation with 2004 global annual sales of US$39.79 billion and 71,553 employees in 102 countries and regions as of July 2006. It develops, manufactures, licenses, and supports a wide range of software products for computing devices.
Intel	Intel Corporation, founded in 1968 and based in Santa Clara, California, USA, is the world's largest semiconductor company. Intel is best known for its PC microprocessors, where it maintains roughly 80% market share.
Exchange	The trade of things of value between buyer and seller so that each is better off after the trade is called the exchange.
Liaison	An individual who serves as a bridge between groups, tying groups together and facilitating the communication flow needed to integrate group activities is a liaison.
Vendor	A person who sells property to a vendee is a vendor. The words vendor and vendee are more commonly applied to the seller and purchaser of real estate, and the words seller and buyer are more commonly applied to the seller and purchaser of personal property.
Balance	In banking and accountancy, the outstanding balance is the amount of money owned, (or due), that remains in a deposit account (or a loan account) at a given date, after all past remittances, payments and withdrawal have been accounted for. It can be positive (then, in the balance sheet of a firm, it is an asset) or negative (a liability).
Entrepreneur	The owner/operator. The person who organizes, manages, and assumes the risks of a firm, taking a new idea or a new product and turning it into a successful business is an entrepreneur.
Forming	The first stage of team development, where the team is formed and the objectives for the team are set is referred to as forming.
Matching	Matching refers to an accounting concept that establishes when expenses are recognized. Expenses are matched with the revenues they helped to generate and are recognized when those revenues are recognized.
Product line	A group of products that are physically similar or are intended for a similar market are called the product line.
Agent	A person who makes economic decisions for another economic actor. A hired manager operates as an agent for a firm's owner.
Storming stage	The storming stage follows the forming stage and isrefered to as the most difficult stage for a team. In this stage the team members are starting to trust one another enough to air differences, and control becomes the main issue.
Norming	The third stage of team development, where the team becomes a cohesive unit, and interdependence, trust, and cooperation are built is called norming.
Performing stage	The final stage of team developement is the performing stage. Some teams will reach the performing stage. These high-performing teams are able to function as a unit as they find ways to get the job done smoothly and effectively without inappropriate conflict or the need for external supervision.

Contribution	In business organization law, the cash or property contributed to a business by its owners is referred to as contribution.
Adjourning	The stage of team development that involves completing the task and breaking up the team is called adjourning.
Alcoa	Alcoa (NYSE: AA) is the world's leading producer of alumina, primary and fabricated aluminum, with operations in 43 countries. (It is followed in this by a former subsidiary, Alcan, the second-leading producer.)
Advertising agency	A firm that specializes in the creation, production, and placement of advertising messages and may provide other services that facilitate the marketing communications process is an advertising agency.
Advertising	Advertising refers to paid, nonpersonal communication through various media by organizations and individuals who are in some way identified in the advertising message.
Openness	Openness refers to the extent to which an economy is open, often measured by the ratio of its trade to GDP.
Common area	Common area is area on a piece of property or part of a building that is available for use to all owners or tenents. Examples include: hallways, swimming pools, parking garage, and cummunity centers.
Conflict resolution	Conflict resolution is the process of resolving a dispute or a conflict. Successful conflict resolution occurs by providing each side's needs, and adequately addressing their interests so that they are each satisfied with the outcome. Conflict resolution aims to end conflicts before they start or lead to physical fighting.
Cooperative	A business owned and controlled by the people who use it, producers, consumers, or workers with similar needs who pool their resources for mutual gain is called cooperative.
Manufacturing	Production of goods primarily by the application of labor and capital to raw materials and other intermediate inputs, in contrast to agriculture, mining, forestry, fishing, and services a manufacturing.
Quota	A government-imposed restriction on quantity, or sometimes on total value, used to restrict the import of something to a specific quantity is called a quota.
Closing	The finalization of a real estate sales transaction that passes title to the property from the seller to the buyer is referred to as a closing. Closing is a sales term which refers to the process of making a sale. It refers to reaching the final step, which may be an exchange of money or acquiring a signature.
Brand	A name, symbol, or design that identifies the goods or services of one seller or group of sellers and distinguishes them from the goods and services of competitors is a brand.
Press release	A written public news announcement normally distributed to major news services is referred to as press release.
Journal	Book of original entry, in which transactions are recorded in a general ledger system, is referred to as a journal.
Wall Street Journal	Dow Jones & Company was founded in 1882 by reporters Charles Dow, Edward Jones and Charles Bergstresser. Jones converted the small Customers' Afternoon Letter into The Wall Street Journal, first published in 1889, and began delivery of the Dow Jones News Service via telegraph. The Journal featured the Jones 'Average', the first of several indexes of stock and bond prices on the New York Stock Exchange.
Negotiation	Negotiation is the process whereby interested parties resolve disputes, agree upon courses of action, bargain for individual or collective advantage, and/or attempt to craft outcomes

	which serve their mutual interests.
Corporation	A legal entity chartered by a state or the Federal government that is distinct and separate from the individuals who own it is a corporation. This separation gives the corporation unique powers which other legal entities lack.
Dell Computer	Dell Computer, formerly PC's Limited, was founded on the principle that by selling personal computer systems directly to customers, PC's Limited could best understand their needs and provide the most effective computing solutions to meet those needs.
Business Week	Business Week is a business magazine published by McGraw-Hill. It was first published in 1929 under the direction of Malcolm Muir, who was serving as president of the McGraw-Hill Publishing company at the time. It is considered to be the standard both in industry and among students.

Empowerment	Giving employees the authority and responsibility to respond quickly to customer requests is called empowerment.
Teamwork	That which occurs when group members work together in ways that utilize their skills well to accomplish a purpose is called teamwork.
Users	Users refer to people in the organization who actually use the product or service purchased by the buying center.
Service	Service refers to a "non tangible product" that is not embodied in a physical good and that typically effects some change in another product, person, or institution. Contrasts with good.
Marketing	Promoting and selling products or services to customers, or prospective customers, is referred to as marketing.
Technology	The body of knowledge and techniques that can be used to combine economic resources to produce goods and services is called technology.
Merrill Lynch	Merrill Lynch through its subsidiaries and affiliates, provides capital markets services, investment banking and advisory services, wealth management, asset management, insurance, banking and related products and services on a global basis. It is best known for its Global Private Client services and its strong sales force.
Exchange	The trade of things of value between buyer and seller so that each is better off after the trade is called the exchange.
Fraud	Tax fraud falls into two categories: civil and criminal. Under civil fraud, the IRS may impose as a penalty of an amount equal to as much as 75 percent of the underpayment.
Credit	Credit refers to a recording as positive in the balance of payments, any transaction that gives rise to a payment into the country, such as an export, the sale of an asset, or borrowing from abroad.
American Express	From the early 1980s until the late 1990s, American Express was known for cutting its merchant fees (also known as a "discount rate") to fine merchants and restaurants if they only accepted American Express and no other credit or charge cards. This prompted competitors such as Visa and MasterCard to cry foul for a while, as the tactics "locked" restaurants into American Express.
Security	Security refers to a claim on the borrower future income that is sold by the borrower to the lender. A security is a type of transferable interest representing financial value.
Innovation	Innovation refers to the first commercially successful introduction of a new product, the use of a new method of production, or the creation of a new form of business organization.
Advertising agency	A firm that specializes in the creation, production, and placement of advertising messages and may provide other services that facilitate the marketing communications process is an advertising agency.
Advertising	Advertising refers to paid, nonpersonal communication through various media by organizations and individuals who are in some way identified in the advertising message.
Franchise	A contractual right to sell certain products or services, use certain trademarks, or perform activities in a geographical region is called a franchise.
Operations management	A specialized area in management that converts or transforms resources into goods and services is operations management.
Production	The creation of finished goods and services using the factors of production: land, labor, capital, entrepreneurship, and knowledge.

189

Management	Management characterizes the process of leading and directing all or part of an organization, often a business, through the deployment and manipulation of resources. Early twentieth-century management writer Mary Parker Follett defined management as "the art of getting things done through people."
Operation	A standardized method or technique that is performed repetitively, often on different materials resulting in different finished goods is called an operation.
Layout	Layout refers to the physical arrangement of the various parts of an advertisement including the headline, subheads, illustrations, body copy, and any identifying marks.
Inventory	Tangible property held for sale in the normal course of business or used in producing goods or services for sale is an inventory.
Manufacturing	Production of goods primarily by the application of labor and capital to raw materials and other intermediate inputs, in contrast to agriculture, mining, forestry, fishing, and services a manufacturing.
Management consulting	Management consulting refers to both the practice of helping companies to improve performance through analysis of existing business problems and development of future plans, as well as to the firms that specialize in this sort of consulting.
Firm	An organization that employs resources to produce a good or service for profit and owns and operates one or more plants is referred to as a firm.
Fortune magazine	Fortune magazine is America's longest-running business magazine. Currently owned by media conglomerate Time Warner, it was founded in 1930 by Henry Luce. It is known for its regular features ranking companies by revenue.
Continuous improvement	The constant effort to eliminate waste, reduce response time, simplify the design of both products and processes, and improve quality and customer service is referred to as continuous improvement.
Production line	A production line is a set of sequential operations established in a factory whereby materials are put through a refining process to produce an end-product that is suitable for onward consumption; or components are assembled to make a finished article.
Supply	Supply is the aggregate amount of any material good that can be called into being at a certain price point; it comprises one half of the equation of supply and demand. In classical economic theory, a curve representing supply is one of the factors that produce price.
Raw material	Raw material refers to a good that has not been transformed by production; a primary product.
Vendor	A person who sells property to a vendee is a vendor. The words vendor and vendee are more commonly applied to the seller and purchaser of real estate, and the words seller and buyer are more commonly applied to the seller and purchaser of personal property.
Standing	Standing refers to the legal requirement that anyone seeking to challenge a particular action in court must demonstrate that such action substantially affects his legitimate interests before he will be entitled to bring suit.
Inputs	The inputs used by a firm or an economy are the labor, raw materials, electricity and other resources it uses to produce its outputs.
Utility	Utility refers to the want-satisfying power of a good or service; the satisfaction or pleasure a consumer obtains from the consumption of a good or service.
Form utility	The value added by the creation of finished goods and services, such as the value added by taking silicon and making computer chips or putting services together to create a vacation package is referred to as form utility.

Go to **Cram101.com** for the Practice Tests for this Chapter.

Finished goods	Completed products awaiting sale are called finished goods. An item considered a finished good in a supplying plant might be considered a component or raw material in a receiving plant.
Industry	A group of firms that produce identical or similar products is an industry. It is also used specifically to refer to an area of economic production focused on manufacturing which involves large amounts of capital investment before any profit can be realized, also called "heavy industry".
Tangible	Having a physical existence is referred to as the tangible. Personal property other than real estate, such as cars, boats, stocks, or other assets.
Production function	Production function refers to a function that specifies the output in an industry for all combinations of inputs.
Human resource management	The process of evaluating human resource needs, finding people to fill those needs, and getting the best work from each employee by providing the right incentives and job environment, all with the goal of meeting the needs of the firm are called human resource management.
Resource management	Resource management is the efficient and effective deployment of an organization's resources when they are needed. Such resources may include financial resources, inventory, human skills, production resources, or information technology.
Lender	Suppliers and financial institutions that lend money to companies is referred to as a lender.
Stockholder	A stockholder is an individual or company (including a corporation) that legally owns one or more shares of stock in a joined stock company. The shareholders are the owners of a corporation. Companies listed at the stock market strive to enhance shareholder value.
Automation	Automation allows machines to do work previously accomplished by people.
Mass production	The process of making a large number of a limited variety of products at very low cost is referred to as mass production.
Stock	In financial terminology, stock is the capital raized by a corporation, through the issuance and sale of shares.
Personnel	A collective term for all of the employees of an organization. Personnel is also commonly used to refer to the personnel management function or the organizational unit responsible for administering personnel programs.
Mechanization	Mechanization is the use of machines to replace manual labor or animals and can also refer to the use of powered machinery to help a human operator in some task.
Labor	People's physical and mental talents and efforts that are used to help produce goods and services are called labor.
Standardization	Standardization, in the context related to technologies and industries, is the process of establishing a technical standard among competing entities in a market, where this will bring benefits without hurting competition.
Assembly line	An assembly line is a manufacturing process in which interchangeable parts are added to a product in a sequential manner to create a finished product.
Extension	Extension refers to an out-of-court settlement in which creditors agree to allow the firm more time to meet its financial obligations. A new repayment schedule will be developed, subject to the acceptance of creditors.
Ford	Ford is an American company that manufactures and sells automobiles worldwide. Ford introduced methods for large-scale manufacturing of cars, and large-scale management of an

Go to **Cram101.com** for the Practice Tests for this Chapter.

	industrial workforce, especially elaborately engineered manufacturing sequences typified by the moving assembly lines.
Henry Ford	Henry Ford was the founder of the Ford Motor Company. His introduction of the Model T automobile revolutionized transportation and American industry.
General Motors	General Motors is the world's largest automaker. Founded in 1908, today it employs about 327,000 people around the world. With global headquarters in Detroit, it manufactures its cars and trucks in 33 countries.
Partnership	In the common law, a partnership is a type of business entity in which partners share with each other the profits or losses of the business undertaking in which they have all invested.
Information technology	Information technology refers to technology that helps companies change business by allowing them to use new methods.
Xerox	Xerox was founded in 1906 as "The Haloid Company" manufacturing photographic paper and equipment. The company came to prominence in 1959 with the introduction of the first plain paper photocopier using the process of xerography (electrophotography) developed by Chester Carlson, the Xerox 914.
Bertelsmann	Bertelsmann is a transnational media corporation founded in 1835, based in Gütersloh, Germany. Bertelsmann made headlines on May 17, 2002, when it announced it would acquire the assets of Napster for $8 million.
Distribution	Distribution in economics, the manner in which total output and income is distributed among individuals or factors.
Warehouse	Warehouse refers to a location, often decentralized, that a firm uses to store, consolidate, age, or mix stock; house product-recall programs; or ease tax burdens.
Buyer	A buyer refers to a role in the buying center with formal authority and responsibility to select the supplier and negotiate the terms of the contract.
Investment	Investment refers to spending for the production and accumulation of capital and additions to inventories. In a financial sense, buying an asset with the expectation of making a return.
Option	A contract that gives the purchaser the option to buy or sell the underlying financial instrument at a specified price, called the exercise price or strike price, within a specific period of time.
Supervisor	A Supervisor is an employee of an organization with some of the powers and responsibilities of management, occupying a role between true manager and a regular employee. A Supervisor position is typically the first step towards being promoted into a management role.
Honda	With more than 14 million internal combustion engines built each year, Honda is the largest engine-maker in the world. In 2004, the company began to produce diesel motors, which were both very quiet whilst not requiring particulate filters to pass pollution standards. It is arguable, however, that the foundation of their success is the motorcycle division.
Research and development	The use of resources for the deliberate discovery of new information and ways of doing things, together with the application of that information in inventing new products or processes is referred to as research and development.
Intermittent process	Intermittent process refers to a production process in which the production run is short and the machines are changed frequently to make different products.
Continuous production	Continuous production is a method used to produce or process any product without interruption. There is no discrete rate at which goods are produced, as opposed to a batch production process, or a one-time production.

Go to **Cram101.com** for the Practice Tests for this Chapter.

Configuration	An organization's shape, which reflects the division of labor and the means of coordinating the divided tasks is configuration.
Flexible manufacturing system	A series of manufacturing machines, controlled and integrated by a computer, which is designed to perform a series of manufacturing operations automatically are referred to as a flexible manufacturing system.
Flexible manufacturing	Flexible manufacturing refers to designing machines to do multiple tasks so that they can produce a variety of products.
Assignment	A transfer of property or some right or interest is referred to as assignment.
Fixture	Fixture refers to a thing that was originally personal property and that has been actually or constructively affixed to the soil itself or to some structure legally a part of the land.
Occupational Safety and Health Administration	The United States Occupational Safety and Health Administration is an agency of the United States Department of Labor. It was created by Congress under the Occupational Safety and Health Act, signed by President Richard M. Nixon, on December 29, 1970.
Administration	Administration refers to the management and direction of the affairs of governments and institutions; a collective term for all policymaking officials of a government; the execution and implementation of public policy.
Bureau of Labor Statistics	The Bureau of Labor Statistics is a unit of the United States Department of Labor, is the principal fact-finding agency for the U.S. government in the field of labor economics and statistics.
Regulation	Regulation refers to restrictions state and federal laws place on business with regard to the conduct of its activities.
Market	A market is, as defined in economics, a social arrangement that allows buyers and sellers to discover information and carry out a voluntary exchange of goods or services.
Policy	Similar to a script in that a policy can be a less than completely rational decision-making method. Involves the use of a pre-existing set of decision steps for any problem that presents itself.
Foundation	A Foundation is a type of philanthropic organization set up by either individuals or institutions as a legal entity (either as a corporation or trust) with the purpose of distributing grants to support causes in line with the goals of the foundation.
Long run	In economic models, the long run time frame assumes no fixed factors of production. Firms can enter or leave the marketplace, and the cost (and availability) of land, labor, raw materials, and capital goods can be assumed to vary.
Productivity	Productivity refers to the total output of goods and services in a given period of time divided by work hours.
Insurance	Insurance refers to a system by which individuals can reduce their exposure to risk of large losses by spreading the risks among a large number of persons.
Turnover	Turnover in a financial context refers to the rate at which a provider of goods cycles through its average inventory. Turnover in a human resources context refers to the characteristic of a given company or industry, relative to rate at which an employer gains and loses staff.
Enabling	Enabling refers to giving workers the education and tools they need to assume their new decision-making powers.
Computer	Computer Numerical Control refers specifically to the computer control of machine tools for

Go to **Cram101.com** for the Practice Tests for this Chapter.

Numerical Control	the purpose of (repeatedly) manufacturing complex parts in metal as well as other materials, using a program written in a notation conforming to the EIA-274-D standard and commonly called G-code.
Cessna	Cessna, located in Wichita, Kansas, is a manufacturer of general aviation aircraft, from small two-seat, single-engine aircraft to business jets. The company traces its history to June 1911, when Clyde Cessna, a farmer in Rago, Kansas, built a wood-and-fabric plane and became the first person to build and fly an aircraft between the Mississippi River and the Rocky Mountains.
Holding	The holding is a court's determination of a matter of law based on the issue presented in the particular case. In other words: under this law, with these facts, this result.
Integration	Economic integration refers to reducing barriers among countries to transactions and to movements of goods, capital, and labor, including harmonization of laws, regulations, and standards. Integrated markets theoretically function as a unified market.
Partition	Partition refers to proceeding the object of which is to enable those who own property as joint tenants or tenants in common to put an end to the tenancy so as to vest in each a sole estate in specific property or an allotment of the lands and tenements. If a division of the estate is impracticable, the estate ought to be sold and the proceeds divided.
Regulatory agency	Regulatory agency refers to an agency, commission, or board established by the Federal government or a state government to regulates businesses in the public interest.
Labor supply	The number of workers available to an economy. The principal determinants of labor supply are population, real wages, and social traditions.
Economy	The income, expenditures, and resources that affect the cost of running a business and household are called an economy.
Wage	The payment for the service of a unit of labor, per unit time. In trade theory, it is the only payment to labor, usually unskilled labor. In empirical work, wage data may exclude other compenzation, which must be added to get the total cost of employment.
Trend	Trend refers to the long-term movement of an economic variable, such as its average rate of increase or decrease over enough years to encompass several business cycles.
Gross domestic product	Gross domestic product refers to the total value of new goods and services produced in a given year within the borders of a country, regardless of by whom.
Domestic	From or in one's own country. A domestic producer is one that produces inside the home country. A domestic price is the price inside the home country. Opposite of 'foreign' or 'world.'.
Control process	A process involving gathering processed data, analyzing processed data, and using this information to make adjustments to the process is a control process.
Evaluation	The consumer's appraisal of the product or brand on important attributes is called evaluation.
Marketing research	Marketing research refers to the analysis of markets to determine opportunities and challenges, and to find the information needed to make good decisions.
Prototype	A prototype is built to test the function of a new design before starting production of a product.
Product concept	The verbal and perhaps pictorial description of the benefits and features of a proposed product; also the early stage of the product development process in which only the product concept exists.

Go to **Cram101.com** for the Practice Tests for this Chapter.

Fund	Independent accounting entity with a self-balancing set of accounts segregated for the purposes of carrying on specific activities is referred to as a fund.
Chrysler	The Chrysler Corporation was an American automobile manufacturer that existed independently from 1925–1998. The company was formed by Walter Percy Chrysler on June 6, 1925, with the remaining assets of Maxwell Motor Company.
Dealer	People who link buyers with sellers by buying and selling securities at stated prices are referred to as a dealer.
Disney	Disney is one of the largest media and entertainment corporations in the world. Founded on October 16, 1923 by brothers Walt and Roy Disney as a small animation studio, today it is one of the largest Hollywood studios and also owns nine theme parks and several television networks, including the American Broadcasting Company (ABC).
Discount	The difference between the face value of a bond and its selling price, when a bond is sold for less than its face value it's referred to as a discount.
Walt Disney	As the co-founder of Walt Disney Productions, Walt became one of the most well-known motion picture producers in the world. The corporation he co-founded, now known as The Walt Disney Company, today has annual revenues of approximately US $30 billion.
Merger	Merger refers to the combination of two firms into a single firm.
Unused capacity	Unused capacity refers to the amount of productive capacity available over and above the productive capacity employed to meet consumer demand in the current period.
Overtime	Overtime is the amount of time someone works beyond normal working hours.
Avon	Avon is an American cosmetics, perfume and toy seller with markets in over 135 countries across the world and a sales of $7.74 billion worldwide.
Preventive maintenance	Maintaining scheduled upkeep and improvement to equipment so equipment can actually improve with age is called the preventive maintenance.
Premium	Premium refers to the fee charged by an insurance company for an insurance policy. The rate of losses must be relatively predictable: In order to set the premium (prices) insurers must be able to estimate them accurately.
Facility layout	The physical arrangement of resources in the production process is called facility layout.
Process layout	A method of organizing the elements of a production process, in which similar processes and functions are grouped together is called process layout.
Product layout	Product layout refers to a facilities layout in which machines and tasks are arranged according to the sequence of steps in the production of a single product.
Lease	A contract for the possession and use of land or other property, including goods, on one side, and a recompense of rent or other income on the other is the lease.
Union	A worker association that bargains with employers over wages and working conditions is called a union.
Churning	Churning is the practice of executing trades for an investment account by a salesman or broker in order to generate commissions from the account. It is a breach of securities law in many jurisdictions, and it is generally actionable by the account holder for the return of the commissions paid.
Chief operating officer	A chief operating officer is a corporate officer responsible for managing the day-to-day activities of the corporation. The chief operating officer is one of the highest ranking members of an organization, monitoring the daily operations of the company and reporting to the chief executive officer directly.

Extranet	An extension of the Internet that connects suppliers, customers, and other organizations via secure websites is an extranet.
Invoice	The itemized bill for a transaction, stating the nature of the transaction and its cost. In international trade, the invoice price is often the preferred basis for levying an ad valorem tariff.
Reengineering	The fundamental rethinking and redesign of business processes to achieve improvements in critical measures of performance, such as cost, quality, service, speed, and customer satisfaction is referred to as reengineering.
Accounting	A system that collects and processes financial information about an organization and reports that information to decision makers is referred to as accounting.
Competitor	Other organizations in the same industry or type of business that provide a good or service to the same set of customers is referred to as a competitor.
Management system	A management system is the framework of processes and procedures used to ensure that an organization can fulfill all tasks required to achieve its objectives.
Materials requirement planning	A computer-based production management system that uses sales forecasts to make sure that needed parts and materials are available at the right time and place is referred to as materials requirement planning.
Inventory control	Inventory control, in the field of loss prevention, are systems designed to introduce technical barriers to shoplifting.
Controlling	A management function that involves determining whether or not an organization is progressing toward its goals and objectives, and taking corrective action if it is not is called controlling.
Production efficiency	A situation in which the economy cannot produce more of one good without producing less of some other good is referred to as production efficiency.
Bill of materials	A bill of materials describes a product in terms of its assemblies, sub-assemblies, and basic parts. Basically consisting of a list of parts, a bill of materials is an essential part of the design and manufacture of any product.
Bill of material	A bill of material is a list of all the materials needed to manufacture a product or product component.
Purchasing	Purchasing refers to the function in a firm that searches for quality material resources, finds the best suppliers, and negotiates the best price for goods and services.
Human resources	Human resources refers to the individuals within the firm, and to the portion of the firm's organization that deals with hiring, firing, training, and other personnel issues.
Gantt chart	Bar graph showing production managers what projects are being worked on and what stage they are in at any given time is a gantt chart.
Program Evaluation and Review Technique	Program evaluation and review technique refers to a method for analyzing the tasks involved in completing a given project, estimating the time needed to complete each task, and identifying the minimum time needed to complete the total project.
Critical path	The sequence of tasks that limit how quickly a project can be completed is referred to as critical path.
Bottleneck	An operation where the work to be performed approaches or exceeds the capacity available to do it is a bottleneck.
General manager	A manager who is responsible for several departments that perform different functions is

Go to **Cram101.com** for the Practice Tests for this Chapter.

called general manager.

Corporation	A legal entity chartered by a state or the Federal government that is distinct and separate from the individuals who own it is a corporation. This separation gives the corporation unique powers which other legal entities lack.
Business plan	A detailed written statement that describes the nature of the business, the target market, the advantages the business will have in relation to competition, and the resources and qualifications of the owner is referred to as a business plan.
Sales forecast	Sales forecast refers to the maximum total sales of a product that a firm expects to sell during a specified time period under specified environmental conditions and its own marketing efforts.
Product design	Product Design is defined as the idea generation, concept development, testing and manufacturing or implementation of a physical object or service. It is possibly the evolution of former discipline name - Industrial Design.
Costs of quality	Costs incurred to prevent, or costs arising as a result of, producing a low-quality product are called costs of quality.
EBay	eBay manages an online auction and shopping website, where people buy and sell goods and services worldwide.
Quality control	The measurement of products and services against set standards is referred to as quality control.
Publicity	Publicity refers to any information about an individual, product, or organization that's distributed to the public through the media and that's not paid for or controlled by the seller.
Mistake	In contract law a mistake is incorrect understanding by one or more parties to a contract and may be used as grounds to invalidate the agreement. Common law has identified three different types of mistake in contract: unilateral mistake, mutual mistake, and common mistake.
Budget	Budget refers to an account, usually for a year, of the planned expenditures and the expected receipts of an entity. For a government, the receipts are tax revenues.
Operating budget	An operating budget is the annual budget of an activity stated in terms of Budget Classification Code, functional/subfunctional categories and cost accounts. It contains estimates of the total value of resources required for the performance of the operation including reimbursable work or services for others.
Six sigma	A means to 'delight the customer' by achieving quality through a highly disciplined process to focus on developing and delivering near-perfect products and services is called six sigma. Originally, it was defined as a metric for measuring defects and improving quality; and a methodology to reduce defect levels below 3.4 Defects Per (one) Million Opportunities (DPMO).
Standardized product	Standardized product refers to a product whose buyers are indifferent to the seller from whom they purchase it, as long as the price charged by all sellers is the same; a product all units of which are identical and thus are perfect substitutes.
American National Standards Institute	The American National Standards Institute or ANSI is a nonprofit organization that oversees the development of standards for products, services, processes and systems in the United States. The organization also coordinates U.S. standards with international standards so that American products can be used worldwide.
ISO 9000	ISO 9000 is a family of ISO standards for Quality Management Systems. It does not guarantee the quality of end products and services; rather, it certifies that consistent business processes are being applied.

Go to **Cram101.com** for the Practice Tests for this Chapter.

205

Audit	An examination of the financial reports to ensure that they represent what they claim and conform with generally accepted accounting principles is referred to as audit.
Customer satisfaction	Customer satisfaction is a business term which is used to capture the idea of measuring how satisfied an enterprise's customers are with the organization's efforts in a marketplace.
Goodyear	Goodyear was founded in 1898 by German immigrants Charles and Frank Seiberling. Today it is the third largest tire and rubber company in the world.
Conversion	Conversion refers to any distinct act of dominion wrongfully exerted over another's personal property in denial of or inconsistent with his rights therein. That tort committed by a person who deals with chattels not belonging to him in a manner that is inconsistent with the ownership of the lawful owner.
Strike	The withholding of labor services by an organized group of workers is referred to as a strike.
Balance	In banking and accountancy, the outstanding balance is the amount of money owned, (or due), that remains in a deposit account (or a loan account) at a given date, after all past remittances, payments and withdrawal have been accounted for. It can be positive (then, in the balance sheet of a firm, it is an asset) or negative (a liability).
Profit	Profit refers to the return to the resource entrepreneurial ability; total revenue minus total cost.
Management philosophy	Management philosophy refers to a philosophy that links key goal-related issues with key collaboration issues to come up with general ways by which the firm will manage its affairs.
Customer service	The ability of logistics management to satisfy users in terms of time, dependability, communication, and convenience is called the customer service.
Brief	Brief refers to a statement of a party's case or legal arguments, usually prepared by an attorney. Also used to make legal arguments before appellate courts.
Boeing	Boeing is the world's largest aircraft manufacturer by revenue. Headquartered in Chicago, Illinois, Boeing is the second-largest defense contractor in the world. In 2005, the company was the world's largest civil aircraft manufacturer in terms of value.
Proprietary	Proprietary indicates that a party, or proprietor, exercises private ownership, control or use over an item of property, usually to the exclusion of other parties. Where a party, holds or claims proprietary interests in relation to certain types of property (eg. a creative literary work, or software), that property may also be the subject of intellectual property law (eg. copyright or patents).
Kraft Foods	Kraft Foods is the largest food and beverage company headquartered in North America and the second largest in the world. In 1993 the Kraft Foods plant in Boston was hit with a $250,000 fine for violating the Clean Air Act of 1970.
Shares	Shares refer to an equity security, representing a shareholder's ownership of a corporation. Shares are one of a finite number of equal portions in the capital of a company, entitling the owner to a proportion of distributed, non-reinvested profits known as dividends and to a portion of the value of the company in case of liquidation.
Investment management	Investment management is a branch of investment analysis that looks into the process of managing money. Investment portfolios can be managed through decisions about security purchases and sales.
Analyst	Analyst refers to a person or tool with a primary function of information analysis, generally with a more limited, practical and short term set of goals than a researcher.
Volatility	Volatility refers to the extent to which an economic variable, such as a price or an exchange

Go to **Cram101.com** for the Practice Tests for this Chapter.

	rate, moves up and down over time.
Digital technology	Technology characterized by use of the Internet and other digital processes to conduct or support business operations is referred to as digital technology.
Federal Express	The company officially began operations on April 17, 1973, utilizing a network of 14 Dassault Falcon 20s which connected 25 U.S. cities. FedEx, the first cargo airline to use jet aircraft for its services, expanded greatly after the deregulation of the cargo airlines sector. Federal Express use of the hub-spoke distribution paradigm in air freight enabled it to become a world leader in its field.

Customer satisfaction	Customer satisfaction is a business term which is used to capture the idea of measuring how satisfied an enterprise's customers are with the organization's efforts in a marketplace.
Marketing	Promoting and selling products or services to customers, or prospective customers, is referred to as marketing.
Market	A market is, as defined in economics, a social arrangement that allows buyers and sellers to discover information and carry out a voluntary exchange of goods or services.
Marketing strategy	Marketing strategy refers to the means by which a marketing goal is to be achieved, usually characterized by a specified target market and a marketing program to reach it.
Buyer	A buyer refers to a role in the buying center with formal authority and responsibility to select the supplier and negotiate the terms of the contract.
Consumer behavior	Consumer behavior refers to the actions a person takes in purchasing and using products and services, including the mental and social processes that precede and follow these actions.
Relationship marketing	Marketing whose goal is to keep individual customers over time by offering them products that exactly meet their requirements is called relationship marketing.
Strategic planning	The process of determining the major goals of the organization and the policies and strategies for obtaining and using resources to achieve those goals is called strategic planning.
Shares	Shares refer to an equity security, representing a shareholder's ownership of a corporation. Shares are one of a finite number of equal portions in the capital of a company, entitling the owner to a proportion of distributed, non-reinvested profits known as dividends and to a portion of the value of the company in case of liquidation.
Stock	In financial terminology, stock is the capital raized by a corporation, through the issuance and sale of shares.
Voting shares	Voting shares are shares that give the stockholder the right to vote on matters of corporate policy making as well as who will compose the members of the board of directors.
Promoter	A person who incorporates a business, organizes its initial management, and raises its initial capital is a promoter.
Operation	A standardized method or technique that is performed repetitively, often on different materials resulting in different finished goods is called an operation.
Chief executive officer	A chief executive officer is the highest-ranking corporate officer or executive officer of a corporation, or agency. In closely held corporations, it is general business culture that the office chief executive officer is also the chairman of the board.
Publicity	Publicity refers to any information about an individual, product, or organization that's distributed to the public through the media and that's not paid for or controlled by the seller.
Chief operating officer	A chief operating officer is a corporate officer responsible for managing the day-to-day activities of the corporation. The chief operating officer is one of the highest ranking members of an organization, monitoring the daily operations of the company and reporting to the chief executive officer directly.
Target audience	That group that composes the present and potential prospects for a product or service is called the target audience.
Target market	One or more specific groups of potential consumers toward which an organization directs its marketing program are a target market.
Advertising	Advertising refers to paid, nonpersonal communication through various media by organizations

and individuals who are in some way identified in the advertising message.

Management	Management characterizes the process of leading and directing all or part of an organization, often a business, through the deployment and manipulation of resources. Early twentieth-century management writer Mary Parker Follett defined management as "the art of getting things done through people."
Firm	An organization that employs resources to produce a good or service for profit and owns and operates one or more plants is referred to as a firm.
Profit	Profit refers to the return to the resource entrepreneurial ability; total revenue minus total cost.
Service	Service refers to a "non tangible product" that is not embodied in a physical good and that typically effects some change in another product, person, or institution. Contrasts with good.
Customer orientation	Customer orientation is a set of beliefs/ strategy that customer needs and satisfaction are the priority of an organization. It focuses on dynamic interactions between the organization and customers as well as competitors in the market and its internal stakeholders.
Technology	The body of knowledge and techniques that can be used to combine economic resources to produce goods and services is called technology.
Exchange	The trade of things of value between buyer and seller so that each is better off after the trade is called the exchange.
Utility	Utility refers to the want-satisfying power of a good or service; the satisfaction or pleasure a consumer obtains from the consumption of a good or service.
Inputs	The inputs used by a firm or an economy are the labor, raw materials, electricity and other resources it uses to produce its outputs.
Production function	Production function refers to a function that specifies the output in an industry for all combinations of inputs.
Finished goods	Completed products awaiting sale are called finished goods. An item considered a finished good in a supplying plant might be considered a component or raw material in a receiving plant.
Form utility	The value added by the creation of finished goods and services, such as the value added by taking silicon and making computer chips or putting services together to create a vacation package is referred to as form utility.
Raw material	Raw material refers to a good that has not been transformed by production; a primary product.
Production	The creation of finished goods and services using the factors of production: land, labor, capital, entrepreneurship, and knowledge.
Time utility	Adding value to products by making them available when they're needed is referred to as time utility.
Place utility	Adding value to products by having them where people want them is called place utility.
Trial	An examination before a competent tribunal, according to the law of the land, of the facts or law put in issue in a cause, for the purpose of determining such issue is a trial. When the court hears and determines any issue of fact or law for the purpose of determining the rights of the parties, it may be considered a trial.
Product line	A group of products that are physically similar or are intended for a similar market are called the product line.

Go to **Cram101.com** for the Practice Tests for this Chapter.

Promotion	Promotion refers to all the techniques sellers use to motivate people to buy products or services. An attempt by marketers to inform people about products and to persuade them to participate in an exchange.
Nike	Because Nike creates goods for a wide range of sports, they have competition from every sports and sports fashion brand there is. Nike has no direct competitors because there is no single brand which can compete directly with their range of sports and non-sports oriented gear, except for Reebok.
Innovation	Innovation refers to the first commercially successful introduction of a new product, the use of a new method of production, or the creation of a new form of business organization.
Preference	The act of a debtor in paying or securing one or more of his creditors in a manner more favorable to them than to other creditors or to the exclusion of such other creditors is a preference. In the absence of statute, a preference is perfectly good, but to be legal it must be bona fide, and not a mere subterfuge of the debtor to secure a future benefit to himself or to prevent the application of his property to his debts.
Enabling	Enabling refers to giving workers the education and tools they need to assume their new decision-making powers.
Production orientation	A production orientation era dominated business thought from the beginning of capitalism to the mid 1950's. Business concerned itself primarily with production, manufacturing, and efficiency issues.
Sales orientation	The sales orientation era ran from the mid-1950s to the early 1970s, and is therefore after the production orientation era but before the marketing orientation era. During WWII world industry geared up for accelerated wartime production. When the war was over this stimulated industrial machine turned to producing consumer products.
Competitor	Other organizations in the same industry or type of business that provide a good or service to the same set of customers is referred to as a competitor.
Loyalty	Marketers tend to define customer loyalty as making repeat purchases. Some argue that it should be defined attitudinally as a strongly positive feeling about the brand.
Balance	In banking and accountancy, the outstanding balance is the amount of money owned, (or due), that remains in a deposit account (or a loan account) at a given date, after all past remittances, payments and withdrawal have been accounted for. It can be positive (then, in the balance sheet of a firm, it is an asset) or negative (a liability).
Customer service	The ability of logistics management to satisfy users in terms of time, dependability, communication, and convenience is called the customer service.
Competitive advantage	A business is said to have a competitive advantage when its unique strengths, often based on cost, quality, time, and innovation, offer consumers a greater percieved value and there by differtiating it from its competitors.
Tangible	Having a physical existence is referred to as the tangible. Personal property other than real estate, such as cars, boats, stocks, or other assets.
Level of service	The degree of service provided to the customer by self, limited, and full-service retailers is referred to as the level of service.
Appeal	Appeal refers to the act of asking an appellate court to overturn a decision after the trial court's final judgment has been entered.
American Express	From the early 1980s until the late 1990s, American Express was known for cutting its merchant fees (also known as a "discount rate") to fine merchants and restaurants if they only accepted American Express and no other credit or charge cards. This prompted competitors

	such as Visa and MasterCard to cry foul for a while, as the tactics "locked" restaurants into American Express.
Polaroid	The Polaroid Corporation was founded in 1937 by Edwin H. Land. It is most famous for its instant film cameras, which reached the market in 1948, and continue to be the company's flagship product line.
Revenue	Revenue is a U.S. business term for the amount of money that a company receives from its activities, mostly from sales of products and/or services to customers.
Pillsbury	Pillsbury the company was the first in the United States to use steam rollers for processing grain. The finished product required transportation, so the Pillsburys assisted in funding railroad development in Minnesota.
Complaint	The pleading in a civil case in which the plaintiff states his claim and requests relief is called complaint. In the common law, it is a formal legal document that sets out the basic facts and legal reasons that the filing party (the plaintiffs) believes are sufficient to support a claim against another person, persons, entity or entities (the defendants) that entitles the plaintiff(s) to a remedy (either money damages or injunctive relief).
Foundation	A Foundation is a type of philanthropic organization set up by either individuals or institutions as a legal entity (either as a corporation or trust) with the purpose of distributing grants to support causes in line with the goals of the foundation.
United Nations	An international organization created by multilateral treaty in 1945 to promote social and economic cooperation among nations and to protect human rights is the United Nations.
Distribution	Distribution in economics, the manner in which total output and income is distributed among individuals or factors.
Private sector	The households and business firms of the economy are referred to as private sector.
Government units	The federal, state, and local agencies that buy goods and services for the constituents they serve is a government units.
Ordinance	Ordinance refers to a legislative enactment of a county or an incorporated city or town. A law made by a non-sovereign body such as a city council or a colony.
Labor	People's physical and mental talents and efforts that are used to help produce goods and services are called labor.
Union	A worker association that bargains with employers over wages and working conditions is called a union.
Labor union	A group of workers organized to advance the interests of the group is called a labor union.
Expense	In accounting, an expense represents an event in which an asset is used up or a liability is incurred. In terms of the accounting equation, expenses reduce owners' equity.
Fund	Independent accounting entity with a self-balancing set of accounts segregated for the purposes of carrying on specific activities is referred to as a fund.
Organizational mission	A organizational mission is a retailer's commitment to a type of business and to a distinctive role in the marketplace. It is reflected in the firm's attitudes to consumers, employees, suppliers, competitors, government, and others.
Public relations	Public relations refers to the management function that evaluates public attitudes, changes policies and procedures in response to the public's requests, and executes a program of action and information to earn public understanding and acceptance.
Partnership	In the common law, a partnership is a type of business entity in which partners share with each other the profits or losses of the business undertaking in which they have all invested.

Sponsorship	When the advertiser assumes responsibility for the production and usually the content of a television program as well as the advertising that appears within it, we have sponsorship.
Corporation	A legal entity chartered by a state or the Federal government that is distinct and separate from the individuals who own it is a corporation. This separation gives the corporation unique powers which other legal entities lack.
Postal Service	The postal service was created in Philadelphia under Benjamin Franklin on July 26, 1775 by decree of the Second Continental Congress. Based on a clause in the United States Constitution empowering Congress "To establish Post Offices and post Roads."
Committee	A long-lasting, sometimes permanent team in the organization structure created to deal with tasks that recur regularly is the committee.
Tactic	A short-term immediate decision that, in its totality, leads to the achievement of strategic goals is called a tactic.
Interest	In finance and economics, interest is the price paid by a borrower for the use of a lender's money. In other words, interest is the amount of paid to "rent" money for a period of time.
Policy	Similar to a script in that a policy can be a less than completely rational decision-making method. Involves the use of a pre-existing set of decision steps for any problem that presents itself.
Advertising campaign	A comprehensive advertising plan that consists of a series of messages in a variety of media that center on a single theme or idea is referred to as an advertising campaign.
Marketing research	Marketing research refers to the analysis of markets to determine opportunities and challenges, and to find the information needed to make good decisions.
Marketing Plan	Marketing plan refers to a road map for the marketing activities of an organization for a specified future period of time, such as one year or five years.
Business plan	A detailed written statement that describes the nature of the business, the target market, the advantages the business will have in relation to competition, and the resources and qualifications of the owner is referred to as a business plan.
Budget	Budget refers to an account, usually for a year, of the planned expenditures and the expected receipts of an entity. For a government, the receipts are tax revenues.
Marketing mix	The marketing mix approach to marketing is a model of crafting and implementing marketing strategies. It stresses the "mixing" or blending of various factors in such a way that both organizational and consumer (target markets) objectives are attained.
Purchasing power	The amount of goods that money will buy, usually measured by the CPI is referred to as purchasing power.
Purchasing	Purchasing refers to the function in a firm that searches for quality material resources, finds the best suppliers, and negotiates the best price for goods and services.
Authority	Authority in agency law, refers to an agent's ability to affect his principal's legal relations with third parties. Also used to refer to an actor's legal power or ability to do something. In addition, sometimes used to refer to a statute, case, or other legal source that justifies a particular result.
Users	Users refer to people in the organization who actually use the product or service purchased by the buying center.
End user	End user refers to the ultimate user of a product or service.
Product strategy	Decisions on the management of products or services based on the conditions of a given market is product strategy. Two general strategies that are well known in the marketing discipline

are marketing mix and relational marketing.

Brand	A name, symbol, or design that identifies the goods or services of one seller or group of sellers and distinguishes them from the goods and services of competitors is a brand.
Warranty	An obligation of a company to replace defective goods or correct any deficiencies in performance or quality of a product is called a warranty.
Pricing strategy	The process in which the price of a product can be determined and is decided upon is a pricing strategy.
Perceived quality	A dimension of quality identified by David Garvin that refers to a subjective assessment of a product's quality based on criteria defined by the observer is a perceived quality.
Channel	Channel, in communications (sometimes called communications channel), refers to the medium used to convey information from a sender (or transmitter) to a receiver.
Distribution channel	A distribution channel is a chain of intermediaries, each passing a product down the chain to the next organization, before it finally reaches the consumer or end-user.
Premium	Premium refers to the fee charged by an insurance company for an insurance policy. The rate of losses must be relatively predictable: In order to set the premium (prices) insurers must be able to estimate them accurately.
Basket	A basket is an economic term for a group of several securities created for the purpose of simultaneous buying or selling. Baskets are frequently used for program trading.
Asset	An item of property, such as land, capital, money, a share in ownership, or a claim on others for future payment, such as a bond or a bank deposit is an asset.
Intranet	Intranet refers to a companywide network, closed to public access, that uses Internet-type technology. A set of communications links within one company that travel over the Internet but are closed to public access.
Time Warner	Time Warner is the world's largest media company with major Internet, publishing, film, telecommunications and television divisions.
Discount	The difference between the face value of a bond and its selling price, when a bond is sold for less than its face value it's referred to as a discount.
Standardization	Standardization, in the context related to technologies and industries, is the process of establishing a technical standard among competing entities in a market, where this will bring benefits without hurting competition.
Prime minister	The Prime Minister of the United Kingdom of Great Britain and Northern Ireland is the head of government and so exercises many of the executive functions nominally vested in the Sovereign, who is head of state. According to custom, the Prime Minister and the Cabinet (which he or she heads) are accountable for their actions to Parliament, of which they are members by (modern) convention.
Domestic	From or in one's own country. A domestic producer is one that produces inside the home country. A domestic price is the price inside the home country. Opposite of 'foreign' or 'world.'.
Mass customization	A manufacturing environment in which many standardized components are combined to produce custommade products to customer order is referred to as mass customization.
Option	A contract that gives the purchaser the option to buy or sell the underlying financial instrument at a specified price, called the exercise price or strike price, within a specific period of time.
Industry	A group of firms that produce identical or similar products is an industry. It is also used

	specifically to refer to an area of economic production focused on manufacturing which involves large amounts of capital investment before any profit can be realized, also called "heavy industry".
Gain	In finance, gain is a profit or an increase in value of an investment such as a stock or bond. Gain is calculated by fair market value or the proceeds from the sale of the investment minus the sum of the purchase price and all costs associated with it.
Inventory	Tangible property held for sale in the normal course of business or used in producing goods or services for sale is an inventory.
Trade association	An industry trade group or trade association is generally a public relations organization founded and funded by corporations that operate in a specific industry. Its purpose is generally to promote that industry through PR activities such as advertizing, education, political donations, political pressure, publishing, and astroturfing.
Advertising agency	A firm that specializes in the creation, production, and placement of advertising messages and may provide other services that facilitate the marketing communications process is an advertising agency.
Composition	An out-of-court settlement in which creditors agree to accept a fractional settlement on their original claim is referred to as composition.
Household	An economic unit that provides the economy with resources and uses the income received to purchase goods and services that satisfy economic wants is called household.
Primary data	Facts and figures that are newly collected for the project are referred to as primary data.
Focus group	A small group of people who meet under the direction of a discussion leader to communicate their opinions about an organization, its products, or other given issues is a focus group.
Applied research	Applied research is conducted to solve particular problems or answer specific questions.
Universal product code	Universal product code refers to a number assigned to identify each product, represented by a series of bars of varying widths for scanning by optical readers.
Bar code	Bar code refers to a printed code that makes use of lines of various widths to encode data about products.
Nielsen	When TV viewers or entertainment professionals in the United States mention "ratings" they are generally referring to Nielsen Ratings, a system developed by Nielsen Media Research to determine the audience size and composition of television programming. Nielsen Ratings are offered in over forty countries.
Market research	Market research is the process of systematic gathering, recording and analyzing of data about customers, competitors and the market. Market research can help create a business plan, launch a new product or service, fine tune existing products and services, expand into new markets etc. It can be used to determine which portion of the population will purchase the product/service, based on variables like age, gender, location and income level. It can be found out what market characteristics your target market has.
Demographic segmentation	Demographic segmentation refers to dividing the market by age, income, and education level.
Market segmentation	The process of dividing the total market into several groups whose members have similar characteristics is market segmentation.
Demographic	A demographic is a term used in marketing and broadcasting, to describe a demographic grouping or a market segment.
Family life	Family life cycle refers to concept that demonstrates changing purchasing behavior as a

Go to **Cram101.com** for the Practice Tests for this Chapter.

cycle	person or a family matures.
Advertisement	Advertisement is the promotion of goods, services, companies and ideas, usually by an identified sponsor. Marketers see advertising as part of an overall promotional strategy.
Targeting	In advertizing, targeting is to select a demographic or other group of people to advertise to, and create advertisements appropriately.
Hasbro	Hasbro originated with the Mr. Potato Head toy. Mr. Potato Head was the invention of George Lerner in the late 1940s. The idea was originally sold to a breakfast cereal manufacturer so that the separate parts could be distributed as cereal package premiums.
Churning	Churning is the practice of executing trades for an investment account by a salesman or broker in order to generate commissions from the account. It is a breach of securities law in many jurisdictions, and it is generally actionable by the account holder for the return of the commissions paid.
Boycott	To protest by refusing to purchase from someone, or otherwise do business with them. In international trade, a boycott most often takes the form of refusal to import a country's goods.
Trademark	A distinctive word, name, symbol, device, or combination thereof, which enables consumers to identify favored products or services and which may find protection under state or federal law is a trademark.
Merchandising	Merchandising refers to the business of acquiring finished goods for resale, either in a wholesale or a retail operation.
Ford	Ford is an American company that manufactures and sells automobiles worldwide. Ford introduced methods for large-scale manufacturing of cars, and large-scale management of an industrial workforce, especially elaborately engineered manufacturing sequences typified by the moving assembly lines.
Toyota	Toyota is a Japanese multinational corporation that manufactures automobiles, trucks and buses. Toyota is the world's second largest automaker by sales. Toyota also provides financial services through its subsidiary, Toyota Financial Services, and participates in other lines of business.
Better Business Bureau	An organization established and funded by businesses that operates primarily at the local level to monitor activities of companies and promote fair advertising and selling practices is a better business bureau.
Vendor	A person who sells property to a vendee is a vendor. The words vendor and vendee are more commonly applied to the seller and purchaser of real estate, and the words seller and buyer are more commonly applied to the seller and purchaser of personal property.
Bid	A bid price is a price offered by a buyer when he/she buys a good. In the context of stock trading on a stock exchange, the bid price is the highest price a buyer of a stock is willing to pay for a share of that given stock.
Procurement	Procurement is the acquisition of goods or services at the best possible total cost of ownership, in the right quantity, at the right time, in the right place for the direct benefit or use of the governments, corporations, or individuals generally via, but not limited to a contract.
Evaluation	The consumer's appraisal of the product or brand on important attributes is called evaluation.
Collaboration	Collaboration occurs when the interaction between groups is very important to goal attainment and the goals are compatible. Wherein people work together —applying both to the work of

Go to **Cram101.com** for the Practice Tests for this Chapter.

225

individuals as well as larger collectives and societies.

Standing	Standing refers to the legal requirement that anyone seeking to challenge a particular action in court must demonstrate that such action substantially affects his legitimate interests before he will be entitled to bring suit.
Positioning	The art and science of fitting the product or service to one or more segments of the market in such a way as to set it meaningfully apart from competition is called positioning.
Commerce	Commerce is the exchange of something of value between two entities. It is the central mechanism from which capitalism is derived.
Contract	A contract is a "promise" or an "agreement" that is enforced or recognized by the law. In the civil law, a contract is considered to be part of the general law of obligations.
Inventory management	The planning, coordinating, and controlling activities related to the flow of inventory into, through, and out of an organization is referred to as inventory management.
Cisco Systems	While Cisco Systems was not the first company to develop and sell a router (a device that forwards computer traffic from one network to another), it did create the first commercially successful multi-protocol router to allow previously incompatible computers to communicate using different network protocols.
Lifetime value	An estimate of the long-term revenue that can be expected from a particular prospect is the lifetime value.
Customer retention	Customer retention refers to the percentage of customers who return to a service provider or continue to purchase a manufactured product.
Holding	The holding is a court's determination of a matter of law based on the issue presented in the particular case. In other words: under this law, with these facts, this result.
Best practice	Best practice is a management idea which asserts that there is a technique, method, process, activity, incentive or reward that is more effective at delivering a particular outcome than any other technique, method, process, etc.
Frequency	Frequency refers to the speed of the up and down movements of a fluctuating economic variable; that is, the number of times per unit of time that the variable completes a cycle of up and down movement.
Points	Loan origination fees that may be deductible as interest by a buyer of property. A seller of property who pays points reduces the selling price by the amount of the points paid for the buyer.
Credit	Credit refers to a recording as positive in the balance of payments, any transaction that gives rise to a payment into the country, such as an export, the sale of an asset, or borrowing from abroad.
Logo	Logo refers to device or other brand name that cannot be spoken.
Intel	Intel Corporation, founded in 1968 and based in Santa Clara, California, USA, is the world's largest semiconductor company. Intel is best known for its PC microprocessors, where it maintains roughly 80% market share.
Credibility	The extent to which a source is perceived as having knowledge, skill, or experience relevant to a communication topic and can be trusted to give an unbiased opinion or present objective information on the issue is called credibility.
Yahoo	Yahoo is an American computer services company. It operates an Internet portal, the Yahoo Directory and a host of other services including the popular Yahoo Mail. Yahoo is the most visited website on the Internet today with more than 400 million unique users. The global

Go to **Cram101.com** for the Practice Tests for this Chapter.

227

network of Yahoo! websites received 3.4 billion page views per day on average as of October 2005.

Sweepstakes	Sales promotions consisting of a game of chance requiring no analytical or creative effort by the consumer is a sweepstakes.
Sweepstake	A sweepstake is technically a lottery in which the prize is financed through the tickets sold. In the United States the word has become associated with promotions where prizes are given away for free.
Enterprise	Enterprise refers to another name for a business organization. Other similar terms are business firm, sometimes simply business, sometimes simply firm, as well as company, and entity.
Manufacturing	Production of goods primarily by the application of labor and capital to raw materials and other intermediate inputs, in contrast to agriculture, mining, forestry, fishing, and services a manufacturing.
Investment	Investment refers to spending for the production and accumulation of capital and additions to inventories. In a financial sense, buying an asset with the expectation of making a return.
Electronic commerce	Electronic commerce or e-commerce, refers to any activity that uses some form of electronic communication in the inventory, exchange, advertisement, distribution, and payment of goods and services.
Customer relationship management	Learning as much as possible about customers and doing everything you can to satisfy them or even delight them with goods and services over time is customer relationship management.
Relationship management	A method for developing long-term associations with customers is referred to as relationship management.
Customer database	Customer database refers to a computer database specifically designed for storage, retrieval, and analysis of customer data by marketers.
Front office	In Business, front office refers to Sales and Marketing divisions of a company. It may also refer to other divisions in a company that involves interactions with customers.
Accounting	A system that collects and processes financial information about an organization and reports that information to decision makers is referred to as accounting.
Demographic characteristic	The vital statistics of a population group or a derived sample, such as: age, sex, education, ethnic heritage, education, income, housing is referred to as a demographic characteristic.
Brand loyalty	The degree to which customers are satisfied, like the brand, and are committed to further purchase is referred to as brand loyalty.
Variable	A variable is something measured by a number; it is used to analyze what happens to other things when the size of that number changes.
Consumer market	All the individuals or households that want goods and services for personal consumption or use are a consumer market.
Ultimate consumers	The people-whether 80 years or 8 months old-who use the goods and services purchased for a household are ultimate consumers.
Information technology	Information technology refers to technology that helps companies change business by allowing them to use new methods.
Homogeneous	In the context of procurement/purchasing, homogeneous is used to describe goods that do not vary in their essential characteristic irrespective of the source of supply.

Action plan	Action plan refers to a written document that includes the steps the trainee and manager will take to ensure that training transfers to the job.
Corporate goal	A strategic performance target that the entire organization must reach to pursue its vision is a corporate goal.

Go to **Cram101.com** for the Practice Tests for this Chapter.

Customer satisfaction	Customer satisfaction is a business term which is used to capture the idea of measuring how satisfied an enterprise's customers are with the organization's efforts in a marketplace.
Management	Management characterizes the process of leading and directing all or part of an organization, often a business, through the deployment and manipulation of resources. Early twentieth-century management writer Mary Parker Follett defined management as "the art of getting things done through people."
Goldman Sachs	Goldman Sachs is widely respected as a financial advisor to some of the most important companies, largest governments, and wealthiest families in the world. It is a primary dealer in the U.S. Treasury securities market. It offers its clients mergers & acquisitions advisory, provides underwriting services, engages in proprietary trading, invests in private equity deals, and also manages the wealth of affluent individuals and families.
Marketing	Promoting and selling products or services to customers, or prospective customers, is referred to as marketing.
Management team	A management team is directly responsible for managing the day-to-day operations (and profitability) of a company.
Channel	Channel, in communications (sometimes called communications channel), refers to the medium used to convey information from a sender (or transmitter) to a receiver.
Relationship marketing	Marketing whose goal is to keep individual customers over time by offering them products that exactly meet their requirements is called relationship marketing.
Business model	A business model is the instrument by which a business intends to generate revenue and profits. It is a summary of how a company means to serve its employees and customers, and involves both strategy (what an business intends to do) as well as an implementation.
Primary factor	Primary factor refers to an input that exists as a stock, providing services that contribute to production. The stock is not used up in production, although it may deteriorate with use, providing a smaller flow of services later.
Buyer	A buyer refers to a role in the buying center with formal authority and responsibility to select the supplier and negotiate the terms of the contract.
Analyst	Analyst refers to a person or tool with a primary function of information analysis, generally with a more limited, practical and short term set of goals than a researcher.
Industry	A group of firms that produce identical or similar products is an industry. It is also used specifically to refer to an area of economic production focused on manufacturing which involves large amounts of capital investment before any profit can be realized, also called "heavy industry".
Brand	A name, symbol, or design that identifies the goods or services of one seller or group of sellers and distinguishes them from the goods and services of competitors is a brand.
Service	Service refers to a "non tangible product" that is not embodied in a physical good and that typically effects some change in another product, person, or institution. Contrasts with good.
Customer service	The ability of logistics management to satisfy users in terms of time, dependability, communication, and convenience is called the customer service.
Interest	In finance and economics, interest is the price paid by a borrower for the use of a lender's money. In other words, interest is the amount of paid to "rent" money for a period of time.
Advertising	Advertising refers to paid, nonpersonal communication through various media by organizations and individuals who are in some way identified in the advertising message.

Go to **Cram101.com** for the Practice Tests for this Chapter.

233

Preference	The act of a debtor in paying or securing one or more of his creditors in a manner more favorable to them than to other creditors or to the exclusion of such other creditors is a preference. In the absence of statute, a preference is perfectly good, but to be legal it must be bona fide, and not a mere subterfuge of the debtor to secure a future benefit to himself or to prevent the application of his property to his debts.
Product life cycle	Product life cycle refers to a series of phases in a product's sales and cash flows over time; these phases, in order of occurrence, are introductory, growth, maturity, and decline.
Product mix	The combination of product lines offered by a manufacturer is referred to as product mix.
Pricing strategy	The process in which the price of a product can be determined and is decided upon is a pricing strategy.
Distribution channel	A distribution channel is a chain of intermediaries, each passing a product down the chain to the next organization, before it finally reaches the consumer or end-user.
Distribution	Distribution in economics, the manner in which total output and income is distributed among individuals or factors.
Commerce	Commerce is the exchange of something of value between two entities. It is the central mechanism from which capitalism is derived.
Public relations	Public relations refers to the management function that evaluates public attitudes, changes policies and procedures in response to the public's requests, and executes a program of action and information to earn public understanding and acceptance.
Personal selling	Personal selling is interpersonal communication, often face to face, between a sales representative and an individual or group, usually with the objective of making a sale.
Promotional mix	Promotional mix refers to the combination of one or more of the promotional elements a firm uses to communicate with consumers. The promotional elements include: advertising, personal selling, sales promotion, public relations, and direct marketing.
Sales promotion	Sales promotion refers to the promotional tool that stimulates consumer purchasing and dealer interest by means of short-term activities.
Promotion	Promotion refers to all the techniques sellers use to motivate people to buy products or services. An attempt by marketers to inform people about products and to persuade them to participate in an exchange.
E*Trade	E*TRADE is a financial services company based in New York City. It is a holding company primarily known as an online discount stock brokerage serving self-directed investors, many of whom are day traders. As a discount brokerage, it charges a much smaller fee on each trade.
Trade show	A type of exhibition or forum where manufacturers can display their products to current as well as prospective buyers is referred to as trade show.
Competitor	Other organizations in the same industry or type of business that provide a good or service to the same set of customers is referred to as a competitor.
Churning	Churning is the practice of executing trades for an investment account by a salesman or broker in order to generate commissions from the account. It is a breach of securities law in many jurisdictions, and it is generally actionable by the account holder for the return of the commissions paid.
Trend	Trend refers to the long-term movement of an economic variable, such as its average rate of increase or decrease over enough years to encompass several business cycles.
Market	A market is, as defined in economics, a social arrangement that allows buyers and sellers to

	discover information and carry out a voluntary exchange of goods or services.
General manager	A manager who is responsible for several departments that perform different functions is called general manager.
Product strategy	Decisions on the management of products or services based on the conditions of a given market is product strategy. Two general strategies that are well known in the marketing discipline are marketing mix and relational marketing.
Marketing strategy	Marketing strategy refers to the means by which a marketing goal is to be achieved, usually characterized by a specified target market and a marketing program to reach it.
Target market	One or more specific groups of potential consumers toward which an organization directs its marketing program are a target market.
Household	An economic unit that provides the economy with resources and uses the income received to purchase goods and services that satisfy economic wants is called household.
Marketing Plan	Marketing plan refers to a road map for the marketing activities of an organization for a specified future period of time, such as one year or five years.
Marketing mix	The marketing mix approach to marketing is a model of crafting and implementing marketing strategies. It stresses the "mixing" or blending of various factors in such a way that both organizational and consumer (target markets) objectives are attained.
Variable	A variable is something measured by a number; it is used to analyze what happens to other things when the size of that number changes.
Chief executive officer	A chief executive officer is the highest-ranking corporate officer or executive officer of a corporation, or agency. In closely held corporations, it is general business culture that the office chief executive officer is also the chairman of the board.
Stockholder	A stockholder is an individual or company (including a corporation) that legally owns one or more shares of stock in a joined stock company. The shareholders are the owners of a corporation. Companies listed at the stock market strive to enhance shareholder value.
Trademark	A distinctive word, name, symbol, device, or combination thereof, which enables consumers to identify favored products or services and which may find protection under state or federal law is a trademark.
Warranty	An obligation of a company to replace defective goods or correct any deficiencies in performance or quality of a product is called a warranty.
Consumer good	Products and services that are ultimately consumed rather than used in the production of another good are a consumer good.
Dealer	People who link buyers with sellers by buying and selling securities at stated prices are referred to as a dealer.
Raw material	Raw material refers to a good that has not been transformed by production; a primary product.
Capital	Capital generally refers to financial wealth, especially that used to start or maintain a business. In classical economics, capital is one of four factors of production, the others being land and labor and entrepreneurship.
Expense	In accounting, an expense represents an event in which an asset is used up or a liability is incurred. In terms of the accounting equation, expenses reduce owners' equity.
Supply	Supply is the aggregate amount of any material good that can be called into being at a certain price point; it comprises one half of the equation of supply and demand. In classical economic theory, a curve representing supply is one of the factors that produce price.

Go to **Cram101.com** for the Practice Tests for this Chapter.

Installations	Support goods, consisting of buildings and fixed equipment are called installations.
Specialist	A specialist is a trader who makes a market in one or several stocks and holds the limit order book for those stocks.
Purchasing	Purchasing refers to the function in a firm that searches for quality material resources, finds the best suppliers, and negotiates the best price for goods and services.
Production	The creation of finished goods and services using the factors of production: land, labor, capital, entrepreneurship, and knowledge.
Firm	An organization that employs resources to produce a good or service for profit and owns and operates one or more plants is referred to as a firm.
Operation	A standardized method or technique that is performed repetitively, often on different materials resulting in different finished goods is called an operation.
Tangible	Having a physical existence is referred to as the tangible. Personal property other than real estate, such as cars, boats, stocks, or other assets.
Product line	A group of products that are physically similar or are intended for a similar market are called the product line.
Profit	Profit refers to the return to the resource entrepreneurial ability; total revenue minus total cost.
Starbucks	Although it has endured much criticism for its purported monopoly on the global coffee-bean market, Starbucks purchases only 3% of the coffee beans grown worldwide. In 2000 the company introduced a line of fair trade products and now offers three options for socially conscious coffee drinkers. According to Starbucks, they purchased 4.8 million pounds of Certified Fair Trade coffee in fiscal year 2004 and 11.5 million pounds in 2005.
Premium	Premium refers to the fee charged by an insurance company for an insurance policy. The rate of losses must be relatively predictable: In order to set the premium (prices) insurers must be able to estimate them accurately.
Gap	In December of 1995, Gap became the first major North American retailer to accept independent monitoring of the working conditions in a contract factory producing its garments. Gap is the largest specialty retailer in the United States.
Maturity	Maturity refers to the final payment date of a loan or other financial instrument, after which point no further interest or principal need be paid.
Trial	An examination before a competent tribunal, according to the law of the land, of the facts or law put in issue in a cause, for the purpose of determining such issue is a trial. When the court hears and determines any issue of fact or law for the purpose of determining the rights of the parties, it may be considered a trial.
Introduction stage	The introduction stage is the first stage in the product life cycle, when a new product is launched into the marketplace. This stage is generally seen as the point of market entry, user trial, and product adoption.
Introductory stage	The first stage of the product life cycle in which sales grow slowly and profit is minimal is the introductory stage.
Users	Users refer to people in the organization who actually use the product or service purchased by the buying center.
Growth stage	The second stage of the product life cycle characterized by rapid increases in sales and by the appearance of competitors is referred to as the growth stage.
Price	Price competition is where a company tries to distinguish its product or service from

Go to **Cram101.com** for the Practice Tests for this Chapter.

competition	competing products on the basis of low price.
Maturity stage	The third stage of the product life cycle is called the maturity stage. This is when sales growth slows due to heavy competition, alternative product options or changing buyer or user preferences.
Appeal	Appeal refers to the act of asking an appellate court to overturn a decision after the trial court's final judgment has been entered.
Dell Computer	Dell Computer, formerly PC's Limited, was founded on the principle that by selling personal computer systems directly to customers, PC's Limited could best understand their needs and provide the most effective computing solutions to meet those needs.
Market share	That fraction of an industry's output accounted for by an individual firm or group of firms is called market share.
Compaq	Compaq was founded in February 1982 by Rod Canion, Jim Harris and Bill Murto, three senior managers from semiconductor manufacturer Texas Instruments. Each invested $1,000 to form the company. Their first venture capital came from Ben Rosen and Sevin-Rosen partners. It is often told that the architecture of the original PC was first sketched out on a placemat by the founders while dining in the Houston restaurant, House of Pies.
Product innovation	The development and sale of a new or improved product is a product innovation. Production of a new product on a commercial basis.
Decline stage	The fourth and last stage of the product life cycle when sales and profits begin to drop is called the decline stage.
Innovation	Innovation refers to the first commercially successful introduction of a new product, the use of a new method of production, or the creation of a new form of business organization.
Frequency	Frequency refers to the speed of the up and down movements of a fluctuating economic variable; that is, the number of times per unit of time that the variable completes a cycle of up and down movement.
Gerber	Gerber is perhaps the most well-known purveyor of baby food and baby products in the world. The company was founded in 1927 in Fremont, Michigan by Daniel Frank Gerber, owner of the Fremont Canning Company.
Logo	Logo refers to device or other brand name that cannot be spoken.
Consumer demand	Consumer demand or consumption is also known as personal consumption expenditure. It is the largest part of aggregate demand or effective demand at the macroeconomic level. There are two variants of consumption in the aggregate demand model, including induced consumption and autonomous consumption.
Marketing research	Marketing research refers to the analysis of markets to determine opportunities and challenges, and to find the information needed to make good decisions.
Screening	Screening in economics refers to a strategy of combating adverse selection, one of the potential decision-making complications in cases of asymmetric information.
Kaizen	Kaizen (Japanese for "change for the better" or "improvement") is an approach to productivity improvement originating in applications of the work of American experts such as Frederick Winslow Taylor, Frank Bunker Gilbreth, Walter Shewhart, and of the War Department's Training Within Industry program by Japanese manufacturers after World War II.
Business analysis	Business analysis is a structured methodology that is focused on completely understanding the customer's needs, identifying how best to meet those needs, and then "reinventing" the stream of processes to meet those needs.

Go to **Cram101.com** for the Practice Tests for this Chapter.

Concept testing	Concept testing is the process of using quantitative methods and qualitative methods to evaluate consumer response to a product idea prior to the introduction of a product to the market. It can also be used to generate communication designed to alter consumer attitudes toward existing products.
Prototype	A prototype is built to test the function of a new design before starting production of a product.
Product development	In business and engineering, new product development is the complete process of bringing a new product to market. There are two parallel aspects to this process : one involves product engineering ; the other marketing analysis. Marketers see new product development as the first stage in product life cycle management, engineers as part of Product Lifecycle Management.
Commercializ-tion	Promoting a product to distributors and retailers to get wide distribution and developing strong advertising and sales campaigns to generate and maintain interest in the product among distributors and consumers is commercialization.
Creep	Creep is a problem in project management where the initial objectives of the project are jeopardized by a gradual increase in overall objectives as the project progresses.
Volkswagen	Volkswagen or VW is an automobile manufacturer based in Wolfsburg, Germany in the state of Lower Saxony. It forms the core of this Group, one of the world's four largest car producers. Its German tagline is "Aus Liebe zum Automobil", which is translated as "For the love of the car" - or, For Love of the People's Cars,".
Cadillac	Cadillac was formed from the remnants of the Henry Ford Company when Henry Ford departed along with several of his key partners. With the intent of liquidating the firm's assets, Ford's financial backers, William Murphy and Lemuel Bowen called in engineer Henry M. Leland to appraise the plant and equipment prior to selling them. Instead, Leland persuaded them to continue in the automobile business.
Market segments	Market segments refer to the groups that result from the process of market segmentation; these groups ideally have common needs and will respond similarly to a marketing action.
General Motors	General Motors is the world's largest automaker. Founded in 1908, today it employs about 327,000 people around the world. With global headquarters in Detroit, it manufactures its cars and trucks in 33 countries.
Equity	Equity is the name given to the set of legal principles, in countries following the English common law tradition, which supplement strict rules of law where their application would operate harshly, so as to achieve what is sometimes referred to as "natural justice."
Brand equity	The combination of factors such as awareness, loyalty, perceived quality, images, and emotions people associate with a given brand name is referred to as brand equity.
Loyalty	Marketers tend to define customer loyalty as making repeat purchases. Some argue that it should be defined attitudinally as a strongly positive feeling about the brand.
Brand loyalty	The degree to which customers are satisfied, like the brand, and are committed to further purchase is referred to as brand loyalty.
Nokia	Nokia Corporation is the world's largest manufacturer of mobile telephones (as of June 2006), with a global market share of approximately 34% in Q2 of 2006. It produces mobile phones for every major market and protocol, including GSM, CDMA, and W-CDMA (UMTS).
Intel	Intel Corporation, founded in 1968 and based in Santa Clara, California, USA, is the world's largest semiconductor company. Intel is best known for its PC microprocessors, where it maintains roughly 80% market share.

Go to **Cram101.com** for the Practice Tests for this Chapter.

Disney	Disney is one of the largest media and entertainment corporations in the world. Founded on October 16, 1923 by brothers Walt and Roy Disney as a small animation studio, today it is one of the largest Hollywood studios and also owns nine theme parks and several television networks, including the American Broadcasting Company (ABC).
Ford	Ford is an American company that manufactures and sells automobiles worldwide. Ford introduced methods for large-scale manufacturing of cars, and large-scale management of an industrial workforce, especially elaborately engineered manufacturing sequences typified by the moving assembly lines.
Microsoft	Microsoft is a multinational computer technology corporation with 2004 global annual sales of US$39.79 billion and 71,553 employees in 102 countries and regions as of July 2006. It develops, manufactures, licenses, and supports a wide range of software products for computing devices.
Texaco	Texaco is the name of an American oil company that was merged into Chevron Corporation in 2001. For many years, Texaco was the only company selling gasoline in all 50 states, but this is no longer true.
Option	A contract that gives the purchaser the option to buy or sell the underlying financial instrument at a specified price, called the exercise price or strike price, within a specific period of time.
Individual branding	Individual branding is the marketing strategy of giving each product in a product portfolio its own unique brand name. The advantage of individual branding is that each product has an image and identity that is unique.
Family branding	Family branding is a marketing strategy that involves selling several related products under one brand name. It is contrasted with individual branding in which each product in a portfolio is given a unique identity and brand name.
Attest	To bear witness to is called attest. To affirm, certify by oath or signature. It is an official act establishing authenticity.
Universal product code	Universal product code refers to a number assigned to identify each product, represented by a series of bars of varying widths for scanning by optical readers.
Bar code	Bar code refers to a printed code that makes use of lines of various widths to encode data about products.
Exchange	The trade of things of value between buyer and seller so that each is better off after the trade is called the exchange.
Relative price	Relative price refers to the price of one thing in terms of another; i.e., the ratio of two prices.
Factors of production	Economic resources: land, capital, labor, and entrepreneurial ability are called factors of production.
Human resources	Human resources refers to the individuals within the firm, and to the portion of the firm's organization that deals with hiring, firing, training, and other personnel issues.
Labor	People's physical and mental talents and efforts that are used to help produce goods and services are called labor.
Wage	The payment for the service of a unit of labor, per unit time. In trade theory, it is the only payment to labor, usually unskilled labor. In empirical work, wage data may exclude other compenzation, which must be added to get the total cost of employment.
Capital expenditure	A substantial expenditure that is used by a company to acquire or upgrade physical assets such as equipment, property, industrial buildings, including those which improve the quality

	and life of an asset is referred to as a capital expenditure.
Interest rate	The rate of return on bonds, loans, or deposits. When one speaks of 'the' interest rate, it is usually in a model where there is only one.
Markup	Markup is a term used in marketing to indicate how much the price of a product is above the cost of producing and distributing the product.
Markup pricing	Markup pricing refers to the pricing method used by many firms in situations of imperfect competition; under this method they estimate average cost and then add some fixed percentage to that cost in order to reach the price they charge.
Total variable Cost	The total of all costs that vary with output in the short run is called total variable cost.
Total fixed costs	The total of all costs that do not change with output, even if output is zero is referred to as total fixed costs. Examples are rent, interest on loans, and insurance
Variable cost	The portion of a firm or industry's cost that changes with output, in contrast to fixed cost is referred to as variable cost.
Fixed cost	The cost that a firm bears if it does not produce at all and that is independent of its output. The presence of a fixed cost tends to imply increasing returns to scale. Contrasts with variable cost.
Total cost	The sum of fixed cost and variable cost is referred to as total cost.
Utility	Utility refers to the want-satisfying power of a good or service; the satisfaction or pleasure a consumer obtains from the consumption of a good or service.
Insurance	Insurance refers to a system by which individuals can reduce their exposure to risk of large losses by spreading the risks among a large number of persons.
Revenue	Revenue is a U.S. business term for the amount of money that a company receives from its activities, mostly from sales of products and/or services to customers.
Total revenue	Total revenue refers to the total number of dollars received by a firm from the sale of a product; equal to the total expenditures for the product produced by the firm; equal to the quantity sold multiplied by the price at which it is sold.
Breakeven point	Breakeven point refers to quantity of output sold at which total revenues equal total costs, that is where the economic profit is zero.
Assessment	Collecting information and providing feedback to employees about their behavior, communication style, or skills is an assessment.
Competitive Pricing	A marketing-oriented strategy whereby a service retailer sets its prices on the basis of the prices charged by competitors is competitive pricing.
Penetration pricing	Setting a low initial price for a new product in order to penetrate the market deeply and gain a large and broad market share is referred to as penetration pricing.
Inventory control	Inventory control, in the field of loss prevention, are systems designed to introduce technical barriers to shoplifting.
Marketing channel	Individuals and firms involved in the process of making a product or service available for use or consumption by consumers or industrial users is a marketing channel.
Inventory	Tangible property held for sale in the normal course of business or used in producing goods or services for sale is an inventory.
Intermediaries	Intermediaries specialize in information either to bring together two parties to a transaction or to buy in order to sell again.

Marketing intermediaries	Independent firms that assist in moving goods and services from producers to industrial and consumer users are marketing intermediaries.
Competitiveness	Competitiveness usually refers to characteristics that permit a firm to compete effectively with other firms due to low cost or superior technology, perhaps internationally.
Ultimate consumers	The people-whether 80 years or 8 months old-who use the goods and services purchased for a household are ultimate consumers.
Clinique	In 1968 Clinique was the first dermatologist-guided, allergy-tested, and fragrance-free cosmetic brand. Clinique was at that time different from most cosmetic companies in that its goal was to meet individual skin care needs by categorizing skin types.
Direct channel	A marketing channel where a producer and ultimate consumer deal directly with each other is a direct channel.
Wholesaling	Wholesaling consists of the sale of goods/merchandise to retailers, to industrial, commercial, institutional, or other professional business users or to other wholesalers and related subordinated services.
Accounting	A system that collects and processes financial information about an organization and reports that information to decision makers is referred to as accounting.
Wholesale	According to the United Nations Statistics Division Wholesale is the resale of new and used goods to retailers, to industrial, commercial, institutional or professional users, or to other wholesalers, or involves acting as an agent or broker in buying merchandise for, or selling merchandise, to such persons or companies.
Kroger	As well as stocking a variety of national brand products, Kroger also employs one of the largest networks of private label manufacturing in the country. Forty-two plants (either wholly owned or used with operating agreements) in seventeen states create about half of the nearly eight thousand private label products. A three-tiered marketing strategy divides the brand names for shoppers' simplicity and understanding.
Sears	Before the Sears catalog, farmers typically bought supplies (often at very high prices) from local general stores. Sears took advantage of this by publishing his catalog with clearly stated prices, so that consumers could know what he was selling and at what price, and order and obtain them conveniently. The catalog business soon grew quickly.
Home Depot	Home Depot has recently added self checkout registers at most of its stores in North America. These automated kiosks allow the customer to scan the barcode of the item they wish to purchase, then insert money to pay for the items, and receive any change automatically. The customer no longer needs to interact with a store employee during checkout.
Retailing	All activities involved in selling, renting, and providing goods and services to ultimate consumers for personal, family, or household use is referred to as retailing.
Enterprise	Enterprise refers to another name for a business organization. Other similar terms are business firm, sometimes simply business, sometimes simply firm, as well as company, and entity.
Direct selling	The direct personal presentation, demonstration, and sale of products and services to consumers usually in their homes or at their jobs is referred to as direct selling.
Retail sale	The sale of goods and services to consumers for their own use is a retail sale.
Warehouse	Warehouse refers to a location, often decentralized, that a firm uses to store, consolidate, age, or mix stock; house product-recall programs; or ease tax burdens.
Wheel of retailing	Wheel of retailing refers to a concept that describes how new retail outlets enter the market as low-status, low-margin stores and gradually add embellishments that raise their prices,

Go to **Cram101.com** for the Practice Tests for this Chapter.
And, **NEVER** highlight a book again!

and status. They now face a new low-status, low-margin operator, and the cycle starts to repeat itself.

Discount	The difference between the face value of a bond and its selling price, when a bond is sold for less than its face value it's referred to as a discount.
Price level	The overall level of prices in a country, as usually measured empirically by a price index, but often captured in theoretical models by a single variable is a price level.
Costco	Costco focuses on selling products at low prices, often at very high volume. These goods are usually bulk-packaged and marketed primarily to large families and small businesses. As a warehouse club, Costco is only open to members and their guests, except for purchases of liquor, gasoline and prescription drugs in some U.S. states due to state law and liquor license restrictions.
Warehouse clubs	Large retail stores that require a yearly fee to shop at the store are called warehouse clubs.
Merchandising	Merchandising refers to the business of acquiring finished goods for resale, either in a wholesale or a retail operation.
Make goods	When a medium falls short of some audience guarantee, advertisers are provided concessions in the form of make goods.
Core	A core is the set of feasible allocations in an economy that cannot be improved upon by subset of the set of the economy's consumers (a coalition). In construction, when the force in an element is within a certain center section, the core, the element will only be under compression.
Advertising campaign	A comprehensive advertising plan that consists of a series of messages in a variety of media that center on a single theme or idea is referred to as an advertising campaign.
Precedent	A previously decided court decision that is recognized as authority for the disposition of future decisions is a precedent.
Broker	In commerce, a broker is a party that mediates between a buyer and a seller. A broker who also acts as a seller or as a buyer becomes a principal party to the deal.
Intensive distribution	Distribution that puts products into as many retail outlets as possible is called intensive distribution.
Selective distribution	Distribution that sends products to only a preferred group of retailers in an area is referred to as selective distribution.
Marketing cost	Marketing cost refers to the cost incurred in selling goods or services. Includes order-getting costs and order-filling or distribution costs.
Exclusive distribution	Distribution that sends products to only one retail outlet in a given geographic area is an exclusive distribution.
Personnel	A collective term for all of the employees of an organization. Personnel is also commonly used to refer to the personnel management function or the organizational unit responsible for administering personnel programs.
License	A license in the sphere of Intellectual Property Rights (IPR) is a document, contract or agreement giving permission or the 'right' to a legally-definable entity to do something (such as manufacture a product or to use a service), or to apply something (such as a trademark), with the objective of achieving commercial gain.
Supply chain	Supply chain refers to the flow of goods, services, and information from the initial sources of materials and services to the delivery of products to consumers.

Go to **Cram101.com** for the Practice Tests for this Chapter.
And, **NEVER** highlight a book again!

Licensing agreement	Detailed and comprehensive written agreement between the licensor and licensee that sets forth the express terms of their agreement is called a licensing agreement.
Licensing	Licensing is a form of strategic alliance which involves the sale of a right to use certain proprietary knowledge (so called intellectual property) in a defined way.
Logistics	Those activities that focus on getting the right amount of the right products to the right place at the right time at the lowest possible cost is referred to as logistics.
Estate	An estate is the totality of the legal rights, interests, entitlements and obligations attaching to property. In the context of wills and probate, it refers to the totality of the property which the deceased owned or in which some interest was held.
Technology	The body of knowledge and techniques that can be used to combine economic resources to produce goods and services is called technology.
Press release	A written public news announcement normally distributed to major news services is referred to as press release.
Finished goods	Completed products awaiting sale are called finished goods. An item considered a finished good in a supplying plant might be considered a component or raw material in a receiving plant.
Consideration	Consideration in contract law, a basic requirement for an enforceable agreement under traditional contract principles, defined in this text as legal value, bargained for and given in exchange for an act or promise. In corporation law, cash or property contributed to a corporation in exchange for shares, or a promise to contribute such cash or property.
Merrill Lynch	Merrill Lynch through its subsidiaries and affiliates, provides capital markets services, investment banking and advisory services, wealth management, asset management, insurance, banking and related products and services on a global basis. It is best known for its Global Private Client services and its strong sales force.
Consultant	A professional that provides expert advice in a particular field or area in which customers occassionaly require this type of knowledge is a consultant.
Complaint	The pleading in a civil case in which the plaintiff states his claim and requests relief is called complaint. In the common law, it is a formal legal document that sets out the basic facts and legal reasons that the filing party (the plaintiffs) believes are sufficient to support a claim against another person, persons, entity or entities (the defendants) that entitles the plaintiff(s) to a remedy (either money damages or injunctive relief).
Mistake	In contract law a mistake is incorrect understanding by one or more parties to a contract and may be used as grounds to invalidate the agreement. Common law has identified three different types of mistake in contract: unilateral mistake, mutual mistake, and common mistake.
Security	Security refers to a claim on the borrower future income that is sold by the borrower to the lender. A security is a type of transferable interest representing financial value.
Integrated Marketing Communication	Integrated Marketing Communication is a management concept that is designed to make all aspects of marketing communication such as advertising, sales promotion, public relations, and direct marketing work together as a unified force.
Marketing communication	The communication components of marketing, which include public relations, advertising, personal selling, and sales promotion is a marketing communication.
Interactive media	A variety of media that allows the consumer to interact with the source of the message, actively receiving information and altering images, responding to questions, and so on is an interactive media.
Event	A type of promotion whereby a company develops sponsorship relations with a particular event

sponsorship	such as a concert, sporting event, or other activity is referred to as event sponsorship.
Sponsorship	When the advertiser assumes responsibility for the production and usually the content of a television program as well as the advertising that appears within it, we have sponsorship.
Brand image	The advertising metric that measures the type and favorability of consumer perceptions of the brand is referred to as the brand image.
Browser	A program that allows a user to connect to the World Wide Web by simply typing in a URL is a browser.
Budget	Budget refers to an account, usually for a year, of the planned expenditures and the expected receipts of an entity. For a government, the receipts are tax revenues.
Philip Morris	Philip Morris, is the world's largest commercial tobacco company by sales. Philip Morris was begun by a London tobacconist of the same name. He was one of the first people to sell hand-rolled cigarettes in the 1860s, selling them under the brand names Oxford and Cambridge Blues, following the adoption of cigarette smoking by British soldiers returning from the Crimean War.
Advertisement	Advertisement is the promotion of goods, services, companies and ideas, usually by an identified sponsor. Marketers see advertising as part of an overall promotional strategy.
Goodwill	Goodwill is an important accounting concept that describes the value of a business entity not directly attributable to its tangible assets and liabilities.
Coupon	In finance, a coupon is "attached" to a bond, either physically (as with old bonds) or electronically. Each coupon represents a predetermined payment promized to the bond-holder in return for his or her loan of money to the bond-issuer. .
Brief	Brief refers to a statement of a party's case or legal arguments, usually prepared by an attorney. Also used to make legal arguments before appellate courts.
Complete information	Complete information refers to the assumption that economic agents know everything that they need to know in order to make optimal decisions. Types of incomplete information are uncertainty and asymmetric information.
Billboard	The most common form of outdoor advertising is called a billboard.
Contribution	In business organization law, the cash or property contributed to a business by its owners is referred to as contribution.
Strike	The withholding of labor services by an organized group of workers is referred to as a strike.
Stock	In financial terminology, stock is the capital raized by a corporation, through the issuance and sale of shares.
Fund	Independent accounting entity with a self-balancing set of accounts segregated for the purposes of carrying on specific activities is referred to as a fund.
Incentive	An incentive is any factor (financial or non-financial) that provides a motive for a particular course of action, or counts as a reason for preferring one choice to the alternatives.
Vendor	A person who sells property to a vendee is a vendor. The words vendor and vendee are more commonly applied to the seller and purchaser of real estate, and the words seller and buyer are more commonly applied to the seller and purchaser of personal property.
Economic development	Increase in the economic standard of living of a country's population, normally accomplished by increasing its stocks of physical and human capital and improving its technology is an economic development.

Environmental protection agency	An administrative agency created by Congress in 1970 to coordinate the implementation and enforcement of the federal environmental protection laws is referred to as the Environmental Protection Agency or EPA.
Holding	The holding is a court's determination of a matter of law based on the issue presented in the particular case. In other words: under this law, with these facts, this result.
Strategic alliance	Strategic alliance refers to a long-term partnership between two or more companies established to help each company build competitive market advantages.
News conference	A publicity tool consisting of an informational meeting with representatives of the media who are sent advance materials on the content is a news conference.
News release	A publicity tool consisting of an announcement regarding changes in the company or the product line is called a news release.
Consumer market	All the individuals or households that want goods and services for personal consumption or use are a consumer market.
Cooperative advertising	Advertising programs by which a manufacturer pays a percentage of the retailer's local advertising expense for advertising the manufacturer's products are called cooperative advertising.
Cooperative	A business owned and controlled by the people who use it, producers, consumers, or workers with similar needs who pool their resources for mutual gain is called cooperative.
Allowance	Reduction in the selling price of goods extended to the buyer because the goods are defective or of lower quality than the buyer ordered and to encourage a buyer to keep merchandise that would otherwise be returned is the allowance.
Shares	Shares refer to an equity security, representing a shareholder's ownership of a corporation. Shares are one of a finite number of equal portions in the capital of a company, entitling the owner to a proportion of distributed, non-reinvested profits known as dividends and to a portion of the value of the company in case of liquidation.
Kmart	Kmart is an international chain of discount department stores in the United States, Australia, and New Zealand. Kmart merged with Sears in early 2005, creating the Sears Holdings Corporation.
PepsiCo	In many ways, PepsiCo differs from its main competitor, having three times as many employees, larger revenues, but a smaller net profit.
Business operations	Business operations are those activities involved in the running of a business for the purpose of producing value for the stakeholders. The outcome of business operations is the harvesting of value from assets owned by a business.
Human resource management	The process of evaluating human resource needs, finding people to fill those needs, and getting the best work from each employee by providing the right incentives and job environment, all with the goal of meeting the needs of the firm are called human resource management.
Resource management	Resource management is the efficient and effective deployment of an organization's resources when they are needed. Such resources may include financial resources, inventory, human skills, production resources, or information technology.
Information system	An information system is a system whether automated or manual, that comprises people, machines, and/or methods organized to collect, process, transmit, and disseminate data that represent user information.
Delta Air Lines	Delta Air Lines currently has the largest route network "footprint" of any airline. The airline also serves Puerto Rico, and the U.S. Virgin Islands, in addition to 95 countries.

Go to **Cram101.com** for the Practice Tests for this Chapter.

Indirect channel	A marketing channel where intermediaries are inserted between the producer and consumers and perform numerous channel functions is an indirect channel.
Amway	Amway is a multi-level marketing company founded in 1959 by Jay Van Andel and Rich DeVos. The company's name is a portmanteau of "American Way." .
Avon	Avon is an American cosmetics, perfume and toy seller with markets in over 135 countries across the world and a sales of $7.74 billion worldwide.
Franchise	A contractual right to sell certain products or services, use certain trademarks, or perform activities in a geographical region is called a franchise.
Honda	With more than 14 million internal combustion engines built each year, Honda is the largest engine-maker in the world. In 2004, the company began to produce diesel motors, which were both very quiet whilst not requiring particulate filters to pass pollution standards. It is arguable, however, that the foundation of their success is the motorcycle division.
Points	Loan origination fees that may be deductible as interest by a buyer of property. A seller of property who pays points reduces the selling price by the amount of the points paid for the buyer.
Competitive advantage	A business is said to have a competitive advantage when its unique strengths, often based on cost, quality, time, and innovation, offer consumers a greater percieved value and there by differtiating it from its competitors.
Patent	The legal right to the proceeds from and control over the use of an invented product or process, granted for a fixed period of time, usually 20 years. Patent is one form of intellectual property that is subject of the TRIPS agreement.
Commodity	Could refer to any good, but in trade a commodity is usually a raw material or primary product that enters into international trade, such as metals or basic agricultural products.
Specialty advertising	An advertising, sales promotion, and motivational communications medium that employs useful articles of merchandise imprinted with an advertiser's name, message, or logo is referred to as specialty advertising.
Promotional products	Promotional Products or Advertising Specialties is the imprinting of company logo or information on literally tens of thousands of different products to help promote their company name or the theme they have on the product. The business is a multi billion dollar industry with sales exceeding $17 billion.
Bid	A bid price is a price offered by a buyer when he/she buys a good. In the context of stock trading on a stock exchange, the bid price is the highest price a buyer of a stock is willing to pay for a share of that given stock.
Reorganization	Reorganization occurs, among other instances, when one corporation acquires another in a merger or acquisition, a single corporation divides into two or more entities, or a corporation makes a substantial change in its capital structure.
Closing	The finalization of a real estate sales transaction that passes title to the property from the seller to the buyer is referred to as a closing. Closing is a sales term which refers to the process of making a sale. It refers to reaching the final step, which may be an exchange of money or acquiring a signature.
Great Depression	The period of severe economic contraction and high unemployment that began in 1929 and continued throughout the 1930s is referred to as the Great Depression.
Depression	Depression refers to a prolonged period characterized by high unemployment, low output and investment, depressed business confidence, falling prices, and widespread business failures. A milder form of business downturn is a recession.

Teamwork	That which occurs when group members work together in ways that utilize their skills well to accomplish a purpose is called teamwork.
Management information system	A computer-based system that provides information and support for effective managerial decision makin is referred to as a management information system.
Recovery	Characterized by rizing output, falling unemployment, rizing profits, and increasing economic activity following a decline is a recovery.
Chief information officer	The chief information officer is a job title for the head of information technology group within an organization. They often report to the chief executive officer or chief financial officer.
Information technology	Information technology refers to technology that helps companies change business by allowing them to use new methods.
Contract	A contract is a "promise" or an "agreement" that is enforced or recognized by the law. In the civil law, a contract is considered to be part of the general law of obligations.
Staffing	Staffing refers to a management function that includes hiring, motivating, and retaining the best people available to accomplish the company's objectives.

Service	Service refers to a "non tangible product" that is not embodied in a physical good and that typically effects some change in another product, person, or institution. Contrasts with good.
Technology	The body of knowledge and techniques that can be used to combine economic resources to produce goods and services is called technology.
Authority	Authority in agency law, refers to an agent's ability to affect his principal's legal relations with third parties. Also used to refer to an actor's legal power or ability to do something. In addition, sometimes used to refer to a statute, case, or other legal source that justifies a particular result.
Information system	An information system is a system whether automated or manual, that comprises people, machines, and/or methods organized to collect, process, transmit, and disseminate data that represent user information.
Management information system	A computer-based system that provides information and support for effective managerial decision makin is referred to as a management information system.
Management	Management characterizes the process of leading and directing all or part of an organization, often a business, through the deployment and manipulation of resources. Early twentieth-century management writer Mary Parker Follett defined management as "the art of getting things done through people."
Operation	A standardized method or technique that is performed repetitively, often on different materials resulting in different finished goods is called an operation.
Firm	An organization that employs resources to produce a good or service for profit and owns and operates one or more plants is referred to as a firm.
Chief information officer	The chief information officer is a job title for the head of information technology group within an organization. They often report to the chief executive officer or chief financial officer.
Chief executive officer	A chief executive officer is the highest-ranking corporate officer or executive officer of a corporation, or agency. In closely held corporations, it is general business culture that the office chief executive officer is also the chairman of the board.
Marketing	Promoting and selling products or services to customers, or prospective customers, is referred to as marketing.
Marketing strategy	Marketing strategy refers to the means by which a marketing goal is to be achieved, usually characterized by a specified target market and a marketing program to reach it.
Consumer demand	Consumer demand or consumption is also known as personal consumption expenditure. It is the largest part of aggregate demand or effective demand at the macroeconomic level. There are two variants of consumption in the aggregate demand model, including induced consumption and autonomous consumption.
Competitor	Other organizations in the same industry or type of business that provide a good or service to the same set of customers is referred to as a competitor.
Regulation	Regulation refers to restrictions state and federal laws place on business with regard to the conduct of its activities.
Microsoft	Microsoft is a multinational computer technology corporation with 2004 global annual sales of US$39.79 billion and 71,553 employees in 102 countries and regions as of July 2006. It develops, manufactures, licenses, and supports a wide range of software products for computing devices.

Go to **Cram101.com** for the Practice Tests for this Chapter.

Cabinet	The heads of the executive departments of a jurisdiction who report to and advise its chief executive; examples would include the president's cabinet, the governor's cabinet, and the mayor's cabinet.
Household	An economic unit that provides the economy with resources and uses the income received to purchase goods and services that satisfy economic wants is called household.
Interest	In finance and economics, interest is the price paid by a borrower for the use of a lender's money. In other words, interest is the amount of paid to "rent" money for a period of time.
Trade association	An industry trade group or trade association is generally a public relations organization founded and funded by corporations that operate in a specific industry. Its purpose is generally to promote that industry through PR activities such as advertizing, education, political donations, political pressure, publishing, and astroturfing.
Prodigy	Prodigy Communications Corporation was a dialup service for personal computers in the United States. The company claimed it was the first consumer online service, differentiating itself from the leading service provider, CompuServe, which was used mostly by technophiles.
Industry	A group of firms that produce identical or similar products is an industry. It is also used specifically to refer to an area of economic production focused on manufacturing which involves large amounts of capital investment before any profit can be realized, also called "heavy industry".
Data mining	The extraction of hidden predictive information from large databases is referred to as data mining.
Complaint	The pleading in a civil case in which the plaintiff states his claim and requests relief is called complaint. In the common law, it is a formal legal document that sets out the basic facts and legal reasons that the filing party (the plaintiffs) believes are sufficient to support a claim against another person, persons, entity or entities (the defendants) that entitles the plaintiff(s) to a remedy (either money damages or injunctive relief).
Decision support system	An interactive, computer-based system that uses decision models and specialized databases to support decision makers is called a decision support system.
Users	Users refer to people in the organization who actually use the product or service purchased by the buying center.
Executive information system	A management information system designed to facilitate strategic decision making at the highest levels of management by providing executives with easy access to timely and relevant information is called executive information system.
Market	A market is, as defined in economics, a social arrangement that allows buyers and sellers to discover information and carry out a voluntary exchange of goods or services.
Trend	Trend refers to the long-term movement of an economic variable, such as its average rate of increase or decrease over enough years to encompass several business cycles.
Stock	In financial terminology, stock is the capital raized by a corporation, through the issuance and sale of shares.
Financial statement	Financial statement refers to a summary of all the transactions that have occurred over a particular period.
Stock market	An organized marketplace in which common stocks are traded. In the United States, the largest stock market is the New York Stock Exchange, on which are traded the stocks of the largest U.S. companies.
Kmart	Kmart is an international chain of discount department stores in the United States, Australia, and New Zealand. Kmart merged with Sears in early 2005, creating the Sears

Go to **Cram101.com** for the Practice Tests for this Chapter.

	Holdings Corporation.
Automation	Automation allows machines to do work previously accomplished by people.
Timex	Timex is the best-known American watch manufacturer, famous for half a century for durable low-cost timepieces. Timex headquarters are located in Middlebury, Connecticut.
Expert system	Computer systems incorporating the decision rules of people recognized as experts in a certain area are refered to as an expert system.
Layout	Layout refers to the physical arrangement of the various parts of an advertisement including the headline, subheads, illustrations, body copy, and any identifying marks.
Credit	Credit refers to a recording as positive in the balance of payments, any transaction that gives rise to a payment into the country, such as an export, the sale of an asset, or borrowing from abroad.
Applicant	In many tribunal and administrative law suits, the person who initiates the claim is called the applicant.
Mortgage	Mortgage refers to a note payable issued for property, such as a house, usually repaid in equal installments consisting of part principle and part interest, over a specified period.
WorldCom	WorldCom was the United States' second largest long distance phone company (AT&T was the largest). WorldCom grew largely by acquiring other telecommunications companies, most notably MCI Communications. It also owned the Tier 1 ISP UUNET, a major part of the Internet backbone.
Enterprise resource planning	Computer-based production and operations system that links multiple firms into one integrated production unit is enterprise resource planning.
Enterprise	Enterprise refers to another name for a business organization. Other similar terms are business firm, sometimes simply business, sometimes simply firm, as well as company, and entity.
Inventory control	Inventory control, in the field of loss prevention, are systems designed to introduce technical barriers to shoplifting.
Inventory	Tangible property held for sale in the normal course of business or used in producing goods or services for sale is an inventory.
Mistake	In contract law a mistake is incorrect understanding by one or more parties to a contract and may be used as grounds to invalidate the agreement. Common law has identified three different types of mistake in contract: unilateral mistake, mutual mistake, and common mistake.
Business operations	Business operations are those activities involved in the running of a business for the purpose of producing value for the stakeholders. The outcome of business operations is the harvesting of value from assets owned by a business.
Knowledge management	Sharing, organizing and disseminating information in the simplest and most relevant way possible for the users of the information is a knowledge management.
Baan	In 1998 the Baan Corporation was exposed to be manipulating profits in a prelude to the big accounting scandals that marked the turn of the century. First Paul Baan left the company as a result of this, shortly after to be followed by brother Jan. The loss of confidence in the Baan Corporation was reflected in a rapidly declining share of the BaaN program in the ERP market.
Project manager	Project manager refers to a manager responsible for a temporary work project that involves the participation of other people from various functions and levels of the organization.

Variable	A variable is something measured by a number; it is used to analyze what happens to other things when the size of that number changes.
Application service provider	An application service provider is a business that provides computer-based services to customers over a network.
Complexity	The technical sophistication of the product and hence the amount of understanding required to use it is referred to as complexity. It is the opposite of simplicity.
Buyer	A buyer refers to a role in the buying center with formal authority and responsibility to select the supplier and negotiate the terms of the contract.
Core	A core is the set of feasible allocations in an economy that cannot be improved upon by subset of the set of the economy's consumers (a coalition). In construction, when the force in an element is within a certain center section, the core, the element will only be under compression.
Core business	The core business of an organization is an idealized construct intended to express that organization's "main" or "essential" activity.
Bill Gates	Bill Gates is the co-founder, chairman, former chief software architect, and former CEO of Microsoft Corporation. He is one of the best-known entrepreneurs of the personal computer revolution and he is widely respected for his foresight and ambition.
Oracle	In 2004, sales at Oracle grew at a rate of 14.5% to $6.2 billion, giving it 41.3% and the top share of the relational-database market. Their main competitors in the database arena are IBM DB2 and Microsoft SQL Server, and to a lesser extent Sybase, Teradata, Informix, and MySQL. In the applications arena, their main competitor is SAP.
Tying	Tying is the practice of making the sale of one good (the tying good) to the de facto or de jure customer conditional on the purchase of a second distinctive good.
Purchasing	Purchasing refers to the function in a firm that searches for quality material resources, finds the best suppliers, and negotiates the best price for goods and services.
Sears	Before the Sears catalog, farmers typically bought supplies (often at very high prices) from local general stores. Sears took advantage of this by publishing his catalog with clearly stated prices, so that consumers could know what he was selling and at what price, and order and obtain them conveniently. The catalog business soon grew quickly.
Chevron	Chevron Corporation is one of the world's largest global energy companies. Headquartered in San Ramon, California, USA and active in more than 180 countries, it is engaged in every aspect of the oil and gas industry, including exploration and production; refining, marketing and transport; chemicals manufacturing and sales; and power generation.
Ford	Ford is an American company that manufactures and sells automobiles worldwide. Ford introduced methods for large-scale manufacturing of cars, and large-scale management of an industrial workforce, especially elaborately engineered manufacturing sequences typified by the moving assembly lines.
Supply chain	Supply chain refers to the flow of goods, services, and information from the initial sources of materials and services to the delivery of products to consumers.
Supply	Supply is the aggregate amount of any material good that can be called into being at a certain price point; it comprises one half of the equation of supply and demand. In classical economic theory, a curve representing supply is one of the factors that produce price.
Supply chain management	Supply chain management deals with the planning and execution issues involved in managing a supply chain. Supply chain management spans all movement and storage of raw materials, work-

Go to **Cram101.com** for the Practice Tests for this Chapter.

	in-process inventory, and finished goods from point-of-origin to point-of-consumption.
Market share	That fraction of an industry's output accounted for by an individual firm or group of firms is called market share.
Hosting	Internet hosting service is a service that runs Internet servers, allowing organizations and individuals to serve content on the Internet.
Disney	Disney is one of the largest media and entertainment corporations in the world. Founded on October 16, 1923 by brothers Walt and Roy Disney as a small animation studio, today it is one of the largest Hollywood studios and also owns nine theme parks and several television networks, including the American Broadcasting Company (ABC).
Customer service	The ability of logistics management to satisfy users in terms of time, dependability, communication, and convenience is called the customer service.
Goldman Sachs	Goldman Sachs is widely respected as a financial advisor to some of the most important companies, largest governments, and wealthiest families in the world. It is a primary dealer in the U.S. Treasury securities market. It offers its clients mergers & acquisitions advisory, provides underwriting services, engages in proprietary trading, invests in private equity deals, and also manages the wealth of affluent individuals and families.
Analyst	Analyst refers to a person or tool with a primary function of information analysis, generally with a more limited, practical and short term set of goals than a researcher.
Outsourcing	Outsourcing refers to a production activity that was previously done inside a firm or plant that is now conducted outside that firm or plant.
Parent company	Parent company refers to the entity that has a controlling influence over another company. It may have its own operations, or it may have been set up solely for the purpose of owning the Subject Company.
Reuters	Reuters is best known as a news service that provides reports from around the world to newspapers and broadcasters. Its main focus is on supplying the financial markets with information and trading products.
Bankruptcy	Bankruptcy is a legally declared inability or impairment of ability of an individual or organization to pay their creditors.
Journal	Book of original entry, in which transactions are recorded in a general ledger system, is referred to as a journal.
Wall Street Journal	Dow Jones & Company was founded in 1882 by reporters Charles Dow, Edward Jones and Charles Bergstresser. Jones converted the small Customers' Afternoon Letter into The Wall Street Journal, first published in 1889, and began delivery of the Dow Jones News Service via telegraph. The Journal featured the Jones 'Average', the first of several indexes of stock and bond prices on the New York Stock Exchange.
Tangible	Having a physical existence is referred to as the tangible. Personal property other than real estate, such as cars, boats, stocks, or other assets.
Revenue	Revenue is a U.S. business term for the amount of money that a company receives from its activities, mostly from sales of products and/or services to customers.
Contract	A contract is a "promise" or an "agreement" that is enforced or recognized by the law. In the civil law, a contract is considered to be part of the general law of obligations.
Appeal	Appeal refers to the act of asking an appellate court to overturn a decision after the trial court's final judgment has been entered.
Nonprofit	An organization whose goals do not include making a personal profit for its owners is a

Go to **Cram101.com** for the Practice Tests for this Chapter.

organization	nonprofit organization.
Sprint	The Sprint Corporation was founded in 1899 by Cleyson Leroy Brown under the name of the "Brown Telephone Company" in the small town of Abilene, Kansas. The company was a landline telephone company that operated as a competitor to the Bell System.
Lease	A contract for the possession and use of land or other property, including goods, on one side, and a recompense of rent or other income on the other is the lease.
Browser	A program that allows a user to connect to the World Wide Web by simply typing in a URL is a browser.
Trial	An examination before a competent tribunal, according to the law of the land, of the facts or law put in issue in a cause, for the purpose of determining such issue is a trial. When the court hears and determines any issue of fact or law for the purpose of determining the rights of the parties, it may be considered a trial.
Apprenticeship	A work-study training method with both on-the-job and classroom training is an apprenticeship.Most of their training is on the job, working for an employer who helps the apprentices learn their trade, art or craft. Less formal, theoretical education is involved.
Franchise	A contractual right to sell certain products or services, use certain trademarks, or perform activities in a geographical region is called a franchise.
Chief operating officer	A chief operating officer is a corporate officer responsible for managing the day-to-day activities of the corporation. The chief operating officer is one of the highest ranking members of an organization, monitoring the daily operations of the company and reporting to the chief executive officer directly.
Interactive media	A variety of media that allows the consumer to interact with the source of the message, actively receiving information and altering images, responding to questions, and so on is an interactive media.
Groupware	Software application that enables multiple users to track, share, and organize information and to work on the same database or document simultaneously is the groupware.
Electronic mail	Electronic mail refers to electronic written communication between individuals using computers connected to the Internet.
Business plan	A detailed written statement that describes the nature of the business, the target market, the advantages the business will have in relation to competition, and the resources and qualifications of the owner is referred to as a business plan.
Freelance	A freelance worker is a self-employed person working in a profession or trade in which full-time employment is also common.
Entrepreneur	The owner/operator. The person who organizes, manages, and assumes the risks of a firm, taking a new idea or a new product and turning it into a successful business is an entrepreneur.
Security	Security refers to a claim on the borrower future income that is sold by the borrower to the lender. A security is a type of transferable interest representing financial value.
Securities and exchange commission	Securities and exchange commission refers to U.S. government agency that determines the financial statements that public companies must provide to stockholders and the measurement rules that they must use in producing those statements.
Exchange	The trade of things of value between buyer and seller so that each is better off after the trade is called the exchange.
Attachment	Attachment in general, the process of taking a person's property under an appropriate

Go to **Cram101.com** for the Practice Tests for this Chapter.

273

	judicial order by an appropriate officer of the court. Used for a variety of purposes, including the acquisition of jurisdiction over the property seized and the securing of property that may be used to satisfy a debt.
Total fixed costs	The total of all costs that do not change with output, even if output is zero is referred to as total fixed costs. Examples are rent, interest on loans, and insurance
Variable cost	The portion of a firm or industry's cost that changes with output, in contrast to fixed cost is referred to as variable cost.
Fixed cost	The cost that a firm bears if it does not produce at all and that is independent of its output. The presence of a fixed cost tends to imply increasing returns to scale. Contrasts with variable cost.
Expense	In accounting, an expense represents an event in which an asset is used up or a liability is incurred. In terms of the accounting equation, expenses reduce owners' equity.
Home Depot	Home Depot has recently added self checkout registers at most of its stores in North America. These automated kiosks allow the customer to scan the barcode of the item they wish to purchase, then insert money to pay for the items, and receive any change automatically. The customer no longer needs to interact with a store employee during checkout.
Aid	Assistance provided by countries and by international institutions such as the World Bank to developing countries in the form of monetary grants, loans at low interest rates, in kind, or a combination of these is called aid. Aid can also refer to assistance of any type rendered to benefit some group or individual.
Virtual reality	Virtual reality refers to computer-based technology that provides trainees with a three-dimensional learning experience. Trainees operate in a simulated environment that responds to their behaviors and reactions.
Product manager	Product manager refers to a person who plans, implements, and controls the annual and long-range plans for the products for which he or she is responsible.
Intranet	Intranet refers to a companywide network, closed to public access, that uses Internet-type technology. A set of communications links within one company that travel over the Internet but are closed to public access.
Virtual private network	A private data network that creates secure connections, or tunnels, over regular Internet lines is called virtual private network.
Broadband technology	Technology that delivers voice, video, and data through the internet is broadband technology.
Administrator	Administrator refers to the personal representative appointed by a probate court to settle the estate of a deceased person who died.
Smart card	A stored-value card that contains a computer chip that allows it to be loaded with digital cash from the owner's bank account whenever needed is called a smart card.
Personnel	A collective term for all of the employees of an organization. Personnel is also commonly used to refer to the personnel management function or the organizational unit responsible for administering personnel programs.
Teamwork	That which occurs when group members work together in ways that utilize their skills well to accomplish a purpose is called teamwork.
Gain	In finance, gain is a profit or an increase in value of an investment such as a stock or bond. Gain is calculated by fair market value or the proceeds from the sale of the investment minus the sum of the purchase price and all costs associated with it.

Go to **Cram101.com** for the Practice Tests for this Chapter.

Market development	Selling existing products to new markets is called market development.
Vendor	A person who sells property to a vendee is a vendor. The words vendor and vendee are more commonly applied to the seller and purchaser of real estate, and the words seller and buyer are more commonly applied to the seller and purchaser of personal property.
Assignment	A transfer of property or some right or interest is referred to as assignment.
Points	Loan origination fees that may be deductible as interest by a buyer of property. A seller of property who pays points reduces the selling price by the amount of the points paid for the buyer.
Asset	An item of property, such as land, capital, money, a share in ownership, or a claim on others for future payment, such as a bond or a bank deposit is an asset.
Utility	Utility refers to the want-satisfying power of a good or service; the satisfaction or pleasure a consumer obtains from the consumption of a good or service.
Recovery	Characterized by rizing output, falling unemployment, rizing profits, and increasing economic activity following a decline is a recovery.
Corporate espionage	Industrial espionage and corporate espionage are phrases used to describe espionage conducted for commercial purposes instead of national security purposes.
Property	Assets defined in the broadest legal sense. Property includes the unrealized receivables of a cash basis taxpayer, but not services rendered.
Fund	Independent accounting entity with a self-balancing set of accounts segregated for the purposes of carrying on specific activities is referred to as a fund.
Marketing research	Marketing research refers to the analysis of markets to determine opportunities and challenges, and to find the information needed to make good decisions.
Internal Revenue Service	In 1862, during the Civil War, President Lincoln and Congress created the office of Commissioner of Internal Revenue and enacted an income tax to pay war expenses. The position of Commissioner still exists today. The Commissioner is the head of the Internal Revenue Service.
PeopleSoft	PeopleSoft, Inc. was a software company that provided HRMS (human resource management), CRM), Manufacturing, Financials, EPM and Student Administration software solutions to large corporations, governments, and organizations. PeopleSoft was acquired in a hostile takeover by the Oracle Corporation.
Generation x	Generation x refers to the 15 percent of the U.S. population born between 1965 and 1976 a period also known as the baby bust.
Corporation	A legal entity chartered by a state or the Federal government that is distinct and separate from the individuals who own it is a corporation. This separation gives the corporation unique powers which other legal entities lack.
Operating results	Operating results refers to measures that are important to monitoring and tracking the effectiveness of a company's operations.
Brief	Brief refers to a statement of a party's case or legal arguments, usually prepared by an attorney. Also used to make legal arguments before appellate courts.
Administration	Administration refers to the management and direction of the affairs of governments and institutions; a collective term for all policymaking officials of a government; the execution and implementation of public policy.
Distribution	Distribution in economics, the manner in which total output and income is distributed among

Go to **Cram101.com** for the Practice Tests for this Chapter.

individuals or factors.

Economics	The social science dealing with the use of scarce resources to obtain the maximum satisfaction of society's virtually unlimited economic wants is an economics.
Commerce	Commerce is the exchange of something of value between two entities. It is the central mechanism from which capitalism is derived.
Recession	A significant decline in economic activity. In the U.S., recession is approximately defined as two successive quarters of falling GDP, as judged by NBER.

Go to **Cram101.com** for the Practice Tests for this Chapter.

Go to **Cram101.com** for the Practice Tests for this Chapter.
And, **NEVER** highlight a book again!

Trend	Trend refers to the long-term movement of an economic variable, such as its average rate of increase or decrease over enough years to encompass several business cycles.
Technology	The body of knowledge and techniques that can be used to combine economic resources to produce goods and services is called technology.
Market	A market is, as defined in economics, a social arrangement that allows buyers and sellers to discover information and carry out a voluntary exchange of goods or services.
Vendor	A person who sells property to a vendee is a vendor. The words vendor and vendee are more commonly applied to the seller and purchaser of real estate, and the words seller and buyer are more commonly applied to the seller and purchaser of personal property.
Competitor	Other organizations in the same industry or type of business that provide a good or service to the same set of customers is referred to as a competitor.
Management	Management characterizes the process of leading and directing all or part of an organization, often a business, through the deployment and manipulation of resources. Early twentieth-century management writer Mary Parker Follett defined management as "the art of getting things done through people."
Enterprise resource planning	Computer-based production and operations system that links multiple firms into one integrated production unit is enterprise resource planning.
Enterprise	Enterprise refers to another name for a business organization. Other similar terms are business firm, sometimes simply business, sometimes simply firm, as well as company, and entity.
Expense	In accounting, an expense represents an event in which an asset is used up or a liability is incurred. In terms of the accounting equation, expenses reduce owners' equity.
Accounting	A system that collects and processes financial information about an organization and reports that information to decision makers is referred to as accounting.
Balance	In banking and accountancy, the outstanding balance is the amount of money owned, (or due), that remains in a deposit account (or a loan account) at a given date, after all past remittances, payments and withdrawal have been accounted for. It can be positive (then, in the balance sheet of a firm, it is an asset) or negative (a liability).
Statement of cash flow	Reports inflows and outflows of cash during the accounting period in the categories of operating, investing, and financing is a statement of cash flow.
Financial statement	Financial statement refers to a summary of all the transactions that have occurred over a particular period.
Income statement	Income statement refers to a financial statement that presents the revenues and expenses and resulting net income or net loss of a company for a specific period of time.
Balance sheet	A statement of the assets, liabilities, and net worth of a firm or individual at some given time often at the end of its "fiscal year," is referred to as a balance sheet.
Principal	In agency law, one under whose direction an agent acts and for whose benefit that agent acts is a principal.
Cash flow	In finance, cash flow refers to the amounts of cash being received and spent by a business during a defined period of time, sometimes tied to a specific project. Most of the time they are being used to determine gaps in the liquid position of a company.
Firm	An organization that employs resources to produce a good or service for profit and owns and operates one or more plants is referred to as a firm.

Financial ratio	A financial ratio is a ratio of two numbers of reported levels or flows of a company. It may be two financial flows categories divided by each other (profit margin, profit/revenue). It may be a level divided by a financial flow (price/earnings). It may be a flow divided by a level (return on equity or earnings/equity). The numerator or denominator may itself be a ratio (PEG ratio).
Stock	In financial terminology, stock is the capital raized by a corporation, through the issuance and sale of shares.
Bull market	A rising stock market. A bull market exists when stock prices are strong and rising and investors are optimistic about future market performance.
Preparation	Preparation refers to usually the first stage in the creative process. It includes education and formal training.
Profit	Profit refers to the return to the resource entrepreneurial ability; total revenue minus total cost.
Revenue	Revenue is a U.S. business term for the amount of money that a company receives from its activities, mostly from sales of products and/or services to customers.
Securities and exchange commission	Securities and exchange commission refers to U.S. government agency that determines the financial statements that public companies must provide to stockholders and the measurement rules that they must use in producing those statements.
A share	In finance the term A share has two distinct meanings, both relating to securities. The first is a designation for a 'class' of common or preferred stock. A share of common or preferred stock typically has enhanced voting rights or other benefits compared to the other forms of shares that may have been created. The equity structure, or how many types of shares are offered, is determined by the corporate charter.
Independent auditor	Independent auditor refers to certified public accountant licensed to perform audits who is not an employee and does not have ownership or interest in the company being audited.
Stock market	An organized marketplace in which common stocks are traded. In the United States, the largest stock market is the New York Stock Exchange, on which are traded the stocks of the largest U.S. companies.
Exchange	The trade of things of value between buyer and seller so that each is better off after the trade is called the exchange.
Security	Security refers to a claim on the borrower future income that is sold by the borrower to the lender. A security is a type of transferable interest representing financial value.
Contract	A contract is a "promise" or an "agreement" that is enforced or recognized by the law. In the civil law, a contract is considered to be part of the general law of obligations.
Economy	The income, expenditures, and resources that affect the cost of running a business and household are called an economy.
New economy	New economy, this term was used in the late 1990's to suggest that globalization and/or innovations in information technology had changed the way that the world economy works.
Industrial revolution	The Industrial Revolution is the stream of new technology and the resulting growth of output that began in England toward the end of the 18th century.
Annual report	An annual report is prepared by corporate management that presents financial information including financial statements, footnotes, and the management discussion and analysis.
Aid	Assistance provided by countries and by international institutions such as the World Bank to developing countries in the form of monetary grants, loans at low interest rates, in kind, or

Go to **Cram101.com** for the Practice Tests for this Chapter.

a combination of these is called aid. Aid can also refer to assistance of any type rendered to benefit some group or individual.

Operation	A standardized method or technique that is performed repetitively, often on different materials resulting in different finished goods is called an operation.
Budget	Budget refers to an account, usually for a year, of the planned expenditures and the expected receipts of an entity. For a government, the receipts are tax revenues.
Controlling	A management function that involves determining whether or not an organization is progressing toward its goals and objectives, and taking corrective action if it is not is called controlling.
Users	Users refer to people in the organization who actually use the product or service purchased by the buying center.
Trustee	An independent party appointed to represent the bondholders is referred to as a trustee.
Union	A worker association that bargains with employers over wages and working conditions is called a union.
Productivity	Productivity refers to the total output of goods and services in a given period of time divided by work hours.
Negotiation	Negotiation is the process whereby interested parties resolve disputes, agree upon courses of action, bargain for individual or collective advantage, and/or attempt to craft outcomes which serve their mutual interests.
Bottom line	The bottom line is net income on the last line of a income statement.
Lender	Suppliers and financial institutions that lend money to companies is referred to as a lender.
Service	Service refers to a "non tangible product" that is not embodied in a physical good and that typically effects some change in another product, person, or institution. Contrasts with good.
Internal Revenue Service	In 1862, during the Civil War, President Lincoln and Congress created the office of Commissioner of Internal Revenue and enacted an income tax to pay war expenses. The position of Commissioner still exists today. The Commissioner is the head of the Internal Revenue Service.
Contribution	In business organization law, the cash or property contributed to a business by its owners is referred to as contribution.
Communism	Communism refers to an economic system in which capital is owned by private government. Contrasts with capitalism.
Certified Public Accountant	Certified Public Accountant refers to an individual in the United States who have passed the Uniform Certified Public Accountant Examination and have met additional state education and experience requirements for certification as a Certified Public Accountant.
Fund	Independent accounting entity with a self-balancing set of accounts segregated for the purposes of carrying on specific activities is referred to as a fund.
Financing activities	Cash flow activities that include obtaining cash from issuing debt and repaying the amounts borrowed and obtaining cash from stockholders and paying dividends is referred to as financing activities.
Asset	An item of property, such as land, capital, money, a share in ownership, or a claim on others for future payment, such as a bond or a bank deposit is an asset.
Investing	Investing activities refers to cash flow activities that include purchasing and disposing of

activities	investments and productive long-lived assets using cash and lending money and collecting on those loans.
Operating activities	Cash flow activities that include the cash effects of transactions that create revenues and expenses and thus enter into the determination of net income is an operating activities.
Audit	An examination of the financial reports to ensure that they represent what they claim and conform with generally accepted accounting principles is referred to as audit.
Management consulting	Management consulting refers to both the practice of helping companies to improve performance through analysis of existing business problems and development of future plans, as well as to the firms that specialize in this sort of consulting.
Arthur Andersen	Arthur Andersen was once one of the Big Five accounting firms, performing auditing, tax, and consulting services for large corporations. In 2002 the firm voluntarily surrendered its licenses to practice as Certified Public Accountants in the U.S. pending the result of prosecution by the U.S. Department of Justice over the firm's handling of the auditing of Enron.
Consultant	A professional that provides expert advice in a particular field or area in which customers occasionaly require this type of knowledge is a consultant.
Points	Loan origination fees that may be deductible as interest by a buyer of property. A seller of property who pays points reduces the selling price by the amount of the points paid for the buyer.
Effective tax rate	The effective tax rate is the amount of income tax an individual or firm pays divided by the individual or firm's total taxable income. This ratio is usually expressed as a percentage.
Tax accountant	An accountant trained in tax law and responsible for preparing tax returns or developing tax strategies is called a tax accountant.
Internal auditor	An accountant employed within a firm who reviews the accounting procedures, records, and reports in both the controller's and treasurer's areas of responsibility is referred to as an internal auditor.
Regulation	Regulation refers to restrictions state and federal laws place on business with regard to the conduct of its activities.
Master budget	Master budget refers to expression of management's operating and financial plans for a specified period and comprises a set of budgeted financial statements. Also called pro forma statements.
Sales budget	Sales budget refers to a schedule that shows the expected sales of services or goods during a budget period, expressed in both monetary terms and units.
Marketing	Promoting and selling products or services to customers, or prospective customers, is referred to as marketing.
Industry	A group of firms that produce identical or similar products is an industry. It is also used specifically to refer to an area of economic production focused on manufacturing which involves large amounts of capital investment before any profit can be realized, also called "heavy industry".
Cash budget	A projection of anticipated cash flows, usually over a one to two year period is called a cash budget.
Interest	In finance and economics, interest is the price paid by a borrower for the use of a lender's money. In other words, interest is the amount of paid to "rent" money for a period of time.
Marketable	Marketable securities refer to securities that are readily traded in the secondary securities

Go to **Cram101.com** for the Practice Tests for this Chapter.

securities	market.
Cash inflow	Cash coming into the company as the result of a previous investment is a cash inflow.
Tangible	Having a physical existence is referred to as the tangible. Personal property other than real estate, such as cars, boats, stocks, or other assets.
Household	An economic unit that provides the economy with resources and uses the income received to purchase goods and services that satisfy economic wants is called household.
Nestle	Nestle is the world's biggest food and beverage company. In the 1860s, a pharmacist, developed a food for babies who were unable to be breastfed. His first success was a premature infant who could not tolerate his own mother's milk nor any of the usual substitutes. The value of the new product was quickly recognized when his new formula saved the child's life.
Exchange rate	Exchange rate refers to the price at which one country's currency trades for another, typically on the exchange market.
Supply	Supply is the aggregate amount of any material good that can be called into being at a certain price point; it comprises one half of the equation of supply and demand. In classical economic theory, a curve representing supply is one of the factors that produce price.
Supply and demand	The partial equilibrium supply and demand economic model originally developed by Alfred Marshall attempts to describe, explain, and predict changes in the price and quantity of goods sold in competitive markets.
Consolidated financial statement	A consolidated financial statement refers to a financial statement of a parent company and its subsidiaries that has been combined into a single set of financial statements as if the companies were one.
Gain	In finance, gain is a profit or an increase in value of an investment such as a stock or bond. Gain is calculated by fair market value or the proceeds from the sale of the investment minus the sum of the purchase price and all costs associated with it.
International firm	International firm refers to those firms who have responded to stiff competition domestically by expanding their sales abroad. They may start a production facility overseas and send some of their managers, who report to a global division, to that country.
Investment	Investment refers to spending for the production and accumulation of capital and additions to inventories. In a financial sense, buying an asset with the expectation of making a return.
Utility	Utility refers to the want-satisfying power of a good or service; the satisfaction or pleasure a consumer obtains from the consumption of a good or service.
Variable	A variable is something measured by a number; it is used to analyze what happens to other things when the size of that number changes.
Variance	Variance refers to a measure of how much an economic or statistical variable varies across values or observations. Its calculation is the same as that of the covariance, being the covariance of the variable with itself.
Personal finance	Personal finance is the application of the principles of financial economics to an individual's (or a family's) financial decisions.
Cost management	The approaches and activities of managers in short-run and long-run planning and control decisions that increase value for customers and lower costs of products and services are called cost management.
Capital	Capital generally refers to financial wealth, especially that used to start or maintain a business. In classical economics, capital is one of four factors of production, the others

289

being land and labor and entrepreneurship.

Working capital | The dollar difference between total current assets and total current liabilities is called working capital.

291

Supply	Supply is the aggregate amount of any material good that can be called into being at a certain price point; it comprises one half of the equation of supply and demand. In classical economic theory, a curve representing supply is one of the factors that produce price.
Money supply	There are several formal definitions, but all include the quantity of currency in circulation plus the amount of demand deposits. The money supply, together with the amount of real economic activity in a country, is an important determinant of price.
Fund	Independent accounting entity with a self-balancing set of accounts segregated for the purposes of carrying on specific activities is referred to as a fund.
Financial institution	A financial institution acts as an agent that provides financial services for its clients. Financial institutions generally fall under financial regulation from a government authority.
Federal reserve system	The central banking authority responsible for monetary policy in the United States is called federal reserve system or the Fed.
Federal Reserve	The Federal Reserve System was created via the Federal Reserve Act of December 23rd, 1913. All national banks were required to join the system and other banks could join. The Reserve Banks opened for business on November 16th, 1914. Federal Reserve Notes were created as part of the legislation, to provide an elastic supply of currency.
Capital	Capital generally refers to financial wealth, especially that used to start or maintain a business. In classical economics, capital is one of four factors of production, the others being land and labor and entrepreneurship.
Entrepreneur	The owner/operator. The person who organizes, manages, and assumes the risks of a firm, taking a new idea or a new product and turning it into a successful business is an entrepreneur.
Firm	An organization that employs resources to produce a good or service for profit and owns and operates one or more plants is referred to as a firm.
Venture capital firm	A financial intermediary that pools the resources of its partners and uses the funds to help entrepreneurs start up new businesses is referred to as a venture capital firm.
Venture capital	Venture capital is capital provided by outside investors for financing of new, growing or struggling businesses. Venture capital investments generally are high risk investments but offer the potential for above average returns.
Technology	The body of knowledge and techniques that can be used to combine economic resources to produce goods and services is called technology.
Ariba	Ariba is a software and information technology services company, headquartered in Sunnyvale, California, USA. The focus of their products and services is cost savings in procurement via electronic commerce, also known as spend management.
Exchange	The trade of things of value between buyer and seller so that each is better off after the trade is called the exchange.
Venture capitalists	Venture capitalists refer to individuals or companies that invest in new businesses in exchange for partial ownership of those businesses.
Industry	A group of firms that produce identical or similar products is an industry. It is also used specifically to refer to an area of economic production focused on manufacturing which involves large amounts of capital investment before any profit can be realized, also called "heavy industry".
Investment	Investment refers to spending for the production and accumulation of capital and additions to inventories. In a financial sense, buying an asset with the expectation of making a return.

Go to **Cram101.com** for the Practice Tests for this Chapter.

Auction	A preexisting business model that operates successfully on the Internet by announcing an item for sale and permitting multiple purchasers to bid on them under specified rules and condition is an auction.
EBay	eBay manages an online auction and shopping website, where people buy and sell goods and services worldwide.
Michael Dell	Michael Dell is the founder of Dell, Inc., the world's largest computer manufacturer which revolutionized the home computer industry.
Bill Gates	Bill Gates is the co-founder, chairman, former chief software architect, and former CEO of Microsoft Corporation. He is one of the best-known entrepreneurs of the personal computer revolution and he is widely respected for his foresight and ambition.
Subsidiary	A company that is controlled by another company or corporation is a subsidiary.
Market	A market is, as defined in economics, a social arrangement that allows buyers and sellers to discover information and carry out a voluntary exchange of goods or services.
Operation	A standardized method or technique that is performed repetitively, often on different materials resulting in different finished goods is called an operation.
Cooperative	A business owned and controlled by the people who use it, producers, consumers, or workers with similar needs who pool their resources for mutual gain is called cooperative.
Chief executive officer	A chief executive officer is the highest-ranking corporate officer or executive officer of a corporation, or agency. In closely held corporations, it is general business culture that the office chief executive officer is also the chairman of the board.
Stock	In financial terminology, stock is the capital raized by a corporation, through the issuance and sale of shares.
Expense	In accounting, an expense represents an event in which an asset is used up or a liability is incurred. In terms of the accounting equation, expenses reduce owners' equity.
Common stock	Common stock refers to the basic, normal, voting stock issued by a corporation; called residual equity because it ranks after preferred stock for dividend and liquidation distributions.
Profit	Profit refers to the return to the resource entrepreneurial ability; total revenue minus total cost.
Financial manager	Managers who make recommendations to top executives regarding strategies for improving the financial strength of a firm are referred to as a financial manager.
Shareholder	A shareholder is an individual or company (including a corporation) that legally owns one or more shares of stock in a joined stock company.
Revenue	Revenue is a U.S. business term for the amount of money that a company receives from its activities, mostly from sales of products and/or services to customers.
Chief financial officer	Chief financial officer refers to executive responsible for overseeing the financial operations of an organization.
Board of directors	The group of individuals elected by the stockholders of a corporation to oversee its operations is a board of directors.
Audit	An examination of the financial reports to ensure that they represent what they claim and conform with generally accepted accounting principles is referred to as audit.
Financial statement	Financial statement refers to a summary of all the transactions that have occurred over a particular period.

Go to **Cram101.com** for the Practice Tests for this Chapter.

Internal audit	An internal audit is an independent appraisal of operations, conducted under the direction of management, to assess the effectiveness of internal administrative and accounting controls and help ensure conformance with managerial policies.
Controller	Controller refers to the financial executive primarily responsible for management accounting and financial accounting. Also called chief accounting officer.
Financing activities	Cash flow activities that include obtaining cash from issuing debt and repaying the amounts borrowed and obtaining cash from stockholders and paying dividends is referred to as financing activities.
Treasurer	In many governments, a treasurer is the person responsible for running the treasury. Treasurers are also employed by organizations to look after funds.
Security	Security refers to a claim on the borrower future income that is sold by the borrower to the lender. A security is a type of transferable interest representing financial value.
Financial management	The job of managing a firm's resources so it can meet its goals and objectives is called financial management.
Management	Management characterizes the process of leading and directing all or part of an organization, often a business, through the deployment and manipulation of resources. Early twentieth-century management writer Mary Parker Follett defined management as "the art of getting things done through people."
Acquisition	A company's purchase of the property and obligations of another company is an acquisition.
Production	The creation of finished goods and services using the factors of production: land, labor, capital, entrepreneurship, and knowledge.
Sears	Before the Sears catalog, farmers typically bought supplies (often at very high prices) from local general stores. Sears took advantage of this by publishing his catalog with clearly stated prices, so that consumers could know what he was selling and at what price, and order and obtain them conveniently. The catalog business soon grew quickly.
Balance	In banking and accountancy, the outstanding balance is the amount of money owned, (or due), that remains in a deposit account (or a loan account) at a given date, after all past remittances, payments and withdrawal have been accounted for. It can be positive (then, in the balance sheet of a firm, it is an asset) or negative (a liability).
Gain	In finance, gain is a profit or an increase in value of an investment such as a stock or bond. Gain is calculated by fair market value or the proceeds from the sale of the investment minus the sum of the purchase price and all costs associated with it.
Boeing	Boeing is the world's largest aircraft manufacturer by revenue. Headquartered in Chicago, Illinois, Boeing is the second-largest defense contractor in the world. In 2005, the company was the world's largest civil aircraft manufacturer in terms of value.
Financial plan	The financial plan section of a business plan consists of three financial statements (the income statement, the cash flow projection, and the balance sheet) and a brief analysis of these three statements.
Purchasing	Purchasing refers to the function in a firm that searches for quality material resources, finds the best suppliers, and negotiates the best price for goods and services.
Service	Service refers to a "non tangible product" that is not embodied in a physical good and that typically effects some change in another product, person, or institution. Contrasts with good.
Credit	Credit refers to a recording as positive in the balance of payments, any transaction that gives rise to a payment into the country, such as an export, the sale of an asset, or

Go to **Cram101.com** for the Practice Tests for this Chapter.

	borrowing from abroad.
Credit sale	A credit sale occurs when a customer does not pay cash at the time of the sale but instead agrees to pay later. The sale occurs now, with payment from the customer to follow at a later time.
Cash inflow	Cash coming into the company as the result of a previous investment is a cash inflow.
Household	An economic unit that provides the economy with resources and uses the income received to purchase goods and services that satisfy economic wants is called household.
Public relations firm	An organization that develops and implements programs to manage a company's publicity, image, and affairs with consumers and other relevant publics is referred to as a public relations firm.
Public relations	Public relations refers to the management function that evaluates public attitudes, changes policies and procedures in response to the public's requests, and executes a program of action and information to earn public understanding and acceptance.
Small business	Small business refers to a business that is independently owned and operated, is not dominant in its field of operation, and meets certain standards of size in terms of employees or annual receipts.
Vendor	A person who sells property to a vendee is a vendor. The words vendor and vendee are more commonly applied to the seller and purchaser of real estate, and the words seller and buyer are more commonly applied to the seller and purchaser of personal property.
Cash flow	In finance, cash flow refers to the amounts of cash being received and spent by a business during a defined period of time, sometimes tied to a specific project. Most of the time they are being used to determine gaps in the liquid position of a company.
Financial control	A process in which a firm periodically compares its actual revenues, costs, and expenses with its projected ones is called financial control.
Cisco Systems	While Cisco Systems was not the first company to develop and sell a router (a device that forwards computer traffic from one network to another), it did create the first commercially successful multi-protocol router to allow previously incompatible computers to communicate using different network protocols.
Margin	A deposit by a buyer in stocks with a seller or a stockbroker, as security to cover fluctuations in the market in reference to stocks that the buyer has purchased but for which he has not paid is a margin. Commodities are also traded on margin.
Profit margin	Profit margin is a measure of profitability. It is calculated using a formula and written as a percentage or a number. Profit margin = Net income before tax and interest / Revenue.
Users	Users refer to people in the organization who actually use the product or service purchased by the buying center.
Purchasing power	The amount of goods that money will buy, usually measured by the CPI is referred to as purchasing power.
Advertising campaign	A comprehensive advertising plan that consists of a series of messages in a variety of media that center on a single theme or idea is referred to as an advertising campaign.
Advertising	Advertising refers to paid, nonpersonal communication through various media by organizations and individuals who are in some way identified in the advertising message.
Distribution	Distribution in economics, the manner in which total output and income is distributed among individuals or factors.
Interest	In finance and economics, interest is the price paid by a borrower for the use of a lender's

	money. In other words, interest is the amount of paid to "rent" money for a period of time.
Economy	The income, expenditures, and resources that affect the cost of running a business and household are called an economy.
Barter	Barter is a type of trade where goods or services are exchanged for a certain amount of other goods or services; no money is involved in the transaction.
Medium of exchange	Medium of exchange refers to any item sellers generally accept and buyers generally use to pay for a good or service; money; a convenient means of exchanging goods and services without engaging in barter.
Store of value	To act as a store of value, a commodity, a form of money, or financial capital must be able to be reliably saved, stored, and retrieved - and be predictably useful when it is so retrieved.
Value of money	Value of money refers to the quantity of goods and services for which a unit of money can be exchanged; the purchasing power of a unit of money; the reciprocal of the price level.
Liquidity	Liquidity refers to the capacity to turn assets into cash, or the amount of assets in a portfolio that have that capacity.
Union	A worker association that bargains with employers over wages and working conditions is called a union.
Draft	A signed, written order by which one party instructs another party to pay a specified sum to a third party, at sight or at a specific date is a draft.
Asset	An item of property, such as land, capital, money, a share in ownership, or a claim on others for future payment, such as a bond or a bank deposit is an asset.
Financial assets	Financial assets refer to monetary claims or obligations by one party against another party. Examples are bonds, mortgages, bank loans, and equities.
Deposit account	A deposit account is an account at a banking institution that alows money to be held on behalf of the account holder. Some banks charge a fee for this service, while others may pay the client interest on the funds deposited.
Demand deposit	Demand deposit refers to a bank deposit that can be withdrawn 'on demand.' The term usually refers only to checking accounts, even though depositors in many other kinds of accounts may be able to write checks and regard their deposits as readily available.
Credit union	A credit union is a not-for-profit co-operative financial institution that is owned and controlled by its members, through the election of a volunteer Board of Directors elected from the membership itself.
American Express	From the early 1980s until the late 1990s, American Express was known for cutting its merchant fees (also known as a "discount rate") to fine merchants and restaurants if they only accepted American Express and no other credit or charge cards. This prompted competitors such as Visa and MasterCard to cry foul for a while, as the tactics "locked" restaurants into American Express.
Option	A contract that gives the purchaser the option to buy or sell the underlying financial instrument at a specified price, called the exercise price or strike price, within a specific period of time.
Interest rate	The rate of return on bonds, loans, or deposits. When one speaks of 'the' interest rate, it is usually in a model where there is only one.
Issuer	The company that borrows money from investors by issuing bonds is referred to as issuer. They are legally responsible for the obligations of the issue and for reporting financial

	conditions, material developments and any other operational activities as required by the regulations of their jurisdictions.
Fraud	Tax fraud falls into two categories: civil and criminal. Under civil fraud, the IRS may impose as a penalty of an amount equal to as much as 75 percent of the underpayment.
Merchant	Under the Uniform Commercial Code, one who regularly deals in goods of the kind sold in the contract at issue, or holds himself out as having special knowledge or skill relevant to such goods, or who makes the sale through an agent who regularly deals in such goods or claims such knowledge or skill is referred to as merchant.
Smart card	A stored-value card that contains a computer chip that allows it to be loaded with digital cash from the owner's bank account whenever needed is called a smart card.
Debit	Debit refers to recording as negative in the balance of payments, any transaction that gives rise to a payment out of the country, such as an import, the purchase of an asset, or lending to foreigners. Opposite of credit.
Market share	That fraction of an industry's output accounted for by an individual firm or group of firms is called market share.
Corporation	A legal entity chartered by a state or the Federal government that is distinct and separate from the individuals who own it is a corporation. This separation gives the corporation unique powers which other legal entities lack.
Holder	A person in possession of a document of title or an instrument payable or indorsed to him, his order, or to bearer is a holder.
Certificates of deposit	Certificates of deposit refer to a certificate offered by banks, savings and loans, and other financial institutions for the deposit of funds at a given interest rate over a specified time period.
Marketable securities	Marketable securities refer to securities that are readily traded in the secondary securities market.
Repurchase agreement	An arrangement whereby the Fed, or another party, purchases securities with the understanding that the seller will repurchase them in a short period of time, usually less than a week is a repurchase agreement.
Commercial paper	Commercial paper is a money market security issued by large banks and corporations. It is generally not used to finance long-term investments but rather for purchases of inventory or to manage working capital. It is commonly bought by money funds (the issuing amounts are often too high for individual investors), and is generally regarded as a very safe investment.
Treasury bills	Short-term obligations of the federal government are treasury bills. They are like zero coupon bonds in that they do not pay interest prior to maturity; instead they are sold at a discount of the par value to create a positive yield to maturity.
Maturity	Maturity refers to the final payment date of a loan or other financial instrument, after which point no further interest or principal need be paid.
Date of issue	As applied to notes, bonds, and so on of a series, the arbitrary date fixed as the beginning of the term for which they run, without reference to the precise time when convenience or the state of the market may permit their sale or delivery is called the date of issue.
Commercial bank	A firm that engages in the business of banking is a commercial bank.
Time deposit	The technical name for a savings account is a time deposit; the bank can require prior notice before the owner withdraws money from a time deposit.

Go to **Cram101.com** for the Practice Tests for this Chapter.

Go to **Cram101.com** for the Practice Tests for this Chapter.
And, **NEVER** highlight a book again!

Savings bank	A depository institution, owned by its depositors, that accepts savings deposits and makes mortgage loans is a savings bank.
Maturity date	The date on which the final payment on a bond is due from the bond issuer to the investor is a maturity date.
Equity	Equity is the name given to the set of legal principles, in countries following the English common law tradition, which supplement strict rules of law where their application would operate harshly, so as to achieve what is sometimes referred to as "natural justice."
Equity capital	Equity capital refers to money raized from within the firm or through the sale of ownership in the firm.
Debt capital	Debt capital refers to funds raized through various forms of borrowing to finance a company that must be repaid.
Equity financing	Financing that consists of funds that are invested in exchange for ownership in the company is called equity financing.
Debt financing	Obtaining financing by borrowing money is debt financing.
Contribution	In business organization law, the cash or property contributed to a business by its owners is referred to as contribution.
Drawback	Drawback refers to rebate of import duties when the imported good is re-exported or used as input to the production of an exported good.
E*Trade	E*TRADE is a financial services company based in New York City. It is a holding company primarily known as an online discount stock brokerage serving self-directed investors, many of whom are day traders. As a discount brokerage, it charges a much smaller fee on each trade.
Trade credit	Trade credit refers to an amount that is loaned to an exporter to be repaid when the exports are paid for by the foreign importer.
Pledge	In law a pledge (also pawn) is a bailment of personal property as a security for some debt or engagement.
Collateral	Property that is pledged to the lender to guarantee payment in the event that the borrower is unable to make debt payments is called collateral.
Inventory	Tangible property held for sale in the normal course of business or used in producing goods or services for sale is an inventory.
Lender	Suppliers and financial institutions that lend money to companies is referred to as a lender.
Stockholder	A stockholder is an individual or company (including a corporation) that legally owns one or more shares of stock in a joined stock company. The shareholders are the owners of a corporation. Companies listed at the stock market strive to enhance shareholder value.
Creditor	A person to whom a debt or legal obligation is owed, and who has the right to enforce payment of that debt or obligation is referred to as creditor.
Residual	Residual payments can refer to an ongoing stream of payments in respect of the completion of past achievements.
Dividend	Amount of corporate profits paid out for each share of stock is referred to as dividend.
Preference	The act of a debtor in paying or securing one or more of his creditors in a manner more favorable to them than to other creditors or to the exclusion of such other creditors is a preference. In the absence of statute, a preference is perfectly good, but to be legal it must be bona fide, and not a mere subterfuge of the debtor to secure a future benefit to

	himself or to prevent the application of his property to his debts.
Property	Assets defined in the broadest legal sense. Property includes the unrealized receivables of a cash basis taxpayer, but not services rendered.
Pension	A pension is a steady income given to a person (usually after retirement). Pensions are typically payments made in the form of a guaranteed annuity to a retired or disabled employee.
Pension fund	Amounts of money put aside by corporations, nonprofit organizations, or unions to cover part of the financial needs of members when they retire is a pension fund.
Insurance	Insurance refers to a system by which individuals can reduce their exposure to risk of large losses by spreading the risks among a large number of persons.
Bond	Bond refers to a debt instrument, issued by a borrower and promising a specified stream of payments to the purchaser, usually regular interest payments plus a final repayment of principal.
Private placement	Private placement refers to the sale of securities directly to a financial institution by a corporation. This eliminates the middleman and reduces the cost of issue to the corporation.
Regulation	Regulation refers to restrictions state and federal laws place on business with regard to the conduct of its activities.
Yield	The interest rate that equates a future value or an annuity to a given present value is a yield.
Securities market	The securities market is the market for securities, where companies and the government can raise long-term funds.
Institutional investors	Institutional investors refers to large organizations such as pension funds, mutual funds, insurance companies, and banks that invest their own funds or the funds of others.
Management consulting	Management consulting refers to both the practice of helping companies to improve performance through analysis of existing business problems and development of future plans, as well as to the firms that specialize in this sort of consulting.
Interest payment	The payment to holders of bonds payable, calculated by multiplying the stated rate on the face of the bond by the par, or face, value of the bond. If bonds are issued at a discount or premium, the interest payment does not equal the interest expense.
Fixed interest	A fixed interest rate loan is a loan where the interest rate doesn't fluctuate over the life of the loan. This allows the borrower to accurately predict their future payments. When the prevailing interest rate is very low, a fixed rate loan will be slightly higher than variable rate loans because the lender is taking a risk they he could get a higher interest rate by loaning money later.
Leverage	Leverage is using given resources in such a way that the potential positive or negative outcome is magnified. In finance, this generally refers to borrowing.
Rate of return	A rate of return is a comparison of the money earned (or lost) on an investment to the amount of money invested.
Bondholder	The individual or entity that purchases a bond, thus loaning money to the company that issued the bond is the bondholder.
Return on investment	Return on investment refers to the return a businessperson gets on the money he and other owners invest in the firm; for example, a business that earned $100 on a $1,000 investment would have a ROI of 10 percent: 100 divided by 1000.
Financial market	In economics, a financial market is a mechanism which allows people to trade money for

Go to **Cram101.com** for the Practice Tests for this Chapter.

securities or commodities such as gold or other precious metals. In general, any commodity market might be considered to be a financial market, if the usual purpose of traders is not the immediate consumption of the commodity, but rather as a means of delaying or accelerating consumption over time.

Deficit	The deficit is the amount by which expenditure exceed revenue.
Budget	Budget refers to an account, usually for a year, of the planned expenditures and the expected receipts of an entity. For a government, the receipts are tax revenues.
Budget deficit	A budget deficit occurs when an entity (often a government) spends more money than it takes
Inventory financing	The process of using inventory such as raw materials as collateral for a loan is inventory financing. Lenders may require additional collateral and may require an appraisal by a national appraisal firm acceptable to the lender. Depending on the type of inventory, the lender's advance rate can range from 35% to 80% of the orderly liquidation value of the inventory.
Depository institution	A depository institution is a financial institution, such as a savings bank, that is legally allowed to accept monetary deposits from consumers.
Consolidation	The combination of two or more firms, generally of equal size and market power, to form an entirely new entity is a consolidation.
Merger	Merger refers to the combination of two firms into a single firm.
Trend	Trend refers to the long-term movement of an economic variable, such as its average rate of increase or decrease over enough years to encompass several business cycles.
Bank failure	A situation in which a bank cannot satisfy its obligations to pay its depositors and other creditors and so goes out of business is called bank failure.
Niche	In industry, a niche is a situation or an activity perfectly suited to a person. A niche can imply a working position or an area suited to a person who occupies it. Basically, a job where a person is able to succeed and thrive.
Points	Loan origination fees that may be deductible as interest by a buyer of property. A seller of property who pays points reduces the selling price by the amount of the points paid for the buyer.
Comprehensive	A comprehensive refers to a layout accurate in size, color, scheme, and other necessary details to show how a final ad will look. For presentation only, never for reproduction.
Financial transaction	A financial transaction involves a change in the status of the finances of two or more businesses or individuals.
Social Security	Social security primarily refers to a field of social welfare concerned with social protection, or protection against socially recognized conditions, including poverty, old age, disability, unemployment, families with children and others.
Yahoo	Yahoo is an American computer services company. It operates an Internet portal, the Yahoo Directory and a host of other services including the popular Yahoo Mail. Yahoo is the most visited website on the Internet today with more than 400 million unique users. The global network of Yahoo! websites received 3.4 billion page views per day on average as of October 2005.
Great Depression	The period of severe economic contraction and high unemployment that began in 1929 and continued throughout the 1930s is referred to as the Great Depression.
Depression	Depression refers to a prolonged period characterized by high unemployment, low output and investment, depressed business confidence, falling prices, and widespread business failures.

Go to **Cram101.com** for the Practice Tests for this Chapter.

A milder form of business downturn is a recession.

Federal Deposit Insurance Corporation	The Federal Deposit Insurance Corporation is a United States government corporation created by the Glass-Steagall Act of 1933. The vast number of bank failures in the Great Depression spurred the United States Congress into creating an institution which would guarantee banks, inspired by the Commonwealth of Massachusetts and its Deposit Insurance Fund (DIF). It currently guarantees checking and savings deposits in member banks up to $100,000 per depositor.
Deposit insurance	Deposit insurance is a measure taken by banks in many countries to protect their clients' savings, either fully or in part, against any possible situation that would prevent the bank from returning said savings.
Comptroller	A comptroller is an official who supervises expenditures. Comptrollers include both royal-household officials and public comptrollers who audit government accounts and sometimes certify expenditures.
Authority	Authority in agency law, refers to an agent's ability to affect his principal's legal relations with third parties. Also used to refer to an actor's legal power or ability to do something. In addition, sometimes used to refer to a statute, case, or other legal source that justifies a particular result.
State bank	State bank refers to a commercial bank authorized by a state government to engage in the business of banking.
Savings and loan association	A financial institution that accepts both savings and checking deposits and provides home mortgage loans is referred to as savings and loan association.
Thrift institution	A savings and loan association, mutual savings bank, or credit union are called a thrift institution.
Savings deposit	Savings deposit refers to a deposit that is interest-bearing and that the depositor can normally withdraw at any time.
Mortgage	Mortgage refers to a note payable issued for property, such as a house, usually repaid in equal installments consisting of part principle and part interest, over a specified period.
Charter	Charter refers to an instrument or authority from the sovereign power bestowing the right or power to do business under the corporate form of organization. Also, the organic law of a city or town, and representing a portion of the statute law of the state.
Premium	Premium refers to the fee charged by an insurance company for an insurance policy. The rate of losses must be relatively predictable: In order to set the premium (prices) insurers must be able to estimate them accurately.
Underwriting	The process of selling securities and, at the same time, assuring the seller a specified price is underwriting. Underwriting is done by investment bankers and represents a form of risk taking.
Operating expense	In throughput accounting, the cost accounting aspect of Theory of Constraints (TOC), operating expense is the money spent turning inventory into throughput. In TOC, operating expense is limited to costs that vary strictly with the quantity produced, like raw materials and purchased components.
Cash outflow	Cash flowing out of the business from all sources over a period of time is cash outflow.
Commercial finance companies	Organizations that make short-term loans to borrowers who offer tangible assets as collateral are referred to as commercial finance companies.

Go to **Cram101.com** for the Practice Tests for this Chapter.

Accounts receivable	Accounts receivable is one of a series of accounting transactions dealing with the billing of customers which owe money to a person, company or organization for goods and services that have been provided to the customer. This is typically done in a one person organization by writing an invoice and mailing or delivering it to each customer.
Tangible asset	Assets that have physical substance that cannot easily be converted into cash are referd to as a tangible asset.
Tangible	Having a physical existence is referred to as the tangible. Personal property other than real estate, such as cars, boats, stocks, or other assets.
Consumer finance	Consumer finance in the most basic sense of the word refers to any kind of lending to consumers. However, in the United States financial services industry, the term "consumer finance" often refers to a particular type of business, sub prime branch lending (that is lending to people with bad credit).
Policy	Similar to a script in that a policy can be a less than completely rational decision-making method. Involves the use of a pre-existing set of decision steps for any problem that presents itself.
Monetary policy	The use of the money supply and/or the interest rate to influence the level of economic activity and other policy objectives including the balance of payments or the exchange rate is called monetary policy.
Board of Governors	A board of governors is usually the governing board of a public entity; the Board of Governors of the Federal Reserve System; the Federal Reserve Board.
Appropriation	A privacy tort that consists of using a person's name or likeness for commercial gain without the person's permission is an appropriation.
Open market	In economics, the open market is the term used to refer to the environment in which bonds are bought and sold.
Committee	A long-lasting, sometimes permanent team in the organization structure created to deal with tasks that recur regularly is the committee.
Check clearing	The process by which funds are transferred from the checking accounts of the writers of checks to the checking accounts of the recipients of the checks is referred to as check clearing.
Home Depot	Home Depot has recently added self checkout registers at most of its stores in North America. These automated kiosks allow the customer to scan the barcode of the item they wish to purchase, then insert money to pay for the items, and receive any change automatically. The customer no longer needs to interact with a store employee during checkout.
Central Bank	Central bank refers to the institution in a country that is normally responsible for managing the supply of the country's money and the value of its currency on the foreign exchange market.
Controlling	A management function that involves determining whether or not an organization is progressing toward its goals and objectives, and taking corrective action if it is not is called controlling.
Inflation	An increase in the overall price level of an economy, usually as measured by the CPI or by the implicit price deflator is called inflation.
Economic growth	Economic growth refers to the increase over time in the capacity of an economy to produce goods and services and to improve the well-being of its citizens.
Recession	A significant decline in economic activity. In the U.S., recession is approximately defined as two successive quarters of falling GDP, as judged by NBER.

Go to **Cram101.com** for the Practice Tests for this Chapter.

Open market operations	Open market operations are the means of implementing monetary policy by which a central bank controls its national money supply by buying and selling government securities, or other instruments. Monetary targets, such as interest rates or exchange rates, are used to guide this implementation.
Open market operation	Open market operation refers to the sale or purchase of government bonds by a central bank, in exchange for domestic currency or central-bank deposits.
Reserve requirement	The reserve requirement is a bank regulation, that sets the minimum reserves each bank must hold to customer deposits and notes.
Discount rate	Discount rate refers to the rate, per year, at which future values are diminished to make them comparable to values in the present. Can be either subjective or objective .
Discount	The difference between the face value of a bond and its selling price, when a bond is sold for less than its face value it's referred to as a discount.
National bank	A National bank refers to federally chartered banks. They are an ordinary private bank which operates nationally (as opposed to regionally or locally or even internationally).
Federal reserve banks	The 12 district banks in the Federal Reserve System are referred to as federal reserve banks. Each bank is responsible to provide services to a specific geographic region of the United States.
Treasury security	A treasury security is a government bond issued by the United States Department of the Treasury through the Bureau of the Public Debt. They are the debt financing instruments of the U.S. Federal government, and are often referred to simply as Treasuries.
Federal funds rate	The interest rate banks and other depository institutions charge one another on overnight loans made out of their excess reserves is called federal funds rate.
Foreign exchange market	A market for converting the currency of one country into that of another country is called foreign exchange market. It is by far the largest market in the world, in terms of cash value traded, and includes trading between large banks, central banks, currency speculators, multinational corporations, governments, and other financial markets and institutions.
Foreign exchange	In finance, foreign exchange means currencies, such as U.S. Dollars and Euros. These are traded on foreign exchange markets.
Exchange market	Exchange market refers to the market on which national currencies are bought and sold.
Bank reserves	Bank reserves are banks' holdings of deposits in accounts with their central bank, plus currency that is physically held in bank vaults (vault cash). The central bank sets minimum reserve requirements.
Shell	One of the original Seven Sisters, Royal Dutch/Shell is the world's third-largest oil company by revenue, and a major player in the petrochemical industry and the solar energy business. Shell has six core businesses: Exploration and Production, Gas and Power, Downstream, Chemicals, Renewables, and Trading/Shipping, and operates in more than 140 countries.
Federal government	Federal government refers to the government of the United States, as distinct from the state and local governments.
Graduation	Termination of a country's eligibility for GSP tariff preferences on the grounds that it has progressed sufficiently, in terms of per capita income or another measure, that it is no longer in need to special and differential treatment is graduation.
Line of credit	Line of credit refers to a given amount of unsecured short-term funds a bank will lend to a business, provided the funds are readily available.
Secured loan	Secured loan refers to a loan backed by something valuable, such as property.

Go to **Cram101.com** for the Practice Tests for this Chapter.

Estate	An estate is the totality of the legal rights, interests, entitlements and obligations attaching to property. In the context of wills and probate, it refers to the totality of the property which the deceased owned or in which some interest was held.
Margin requirement	Margin requirement refers to a rule that specifies the amount of cash or equity that must be deposited with a brokerage firm or bank, with the balance of funds eligible for borrowing. Margin is set by the Board of Governors of the Federal Reserve Board.
Brief	Brief refers to a statement of a party's case or legal arguments, usually prepared by an attorney. Also used to make legal arguments before appellate courts.
Matching	Matching refers to an accounting concept that establishes when expenses are recognized. Expenses are matched with the revenues they helped to generate and are recognized when those revenues are recognized.
Brokerage firm	A company that conducts various aspects of securities trading, analysis and advisory services is a brokerage firm.
Broker	In commerce, a broker is a party that mediates between a buyer and a seller. A broker who also acts as a seller or as a buyer becomes a principal party to the deal.
Charles Schwab	Charles Schwab is the world's second-largest discount broker. Besides discount brokerage, the firm offers mutual funds, annuities, bond trading, and now mortgages through its Charles Schwab Bank.
Merrill Lynch	Merrill Lynch through its subsidiaries and affiliates, provides capital markets services, investment banking and advisory services, wealth management, asset management, insurance, banking and related products and services on a global basis. It is best known for its Global Private Client services and its strong sales force.

Go to **Cram101.com** for the Practice Tests for this Chapter.

Corporation	A legal entity chartered by a state or the Federal government that is distinct and separate from the individuals who own it is a corporation. This separation gives the corporation unique powers which other legal entities lack.
Management	Management characterizes the process of leading and directing all or part of an organization, often a business, through the deployment and manipulation of resources. Early twentieth-century management writer Mary Parker Follett defined management as "the art of getting things done through people."
Service	Service refers to a "non tangible product" that is not embodied in a physical good and that typically effects some change in another product, person, or institution. Contrasts with good.
Expense	In accounting, an expense represents an event in which an asset is used up or a liability is incurred. In terms of the accounting equation, expenses reduce owners' equity.
E*Trade	E*TRADE is a financial services company based in New York City. It is a holding company primarily known as an online discount stock brokerage serving self-directed investors, many of whom are day traders. As a discount brokerage, it charges a much smaller fee on each trade.
Lender	Suppliers and financial institutions that lend money to companies is referred to as a lender.
Mortgage	Mortgage refers to a note payable issued for property, such as a house, usually repaid in equal installments consisting of part principle and part interest, over a specified period.
Stock	In financial terminology, stock is the capital raized by a corporation, through the issuance and sale of shares.
Financial transaction	A financial transaction involves a change in the status of the finances of two or more businesses or individuals.
Market	A market is, as defined in economics, a social arrangement that allows buyers and sellers to discover information and carry out a voluntary exchange of goods or services.
Bond	Bond refers to a debt instrument, issued by a borrower and promising a specified stream of payments to the purchaser, usually regular interest payments plus a final repayment of principal.
Common stock	Common stock refers to the basic, normal, voting stock issued by a corporation; called residual equity because it ranks after preferred stock for dividend and liquidation distributions.
Money market	The money market, in macroeconomics and international finance, refers to the equilibration of demand for a country's domestic money to its money supply; market for short-term financial instruments.
Instrument	Instrument refers to an economic variable that is controlled by policy makers and can be used to influence other variables, called targets. Examples are monetary and fiscal policies used to achieve external and internal balance.
Security	Security refers to a claim on the borrower future income that is sold by the borrower to the lender. A security is a type of transferable interest representing financial value.
Exchange	The trade of things of value between buyer and seller so that each is better off after the trade is called the exchange.
Fund	Independent accounting entity with a self-balancing set of accounts segregated for the purposes of carrying on specific activities is referred to as a fund.
Mutual fund	A mutual fund is a form of collective investment that pools money from many investors and

Go to **Cram101.com** for the Practice Tests for this Chapter.

	invests the money in stocks, bonds, short-term money market instruments, and/or other securities. In a mutual fund, the fund manager trades the fund's underlying securities, realizing capital gains or loss, and collects the dividend or interest income.
Securities market	The securities market is the market for securities, where companies and the government can raise long-term funds.
Regulation	Regulation refers to restrictions state and federal laws place on business with regard to the conduct of its activities.
Communication network	A communication network refer to networks that form spontaneously and naturally as the interactions among workers continue over time.
NASDAQ	NASDAQ is an American electronic stock exchange. It was founded in 1971 by the National Association of Securities Dealers who divested it in a series of sales in 2000 and 2001.
Buyer	A buyer refers to a role in the buying center with formal authority and responsibility to select the supplier and negotiate the terms of the contract.
Stock exchange	A stock exchange is a corporation or mutual organization which provides facilities for stock brokers and traders, to trade company stocks and other securities.
Stock market	An organized marketplace in which common stocks are traded. In the United States, the largest stock market is the New York Stock Exchange, on which are traded the stocks of the largest U.S. companies.
Market price	Market price is an economic concept with commonplace familiarity; it is the price that a good or service is offered at, or will fetch, in the marketplace; it is of interest mainly in the study of microeconomics.
Shares	Shares refer to an equity security, representing a shareholder's ownership of a corporation. Shares are one of a finite number of equal portions in the capital of a company, entitling the owner to a proportion of distributed, non-reinvested profits known as dividends and to a portion of the value of the company in case of liquidation.
Holding	The holding is a court's determination of a matter of law based on the issue presented in the particular case. In other words: under this law, with these facts, this result.
Competitive market	A market in which no buyer or seller has market power is called a competitive market.
Entrepreneur	The owner/operator. The person who organizes, manages, and assumes the risks of a firm, taking a new idea or a new product and turning it into a successful business is an entrepreneur.
Cisco Systems	While Cisco Systems was not the first company to develop and sell a router (a device that forwards computer traffic from one network to another), it did create the first commercially successful multi-protocol router to allow previously incompatible computers to communicate using different network protocols.
Matching	Matching refers to an accounting concept that establishes when expenses are recognized. Expenses are matched with the revenues they helped to generate and are recognized when those revenues are recognized.
Intermediaries	Intermediaries specialize in information either to bring together two parties to a transaction or to buy in order to sell again.
Merger	Merger refers to the combination of two firms into a single firm.
Layoff	A layoff is the termination of an employee or (more commonly) a group of employees for business reasons, such as the decision that certain positions are no longer necessary.

Go to **Cram101.com** for the Practice Tests for this Chapter.

Capital	Capital generally refers to financial wealth, especially that used to start or maintain a business. In classical economics, capital is one of four factors of production, the others being land and labor and entrepreneurship.
Government bond	A government bond is a bond issued by a national government denominated in the country's own currency. Bonds issued by national governments in foreign currencies are normally referred to as sovereign bonds.
Corporate bond	A Corporate bond is a bond issued by a corporation, as the name suggests. The term is usually applied to longer term debt instruments, generally with a maturity date falling at least 12 months after their issue date (the term "commercial paper" being sometimes used for instruments with a shorter maturity).
Municipal bond	In the United States, a municipal bond is a bond issued by a state, city or other local government, or their agencies. Potential issuers of these include cities, counties, redevelopment agencies, school districts, publicly owned airports and seaports, and any other governmental entity (or group of governments) below the state level. They are guaranteed by a local government, a subdivision thereof, or a group of local governments, and are assessed for risk and rated accordingly.
Debt capital	Debt capital refers to funds raized through various forms of borrowing to finance a company that must be repaid.
Equity	Equity is the name given to the set of legal principles, in countries following the English common law tradition, which supplement strict rules of law where their application would operate harshly, so as to achieve what is sometimes referred to as "natural justice."
Preferred stock	Stock that has specified rights over common stock is a preferred stock.
Equity capital	Equity capital refers to money raized from within the firm or through the sale of ownership in the firm.
Issuer	The company that borrows money from investors by issuing bonds is referred to as issuer. They are legally responsible for the obligations of the issue and for reporting financial conditions, material developments and any other operational activities as required by the regulations of their jurisdictions.
Firm	An organization that employs resources to produce a good or service for profit and owns and operates one or more plants is referred to as a firm.
Primary market	The market for the raising of new funds as opposed to the trading of securities already in existence is called primary market.
Investment	Investment refers to spending for the production and accumulation of capital and additions to inventories. In a financial sense, buying an asset with the expectation of making a return.
Inventory	Tangible property held for sale in the normal course of business or used in producing goods or services for sale is an inventory.
Amgen	Amgen is an international biotechnology company headquartered in Newbury Park, California. Amgen is the largest independent biotech firm, with approx. 15,000 staff members in 2005.
Initial public offering	Firms in the process of becoming publicly traded companies will issue shares of stock using an initial public offering, which is merely the process of selling stock for the first time to interested investors.
Profit	Profit refers to the return to the resource entrepreneurial ability; total revenue minus total cost.
Merrill Lynch	Merrill Lynch through its subsidiaries and affiliates, provides capital markets services, investment banking and advisory services, wealth management, asset management, insurance,

	banking and related products and services on a global basis. It is best known for its Global Private Client services and its strong sales force.
Journal	Book of original entry, in which transactions are recorded in a general ledger system, is referred to as a journal.
Wall Street Journal	Dow Jones & Company was founded in 1882 by reporters Charles Dow, Edward Jones and Charles Bergstresser. Jones converted the small Customers' Afternoon Letter into The Wall Street Journal, first published in 1889, and began delivery of the Dow Jones News Service via telegraph. The Journal featured the Jones 'Average', the first of several indexes of stock and bond prices on the New York Stock Exchange.
Secondary market	Secondary market refers to the market for securities that have already been issued. It is a market in which investors trade back and forth with each other.
Venture capitalists	Venture capitalists refer to individuals or companies that invest in new businesses in exchange for partial ownership of those businesses.
Technology	The body of knowledge and techniques that can be used to combine economic resources to produce goods and services is called technology.
Lease	A contract for the possession and use of land or other property, including goods, on one side, and a recompense of rent or other income on the other is the lease.
Venture capital	Venture capital is capital provided by outside investors for financing of new, growing or struggling businesses. Venture capital investments generally are high risk investments but offer the potential for above average returns.
Revenue	Revenue is a U.S. business term for the amount of money that a company receives from its activities, mostly from sales of products and/or services to customers.
Registration statement	Document that an issuer of securities files with the SEC that contains required information about the issuer, the securities to be issued, and other relevant information so the security may be sold on a national stock exchange is a registration statement.
Working capital	The dollar difference between total current assets and total current liabilities is called working capital.
Auction	A preexisting business model that operates successfully on the Internet by announcing an item for sale and permitting multiple purchasers to bid on them under specified rules and condition is an auction.
Investment banker	Investment banker refers to a financial organization that specializes in selling primary offerings of securities. Investment bankers can also perform other financial functions, such as advising clients, negotiating mergers and takeovers, and selling secondary offerings.
Treasury security	A treasury security is a government bond issued by the United States Department of the Treasury through the Bureau of the Public Debt. They are the debt financing instruments of the U.S. Federal government, and are often referred to simply as Treasuries.
Treasury bills	Short-term obligations of the federal government are treasury bills. They are like zero coupon bonds in that they do not pay interest prior to maturity; instead they are sold at a discount of the par value to create a positive yield to maturity.
Bid	A bid price is a price offered by a buyer when he/she buys a good. In the context of stock trading on a stock exchange, the bid price is the highest price a buyer of a stock is willing to pay for a share of that given stock.
Financial intermediary	Financial intermediary refers to a financial institution, such as a bank or a life insurance company, which directs other people's money into such investments as government and corporate securities.

Deutsche Bank	Deutsche Bank was founded in Germany on January 22, 1870 as a specialist bank for foreign trade. Major projects in its first decades included the Northern Pacific Railroad in the United States (1883) and the Baghdad Railway (1888). It also financed bond offerings of the steel concern Krupp (1885) and introduced the chemical company Bayer on the Berlin stock market.
Discount	The difference between the face value of a bond and its selling price, when a bond is sold for less than its face value it's referred to as a discount.
Negotiable	A negotiable instrument is one that can be bought and sold after being issued - in other words, it is a tradable instrument.
Underwriting	The process of selling securities and, at the same time, assuring the seller a specified price is underwriting. Underwriting is done by investment bankers and represents a form of risk taking.
Financial market	In economics, a financial market is a mechanism which allows people to trade money for securities or commodities such as gold or other precious metals. In general, any commodity market might be considered to be a financial market, if the usual purpose of traders is not the immediate consumption of the commodity, but rather as a means of delaying or accelerating consumption over time.
Margin	A deposit by a buyer in stocks with a seller or a stockbroker, as security to cover fluctuations in the market in reference to stocks that the buyer has purchased but for which he has not paid is a margin. Commodities are also traded on margin.
Nike	Because Nike creates goods for a wide range of sports, they have competition from every sports and sports fashion brand there is. Nike has no direct competitors because there is no single brand which can compete directly with their range of sports and non-sports oriented gear, except for Reebok.
Sun Microsystems	Sun Microsystems is most well known for its Unix systems, which have a reputation for system stability and a consistent design philosophy.
Debt security	Type of security acquired by loaning assets is called a debt security.
Time Warner	Time Warner is the world's largest media company with major Internet, publishing, film, telecommunications and television divisions.
Financial institution	A financial institution acts as an agent that provides financial services for its clients. Financial institutions generally fall under financial regulation from a government authority.
Date of issue	As applied to notes, bonds, and so on of a series, the arbitrary date fixed as the beginning of the term for which they run, without reference to the precise time when convenience or the state of the market may permit their sale or delivery is called the date of issue.
Interest	In finance and economics, interest is the price paid by a borrower for the use of a lender's money. In other words, interest is the amount of paid to "rent" money for a period of time.
Balance	In banking and accountancy, the outstanding balance is the amount of money owned, (or due), that remains in a deposit account (or a loan account) at a given date, after all past remittances, payments and withdrawal have been accounted for. It can be positive (then, in the balance sheet of a firm, it is an asset) or negative (a liability).
Asset	An item of property, such as land, capital, money, a share in ownership, or a claim on others for future payment, such as a bond or a bank deposit is an asset.
Current asset	A current asset is an asset on the balance sheet which is expected to be sold or otherwise used up in the near future, usually within one year.
Balance sheet	A statement of the assets, liabilities, and net worth of a firm or individual at some given

Go to **Cram101.com** for the Practice Tests for this Chapter.

	time often at the end of its "fiscal year," is referred to as a balance sheet.
Microsoft	Microsoft is a multinational computer technology corporation with 2004 global annual sales of US$39.79 billion and 71,553 employees in 102 countries and regions as of July 2006. It develops, manufactures, licenses, and supports a wide range of software products for computing devices.
Bondholder	The individual or entity that purchases a bond, thus loaning money to the company that issued the bond is the bondholder.
Creditor	A person to whom a debt or legal obligation is owed, and who has the right to enforce payment of that debt or obligation is referred to as creditor.
Maturity	Maturity refers to the final payment date of a loan or other financial instrument, after which point no further interest or principal need be paid.
Maturity date	The date on which the final payment on a bond is due from the bond issuer to the investor is a maturity date.
Face value	The nominal or par value of an instrument as expressed on its face is referred to as the face value.
Stockholder	A stockholder is an individual or company (including a corporation) that legally owns one or more shares of stock in a joined stock company. The shareholders are the owners of a corporation. Companies listed at the stock market strive to enhance shareholder value.
Dissolution	Dissolution is the process of admitting or removing a partner in a partnership.
Bankruptcy	Bankruptcy is a legally declared inability or impairment of ability of an individual or organization to pay their creditors.
Default	In finance, default occurs when a debtor has not met its legal obligations according to the debt contract, e.g. it has not made a scheduled payment, or violated a covenant (condition) of the debt contract.
Pledge	In law a pledge (also pawn) is a bailment of personal property as a security for some debt or engagement.
Debenture	A debenture is a long-term debt instrument used by governments and large companies to obtain funds. It is similar to a bond except the securitization conditions are different.
Credit	Credit refers to a recording as positive in the balance of payments, any transaction that gives rise to a payment into the country, such as an export, the sale of an asset, or borrowing from abroad.
Revenue bond	A revenue bond is a special type of municipal bond distinguished by its guarantee of repayment solely from revenues generated by a specified revenue-generating entity associated with the purpose of the bonds.
Authority	Authority in agency law, refers to an agent's ability to affect his principal's legal relations with third parties. Also used to refer to an actor's legal power or ability to do something. In addition, sometimes used to refer to a statute, case, or other legal source that justifies a particular result.
Levy	Levy refers to imposing and collecting a tax or tariff.
Exempt	Employees who are not covered by the Fair Labor Standards Act are exempt. Exempt employees are not eligible for overtime pay.
Interest payment	The payment to holders of bonds payable, calculated by multiplying the stated rate on the face of the bond by the par, or face, value of the bond. If bonds are issued at a discount or premium, the interest payment does not equal the interest expense.

Go to **Cram101.com** for the Practice Tests for this Chapter.

Interest rate	The rate of return on bonds, loans, or deposits. When one speaks of 'the' interest rate, it is usually in a model where there is only one.
Junk bond	In finance, a junk bond is a bond that is rated below investment grade. These bonds have a higher risk of defaulting, but typically pay high yields in order to make them attractive to investors.
Principal	In agency law, one under whose direction an agent acts and for whose benefit that agent acts is a principal.
Serial bonds	Serial bonds refer to bonds in an issue that mature periodically over several years, usually at varying interest rates.
Sinking fund	A sinking fund is a method by which an organization sets aside money over time to retire its indebtedness. More specifically, it is a fund into which money can be deposited, so that over time its preferred stock, debentures or stocks can be retired.
Accrued interest	In finance, accrued interest is the interest that has accumulated since the principal investment, or since the previous interest payment if there has been one already. For a financial instrument such as a bond, interest is calculated and paid in set intervals.
Call provision	Call provision refers to bonds and some preferred stock, in which a call allows the corporation to retire securities before maturity by forcing the bondholders to sell bonds back to it at a set price. The call provisions are included in the bond indenture.
Retailing	All activities involved in selling, renting, and providing goods and services to ultimate consumers for personal, family, or household use is referred to as retailing.
Interest expense	The cost a business incurs to borrow money. With respect to bonds payable, the interest expense is calculated by multiplying the market rate of interest by the carrying value of the bonds on the date of the payment.
Dividend	Amount of corporate profits paid out for each share of stock is referred to as dividend.
Holder	A person in possession of a document of title or an instrument payable or indorsed to him, his order, or to bearer is a holder.
Residual	Residual payments can refer to an ongoing stream of payments in respect of the completion of past achievements.
Market value	Market value refers to the price of an asset agreed on between a willing buyer and a willing seller; the price an asset could demand if it is sold on the open market.
Book value	The book value of an asset or group of assets is sometimes the price at which they were originally acquired, in many cases equal to purchase price.
Liability	A liability is a present obligation of the enterprise arizing from past events, the settlement of which is expected to result in an outflow from the enterprise of resources embodying economic benefits.
Salvage value	In accounting, the salvage value of an asset is its remaining value after depreciation. The estimated value of an asset at the end of its useful life.
Long run	In economic models, the long run time frame assumes no fixed factors of production. Firms can enter or leave the marketplace, and the cost (and availability) of land, labor, raw materials, and capital goods can be assumed to vary.
Variable	A variable is something measured by a number; it is used to analyze what happens to other things when the size of that number changes.
Convertible securities	Securities giving their holders the power to exchange those securities for other securities without paying any additional consideration are convertible securities.

Go to **Cram101.com** for the Practice Tests for this Chapter.

Convertible security	A convertible security is a security that can be converted into another security, for example, a bond that under certain terms can be converted into equity.
Conversion	Conversion refers to any distinct act of dominion wrongfully exerted over another's personal property in denial of or inconsistent with his rights therein. That tort committed by a person who deals with chattels not belonging to him in a manner that is inconsistent with the ownership of the lawful owner.
Convertible bond	A convertible bond is type of bond that can be converted into shares of stock in the issuing company, usually at some pre-announced ratio.
Starbucks	Although it has endured much criticism for its purported monopoly on the global coffee-bean market, Starbucks purchases only 3% of the coffee beans grown worldwide. In 2000 the company introduced a line of fair trade products and now offers three options for socially conscious coffee drinkers. According to Starbucks, they purchased 4.8 million pounds of Certified Fair Trade coffee in fiscal year 2004 and 11.5 million pounds in 2005.
Gain	In finance, gain is a profit or an increase in value of an investment such as a stock or bond. Gain is calculated by fair market value or the proceeds from the sale of the investment minus the sum of the purchase price and all costs associated with it.
Trust	An arrangement in which shareholders of independent firms agree to give up their stock in exchange for trust certificates that entitle them to a share of the trust's common profits.
Pension	A pension is a steady income given to a person (usually after retirement). Pensions are typically payments made in the form of a guaranteed annuity to a retired or disabled employee.
Institutional investors	Institutional investors refers to large organizations such as pension funds, mutual funds, insurance companies, and banks that invest their own funds or the funds of others.
Pension fund	Amounts of money put aside by corporations, nonprofit organizations, or unions to cover part of the financial needs of members when they retire is a pension fund.
Insurance	Insurance refers to a system by which individuals can reduce their exposure to risk of large losses by spreading the risks among a large number of persons.
Liquidity	Liquidity refers to the capacity to turn assets into cash, or the amount of assets in a portfolio that have that capacity.
Bottom line	The bottom line is net income on the last line of a income statement.
Mutual savings bank	A mutual savings bank is a financial institution chartered by a state or federal government to provide a safe place for individuals to save and to invest those savings in mortgages, loans, stocks, Bonds and other securities.
Savings bank	A depository institution, owned by its depositors, that accepts savings deposits and makes mortgage loans is a savings bank.
Preference	The act of a debtor in paying or securing one or more of his creditors in a manner more favorable to them than to other creditors or to the exclusion of such other creditors is a preference. In the absence of statute, a preference is perfectly good, but to be legal it must be bona fide, and not a mere subterfuge of the debtor to secure a future benefit to himself or to prevent the application of his property to his debts.
Tort	In the common law, a tort is a civil wrong, other than a breach of contract, for which the law provides a remedy. A tort is a breach of a non-contractual duty potentially owed to the entire world, imposed by law. The majority of legal claims are brought in tort.
Brokerage firm	A company that conducts various aspects of securities trading, analysis and advisory services is a brokerage firm.

Consultant	A professional that provides expert advice in a particular field or area in which customers occassionaly require this type of knowledge is a consultant.
Industry	A group of firms that produce identical or similar products is an industry. It is also used specifically to refer to an area of economic production focused on manufacturing which involves large amounts of capital investment before any profit can be realized, also called "heavy industry".
Aid	Assistance provided by countries and by international institutions such as the World Bank to developing countries in the form of monetary grants, loans at low interest rates, in kind, or a combination of these is called aid. Aid can also refer to assistance of any type rendered to benefit some group or individual.
Stock dividend	Stock dividend refers to pro rata distributions of stock or stock rights on common stock. They are usually issued in proportion to shares owned.
Inflation	An increase in the overall price level of an economy, usually as measured by the CPI or by the implicit price deflator is called inflation.
Marginal tax rate	The percentage of an additional dollar of earnings that goes to taxes is referred to as the marginal tax rate.
Capital gain	Capital gain refers to the gain in value that the owner of an asset experiences when the price of the asset rises, including when the currency in which the asset is denominated appreciates.
Specialist	A specialist is a trader who makes a market in one or several stocks and holds the limit order book for those stocks.
Dealer	People who link buyers with sellers by buying and selling securities at stated prices are referred to as a dealer.
Market makers	Market makers refer to financial service companies that connect investors and borrowers, either directly or indirectly.
Listing requirements	Financial standards that corporations must meet before their common stock can be traded on a stock exchange are listing requirements. Listing requirements are not standard, but are set by each exchange. The requirements for the NYSE are the most stringent.
Option	A contract that gives the purchaser the option to buy or sell the underlying financial instrument at a specified price, called the exercise price or strike price, within a specific period of time.
Financial instrument	Formal or legal documents in writing, such as contracts, deeds, wills, bonds, leases, and mortgages is referred to as a financial instrument.
Regional stock exchange	Any securities exchange located outside a country's main financial center is a regional stock exchange.
Communism	Communism refers to an economic system in which capital is owned by private government. Contrasts with capitalism.
Committee	A long-lasting, sometimes permanent team in the organization structure created to deal with tasks that recur regularly is the committee.
Stockbroker	A registered representative who works as a market intermediary to buy and sell securities for clients is a stockbroker.
Market order	Instructions to a broker to buy or sell a stock immediately at the best price available is a market order.
Limit order	A limit order is an order to buy a security at no more (or sell at no less) than a specific

Go to **Cram101.com** for the Practice Tests for this Chapter.

price. This gives the customer some control over the price at which the trade is executed.

Volatility	Volatility refers to the extent to which an economic variable, such as a price or an exchange rate, moves up and down over time.
Round lots	Round lots refer to purchases of 100 shares of stock at a time.
Odd lots	Odd lots refer to purchases of less than 100 shares of stock at a time. They are a fractional unit of a share that may result from the allocation of bonus shares. The amounts in cash are paid into deposit accounts. Odd lots resulting from difference sources are not combined.
Account executive	The individual who serves as the liaison between the advertising agency and the client is the account executive. The account executive is responsible for managing all of the services the agency provides to the client and representing the agency's point of view to the client.
Broker	In commerce, a broker is a party that mediates between a buyer and a seller. A broker who also acts as a seller or as a buyer becomes a principal party to the deal.
Charles Schwab	Charles Schwab is the world's second-largest discount broker. Besides discount brokerage, the firm offers mutual funds, annuities, bond trading, and now mortgages through its Charles Schwab Bank.
Mobil	Mobil is a major oil company which merged with the Exxon Corporation in 1999. Today Mobil continues as a major brand name within the combined company.
Exxon	Exxon formally replaced the Esso, Enco, and Humble brands on January 1, 1973, in the USA. The name Esso, pronounced S-O, attracted protests from other Standard Oil spinoffs because of its similarity to the name of the parent company, Standard Oil.
Disney	Disney is one of the largest media and entertainment corporations in the world. Founded on October 16, 1923 by brothers Walt and Roy Disney as a small animation studio, today it is one of the largest Hollywood studios and also owns nine theme parks and several television networks, including the American Broadcasting Company (ABC).
Ford	Ford is an American company that manufactures and sells automobiles worldwide. Ford introduced methods for large-scale manufacturing of cars, and large-scale management of an industrial workforce, especially elaborately engineered manufacturing sequences typified by the moving assembly lines.
Exxon Mobil	Exxon Mobil is the largest publicly traded integrated oil and gas company in the world, formed on November 30, 1999, by the merger of Exxon and Mobil. It is the sixth-largest company in the world as ranked by the Forbes Global 2000 and the largest company in the world (by revenue) as ranked by the Fortune Global 500.
Purchasing	Purchasing refers to the function in a firm that searches for quality material resources, finds the best suppliers, and negotiates the best price for goods and services.
Portfolio	In finance, a portfolio is a collection of investments held by an institution or a private individual. Holding but not always a portfolio is part of an investment and risk-limiting strategy called diversification. By owning several assets, certain types of risk (in particular specific risk) can be reduced.
Dividend reinvestment plans	Plans that provide the investor with an opportunity to buy additional shares of stock with the cash dividends paid by the company are called dividend reinvestment plans.
Direct investment	Direct investment refers to a domestic firm actually investing in and owning a foreign subsidiary or division.
Securities and exchange	Securities and exchange commission refers to U.S. government agency that determines the financial statements that public companies must provide to stockholders and the measurement

commission	rules that they must use in producing those statements.
Yield	The interest rate that equates a future value or an annuity to a given present value is a yield.
Closing	The finalization of a real estate sales transaction that passes title to the property from the seller to the buyer is referred to as a closing. Closing is a sales term which refers to the process of making a sale. It refers to reaching the final step, which may be an exchange of money or acquiring a signature.
Earnings per share	Earnings per share refers to annual profit of the corporation divided by the number of shares outstanding.
Bond certificate	A legal document that indicates the name of the issuer, the face value of the bonds, and such other data as the contractual interest rate and the maturity date of the bond is called a bond certificate.
Current yield	Current yield refers to the rate of return on a bond; the annual interest payment divided by the bond's price.
Dow Jones Industrial Average	Today, the Dow Jones Industrial Average consists of 30 of the largest and most widely held public companies in the United States. The "industrial" portion of the name is largely historical—many of the 30 modern components have little to do with heavy industry. To compensate for the effects of stock splits and other adjustments, it is currently a weighted average, not the actual average of the prices of its component stocks.
Utility	Utility refers to the want-satisfying power of a good or service; the satisfaction or pleasure a consumer obtains from the consumption of a good or service.
Economy	The income, expenditures, and resources that affect the cost of running a business and household are called an economy.
Alcoa	Alcoa (NYSE: AA) is the world's leading producer of alumina, primary and fabricated aluminum, with operations in 43 countries. (It is followed in this by a former subsidiary, Alcan, the second-leading producer.)
American Express	From the early 1980s until the late 1990s, American Express was known for cutting its merchant fees (also known as a "discount rate") to fine merchants and restaurants if they only accepted American Express and no other credit or charge cards. This prompted competitors such as Visa and MasterCard to cry foul for a while, as the tactics "locked" restaurants into American Express.
General Motors	General Motors is the world's largest automaker. Founded in 1908, today it employs about 327,000 people around the world. With global headquarters in Detroit, it manufactures its cars and trucks in 33 countries.
Walt Disney	As the co-founder of Walt Disney Productions, Walt became one of the most well-known motion picture producers in the world. The corporation he co-founded, now known as The Walt Disney Company, today has annual revenues of approximately US $30 billion.
Intel	Intel Corporation, founded in 1968 and based in Santa Clara, California, USA, is the world's largest semiconductor company. Intel is best known for its PC microprocessors, where it maintains roughly 80% market share.
Sears	Before the Sears catalog, farmers typically bought supplies (often at very high prices) from local general stores. Sears took advantage of this by publishing his catalog with clearly stated prices, so that consumers could know what he was selling and at what price, and order and obtain them conveniently. The catalog business soon grew quickly.
Union	A worker association that bargains with employers over wages and working conditions is called

Go to **Cram101.com** for the Practice Tests for this Chapter.

a union.

Chevron	Chevron Corporation is one of the world's largest global energy companies. Headquartered in San Ramon, California, USA and active in more than 180 countries, it is engaged in every aspect of the oil and gas industry, including exploration and production; refining, marketing and transport; chemicals manufacturing and sales; and power generation.
Home Depot	Home Depot has recently added self checkout registers at most of its stores in North America. These automated kiosks allow the customer to scan the barcode of the item they wish to purchase, then insert money to pay for the items, and receive any change automatically. The customer no longer needs to interact with a store employee during checkout.
Goodyear	Goodyear was founded in 1898 by German immigrants Charles and Frank Seiberling. Today it is the third largest tire and rubber company in the world.
Diversified portfolio	Diversified portfolio refers to a portfolio that includes a variety of assets whose prices are not likely all to change together. In international economics, this usually means holding assets denominated in different currencies.
Bond fund	A bond fund is a fund that invests in bonds. This may be a mutual fund or exchange-traded fund.They can be distinguished by several properties. Some invest in government bonds, others in corporate bonds.
Outstanding shares	Total number of shares of stock that are owned by stockholders on any particular date is referred to as outstanding shares.
Net asset value	The Net Asset Value is a term used to describe the value of an entity's assets less the value of its liabilities. The term is commonly used in relation to collective investment schemes.
Load fund	Funds that are a load fund exhibit a "Sales Load" with a percentage charge levied on purchase or sale of shares.
Fraud	Tax fraud falls into two categories: civil and criminal. Under civil fraud, the IRS may impose as a penalty of an amount equal to as much as 75 percent of the underpayment.
Federal government	Federal government refers to the government of the United States, as distinct from the state and local governments.
Civil action	A lawsuit is a civil action brought before a court in which the party commencing the action, the plaintiff, seeks a legal remedy. If the plaintiff is successful, judgment will be given in the plaintiff's favour, and a range of court orders may be issued to enforce a right, impose a penalty, award damages, impose an injunction to prevent an act or compel an act, or to obtain a declaratory judgment to prevent future legal disputes.
Department of Justice	The United States Department of Justice is a Cabinet department in the United States government designed to enforce the law and defend the interests of the United States according to the law and to ensure fair and impartial administration of justice for all Americans. This department is administered by the United States Attorney General, one of the original members of the cabinet.
Prospectus	Prospectus refers to a report detailing a future stock offering containing a set of financial statements; required by the SEC from a company that wishes to make an initial public offering of its stock.
Research and development	The use of resources for the deliberate discovery of new information and ways of doing things, together with the application of that information in inventing new products or processes is referred to as research and development.
Litigation	The process of bringing, maintaining, and defending a lawsuit is litigation.
Disclosure	Disclosure means the giving out of information, either voluntarily or to be in compliance

with legal regulations or workplace rules.

Program trading Giving instructions to computers to automatically sell if the price of a stock dips to a certain point to avoid potential losses is referred to as program trading.

Insider trading Insider trading is the trading of a corporation's stock or other securities (e.g. Bonds or stock options) by corporate insiders such as officers, directors, or holders of more than ten percent of the firm's shares.

Socially responsible investing Socially Responsible Investing is an umbrella term for a philosophy of investing by both financial and social criteria. The investors seek to align their personal values and financial goals by choosing to invest in companies and organizations displaying values comparable to their own.

Labor People's physical and mental talents and efforts that are used to help produce goods and services are called labor.

Appeal Appeal refers to the act of asking an appellate court to overturn a decision after the trial court's final judgment has been entered.

Net assets Net assets refers to portion of the assets remaining after the creditors' claims have been satisfied; also called equity or residual interest.

Annual report An annual report is prepared by corporate management that presents financial information including financial statements, footnotes, and the management discussion and analysis.

Distribution Distribution in economics, the manner in which total output and income is distributed among individuals or factors.

Arbitration Arbitration is a form of mediation or conciliation, where the mediating party is given power by the disputant parties to settle the dispute by making a finding. In practice arbitration is generally used as a substitute for judicial systems, particularly when the judicial processes are viewed as too slow, expensive or biased. Arbitration is also used by communities which lack formal law, as a substitute for formal law.

Shareholder A shareholder is an individual or company (including a corporation) that legally owns one or more shares of stock in a joined stock company.

Publicly traded corporation A corporation whose stock is traded on the stock exchanges is referred to as a publicly traded corporation.

Household An economic unit that provides the economy with resources and uses the income received to purchase goods and services that satisfy economic wants is called household.

Personnel A collective term for all of the employees of an organization. Personnel is also commonly used to refer to the personnel management function or the organizational unit responsible for administering personnel programs.

Audit An examination of the financial reports to ensure that they represent what they claim and conform with generally accepted accounting principles is referred to as audit.

Audit trail An audit trail is a chronological sequence of audit records, each of which contains evidence directly pertaining to and resulting from the execution of a business process or system function.

Analyst Analyst refers to a person or tool with a primary function of information analysis, generally with a more limited, practical and short term set of goals than a researcher.

Policy Similar to a script in that a policy can be a less than completely rational decision-making method. Involves the use of a pre-existing set of decision steps for any problem that presents itself.

Go to **Cram101.com** for the Practice Tests for this Chapter.
And, **NEVER** highlight a book again!

Respondent	Respondent refers to a term often used to describe the party charged in an administrative proceeding. The party adverse to the appellant in a case appealed to a higher court.
Points	Loan origination fees that may be deductible as interest by a buyer of property. A seller of property who pays points reduces the selling price by the amount of the points paid for the buyer.
Uniform Commercial Code	Uniform commercial code refers to a comprehensive commercial law adopted by every state in the United States; it covers sales laws and other commercial laws.
Business law	Business law is the body of law which governs business and commerce and is often considered to be a branch of civil law and deals both with issues of private law and public law. It regulates corporate contracts, hiring practices, and the manufacture and sales of consumer goods.
Contract law	Set of laws that specify what constitutes a legally enforceable agreement is called contract
Contract	A contract is a "promise" or an "agreement" that is enforced or recognized by the law. In the civil law, a contract is considered to be part of the general law of obligations.
Trading securities	All investments in stocks or bonds that are held primarily for the purpose of active trading in the near future are called trading securities.
Dividend yield	Dividends per share divided by market price per share are called a dividend yield. Dividend yield indicates the percentage return that a stockholder will receive on dividends alone.
P/E ratio	In finance, the P/E ratio of a stock is used to measure how cheap or expensive share prices are. It is probably the single most consistent red flag to excessive optimism and over-investment.
A share	In finance the term A share has two distinct meanings, both relating to securities. The first is a designation for a 'class' of common or preferred stock. A share of common or preferred stock typically has enhanced voting rights or other benefits compared to the other forms of shares that may have been created. The equity structure, or how many types of shares are offered, is determined by the corporate charter.
Diversification	Investing in a collection of assets whose returns do not always move together, with the result that overall risk is lower than for individual assets is referred to as diversification.
Operation	A standardized method or technique that is performed repetitively, often on different materials resulting in different finished goods is called an operation.
Takeover	A takeover in business refers to one company (the acquirer) purchasing another (the target). Such events resemble mergers, but without the formation of a new company.
Financial management	The job of managing a firm's resources so it can meet its goals and objectives is called financial management.
Bureaucracy	Bureaucracy refers to an organization with many layers of managers who set rules and regulations and oversee all decisions.
Economics	The social science dealing with the use of scarce resources to obtain the maximum satisfaction of society's virtually unlimited economic wants is an economics.
Loyalty	Marketers tend to define customer loyalty as making repeat purchases. Some argue that it should be defined attitudinally as a strongly positive feeling about the brand.
Promotion	Promotion refers to all the techniques sellers use to motivate people to buy products or services. An attempt by marketers to inform people about products and to persuade them to participate in an exchange.

Go to **Cram101.com** for the Practice Tests for this Chapter.

Accounting	A system that collects and processes financial information about an organization and reports that information to decision makers is referred to as accounting.
Public debt	Public debt refers to the total amount owed by the Federal government to the owners of government securities; equal to the sum of past government budget deficits less government budget surpluses.
Edict	Edict refers to a command or prohibition promulgated by a sovereign and having the effect of
Chief executive officer	A chief executive officer is the highest-ranking corporate officer or executive officer of a corporation, or agency. In closely held corporations, it is general business culture that the office chief executive officer is also the chairman of the board.
Financial plan	The financial plan section of a business plan consists of three financial statements (the income statement, the cash flow projection, and the balance sheet) and a brief analysis of these three statements.
Asset management	Asset management is the method that a company uses to track fixed assets, for example factory equipment, desks and chairs, computers, even buildings. Although the exact details of the task varies widely from company to company, asset management often includes tracking the physical location of assets, managing demand for scarce resources, and accounting tasks such as amortization.
Market position	Market position is a measure of the position of a company or product on a market.

Printed in the United States
100011LV00008B/26/A